How to Survive the Stress of Still Being Black in America

Recognizing Race-Based and Racism-Related Stress in 21st Century America and Strategies for Active Coping

by Joseph R. Gibson, Ed.S.

KITABU Publishing, LLC

KitabuPublishing.com

This book is dedicated to my best friend Keith Handy and my first student Aleax Griffin. Both of whom we lost as I wrote. Love you both, dearly, and pray that you have found peace.

"Let the globe, if nothing else, say this is true. That even as we grieved, we grew."

-Amanda Gorman

"If I remain in this bloody land, I will not live long. I cannot remain where I must hear slaves' chains continually and where I must encounter the insults of their hypocritical enslavers."

-David Walker

But Because It Is Feared[1]
Understanding the Stress of Just Being Black in America

"White privilege doesn't mean your life hasn't been hard. It just means the color of your skin isn't one of the things that makes it harder."
-Jimmy Kimmel

"Nobody ever tells you it's something wrong with being Black, you just start feeling it."
-Ras Kass

"These people have deluded themselves for so long that they really don't think I'm human. I base this on their conduct, not what they say."
-James Baldwin

For much of my life, when someone would ask me, "who are you?" I'd hesitate for a second, trying to figure out a *better* answer, and then rather defiantly reply, "a Black man in America." And then wonder where this sudden urge to be defiant came from and if it was necessary or even appropriate. I already knew where "my" answer came from, at least kind of. It was a line from some movie I had watched; I can't remember exactly *which* movie it was. I do remember that when the character, who I can't remember either, said it, I *felt* it in such a way that I internalized it.

---

[1] Excerpted from the following James Baldwin quote from *The Fire Next Time*: "Black has *become* a beautiful color—not because it is loved but because it is feared."

I was asked this question again recently, and instead of using my standard retort, I hesitated and then candidly admitted that I had no clue. I had lost confidence in the adequacy of "a Black man in America" as a descriptor of me. And instead of feeling embarrassed, I felt curious, like urgently curious. Not knowing "who I am" suddenly became acutely problematic for my self-worth. I needed to figure this thing out. I needed to have a *good* answer, a conclusive self-concept if you will, and I needed it *immediately*.

So, I began brainstorming some possible responses, and realized quickly that I'm a lot of awesome things…

Human.
Son.
Husband.
Father.
Emotion-driven Scorpio.
Anti-racist (since '93).
Rebel.
Revolutionary.
Educator.
Positive Black Male Image.
Passionate Problem Solver.
Author.
Publisher.
World Traveler.
Black Stuff Scholar.
Unabashed Womanist (see Alice Walker's definition).
Louisiana Food Connoisseur.
New Orleans Saints Fanatic.
Proud Graduate of Grambling State University.
Marvel Cinematic Universe Enthusiast.
Southern Hip Hop Zealot.
Borderline Sneakerhead.

General Cinephile with a Particular Fondness for Quoting Black Films.

Last but Not Least, Practicing Survivor of Shit. And by *shit*, I'm rather brazenly referring to a lifetime of exposure to various types of terrible, exhausting experiences, including several forms of racism[2], conditioned Black docility, intergenerational poverty, numerous other childhood trauma, lingering father hunger, a fierce fear of abandonment, compensatory hypersexuality, an involuntary extension of my active-duty military service, some insecure and unnecessarily evil people sporadically placed in my professional life, *President* Trump, 2020, etc. But perhaps most importantly, I'm a survivor of the constant stress of simply *being* what for much of my life I, as aforementioned, primarily identified as—Black in America.

Race[3] (i.e., being Black) as a lived, psychosocial experience is a chronic stressor for a lot of Black people in America. It certainly has been for me. Being a Black person living in an anti-Black, racialized society is stressful. Just being Black in this country, observed Joe Feagin, "means always having to be prepared for anti-black actions," which, as a specific type of constant hypervigilance, can certainly be stressful. Stress can be subtle camouflage for fear, rage, or disappointment. For Black people in America, there's a lot of things we experience that scares us and

---

[2]   Contemporary racism in America can be systemic, individual, institutional, cultural, unconscious, aversive, everyday, anticipated, perceived, or internalized, which radically increases the probability and regularity of experiencing it in some form.

[3]   "It is important to bear in mind that *race* is a social category, not a biological one," wrote Bernard Whitley and Mary Kite. For example, "genetic studies find more differences within traditionally defined racial groups than between them. In statistical terms, the differences between races that do exist are trivial relative to the genetic factors common to all people." However, "its social nature does not diminish the psychological importance of race. It remains a fundamental basis for how people think about and interact with each other."

even more that makes us angry or disappointed; none of which we'd prefer to emotionally acknowledge, but still must somehow survive.

Danielle Williams acknowledged that just "being Black in a racist society is stressful." Being Black in America makes us uniquely, highly, and constantly vulnerable to experiencing *race-based stress*. And we don't necessarily need to experience some form of racism in order to experience race-based stress; merely *being Black* is enough.

Explicit race relations in America may have changed since the Civil Rights Movement, but America remains, to quote Michael Emerson and Christian Smith, an implicitly "racialized society wherein race matters profoundly for differences in life experiences, life opportunities, and social relationships." America continues to be a nation "that allocates differential economic, political, social, and even psychological rewards to groups along racial lines; lines that are socially constructed."

Consequently, being Black in America creates a disproportionate vulnerability to "repetitive stressors, such as high rates of crime, low quality schools, high unemployment, food insecurity, financial difficulties, inadequate housing, disparities in health care, or racism in the community and workplace," explained Ernest Levister.

Historically, explained E. Yvonne Moss and Wornie Reed, the "status of blacks relative to whites has been one of subordination; race has been a primary factor in determining social stratification. Despite improvements in various aspects of American life, racial stratification has not changed in any fundamental sense." Yet, public perception and "policies tend to treat this racial inequality as a product of poor personal decision-making" or relative inferiority and incompetence on the part of Black people as a whole, observed Kate Shuster, "rather than acknowledging it as the result of racialized systems and structures that restrict choice and limit opportunity."

4

In contemporary America, observed Karyn Loscocco, "the dominant group has the power and resources to create a race hierarchy that reflects its preeminence, ordering groups from best to worst, from valued to devalued, from human to 'other.' Perhaps most consequential is that the 'racial other' is seen first and foremost as a racial group member, while their humanity and individuality are ignored," which can be experienced as a chronic stressor.

Philomena Essed recognized that White people, as members of this country's dominant racial/ethnic group, generally tend to "automatically favor members of their own group, not simply because they want to be with those they feel are their own, but because they believe, deep down, that white lives count more, that they are more human."

For what it's worth, I'm totally capable of acknowledging the fault and flaws of Black people and our collective tendency to not only commit but oftentimes glorify certain self-defeating, handicapping, and destructive behavior. Moreover, while I believe it to be unoriginal, inaccurate, and counterproductive to simply blame old-fashioned racism or individual White people (i.e., "the White man") for *our* behavior, contemporary racism[4] and racism-related stress[5] comes in many forms, and much of this behavior is effectively related to (i.e., a direct or secondary consequence of) some of these forms.

---

[4] In its various forms, including individual, institutional, cultural, unconscious, systemic, aversive, everyday, anticipated, perceived, and, perhaps most insidiously, internalized racism.

[5] Shelly Harrell definitively identified six distinct racism-related stressors: "racism-related life events (significant events that may occur infrequently), vicarious racist experiences (stress induced by other people's racism experiences), daily racist microstressors (frequent experiences of minor racist events), chronic-contextual stress (stress due to the macro environment and atmosphere), collective experiences (perception of racist experiences as a group), and transgenerational transmission (historical events that passed down across generations)."

It bothers me that, to quote Brando Starkey, "American culture conditions white folk to not fully grasp how society privileges them," which makes it easier for many of them to maintain their denial of the persistent (if not increasing) significance of race in 21st century America. Far too many continue to not (want to) grasp that "White privilege doesn't mean your life hasn't been hard. It just means," concluded Jimmy Kimmel (yes, *that* Jimmy Kimmel), "the color of your skin isn't one of the things that makes it harder." A common reaction among "White Americans is to presume racial innocence." Tim Wise wrote that "ignorance of how we are shaped racially is the first sign of privilege. In other words, it is a privilege to ignore the consequences of race in America."

It equally concerns me that White people in America collectively "appear to be more supportive of equal rights in principle than of equal rights in practice," as boldly argued by Kristin Anderson (herself White) in *Benign Bigotry*. "When commitment is required to perform specific actions involving their own lives and the status of their own group, they are much less receptive to the idea of equality."

This lack of receptiveness, noted Feagin (also White), "is grounded in white resistance to substantial changes in the status quo. Central to white concerns is a fear whites have of losing status and power because of black attempts to bring change." Privilege is logically preferrable for the privileged. However, there can be no race-based privilege without race-based inequity. Preventing equality by maintaining social boundaries makes privilege possible.

Acknowledging this and the lingering consequence of race in this country is neither anti-White nor synonymous with suggesting that all (or even most) White people are necessarily (or explicitly) racist or that somehow racism or White privilege is necessarily (or explicitly) responsible for all (or most) things impacting Black people, including stress. Black people should still be held accountable as individuals for decisions and habits that may be more self-defeating, handicapping, or destructive than they should be. I have always actively endorsed Dr. King's acknowledgement that "we must not let the fact that we are victims of injustice lull us into abrogating responsibility for our own lives. We must not use our oppression as an excuse for mediocrity and laziness" or poor decision and habit making.

Concurrently, I believe it *should be* normal for most (if not all) White people to accept that there is nothing biologically or genetically that would *automatically* make me (or any other Black person) more likely to be lazy, violent, unintelligent, criminal, irresponsible, incompetent, dangerous, degenerate, disrespectful, apathetic, hostile, unqualified, problematic, self-destructive, excuse-dependent, complaint-oriented, diabolical, flawed, incorrigible, and/or generally inferior simply because I am (we are) Black. I need more White people to somehow *feel* just how awful and infuriating and discouraging this can be; most of us already know. I have known for what seems like forever.

I'm also fully cognizant that, unfortunately, there is something culturally, cognitively, and affectively in this country that tends to make White people (and occasionally even other Black people) consistently presume and expect that I am any combination of the aforementioned negative traits due to the stigma America has socioculturally attached to Blackness. And there's not much I (or any other individual Black person) can do to stop these people from probably applying these negative presumptions and expectations to me, which can be both terrifically and routinely stressful.

Simply *being* Black in America is typically experienced by Black people as a chronic stressor in our daily lives. Existing in a "social environment in which Black Americans bear the stigma burden of their racial group while White Americans are allowed to view themselves as individuals" is stressful, explained Margaret Hicken et al. Having to deal with, possibly to some degree on a daily basis, the negative assumptions and expectations now associated with being Black in America is stressful. Enduring

7

"unequal life experiences and chances based on the socially constructed racial group membership categories" being "woven into our social structure and institutions" is stressful.

Stress is the brain's reaction to any information from our external circumstances that reveal or imply threat, especially threat that we feel we don't have the capacity or resources to cope with. The stress response is also referred to as the "fight or flight" response because it effectively prepares us to either fight or flee from this implied threat. Being Black in America involves the *perpetual* perception of threat (i.e., being physically or psychologically threatened by race-based experiences or being perceived as a threat because of racial stigma or White privilege), which implies a constant possibility of stress. Robert Carter recognized that stress increases if an experience is "ambiguous, negative, unpredictable, and uncontrollable," and race-based experiences typically feature these characteristics.

The chronic stress of being Black is largely rooted in Blackness still being profoundly stigmatized in America. Although fundamentally inaccurate, racial stigma plays a powerful role in shaping who Black people in America are understood or expected to be, or how we are looked at and what people, ourselves included, choose to believe they see. "Because stigma conveys a devalued social identity within a particular context," explained Mark Hatzenbuehler et al., "it creates unique stressors." In other words, stigma, specifically racial stigma (i.e., the stigma of Blackness in America) is stressful.

I doubt that stigma is a concept people are familiar enough with. Stigma, as defined by Erving Goffman, is "a powerfully negative label" that triggers the social perception of members of stigmatized groups as somehow being "negatively different" and "less than fully human" and, therefore, meriting "less valued treatment than 'normal' people" simply because they possess "this socially defined and disfavored attribute" or "negatively evaluated difference." With racial stigma, the negatively evaluated difference *is* the race or just *being* a member of the stigmatized racial group.

"Race is a stigma." Specifically, being Black in America remains to this day a socially defined and disfavored attribute or "undesired differentness" that "conveys a negative social identity." Racial stigma occurs when membership in a particular racial group is identified as undesirably different and this difference is then associated with specific, highly negative stereotypes. Stereotypes can "affect how we acquire and process information about the racially stigmatized," noted Robin Lenhardt. Stereotypes ultimately "perform a self-reinforcing role with respect to racial stigma" by giving "an information-processing advantage for stereotypical traits, ensuring that they always fall in our perceptual foreground rather than background." In other words, stereotypes enable the human brain to see the stigmatized as stigmatized *more automatically* than we would see them as normal or "fully human."

Patrick Corrigan described stigma as "cues that elicit stereotypes, knowledge structures that the general public learns about a marked social group. Stereotypes are especially efficient means of categorizing information about social groups. Stereotypes are considered 'social' because they represent collectively agreed on notions about groups of persons. They are 'efficient' because people can quickly generate impressions and expectations of individuals who belong to a stereotyped group."

Monica Biernat and John Dovidio detailed how "stereotypes generally play an integral role in the devaluation of 'marked' persons. Stereotypes are involved in stigmatization to the extent that the response of perceivers is not simply a negative one (i.e., dislike of 'devalued identity'), but also that a specific set of characteristics is assumed to exist among people sharing the same stigma (i.e., the stigma evokes a social identity)."

"To the extent that stigma is based on membership in a definable group, stereotypes are likely to develop and persevere. This is presumably the case because categories (even diffuse ones

9

such as gender or race) can imply a substantial amount of other information about a person. By categorizing others, we humans 'go beyond' given information and view objects with 'more elaborated, connotative meaning;' categorization generates expectations about individual group members."

Blackness (or being Black) is not naturally stigmatizing (i.e., indicative of somehow being inadequate, highly negative, or "less human"). In fact, racial stigma is an artificial, socially fabricated construct established from "years, even generations, of explicit and implicit cultural messages—gleaned from parents, the media, first-hand experiences, and countless other sources"—that associate Blackness with a host of highly negative assumptions and expectations. These messages, according to Susan Fiske, have "origins in the age of slavery" and are an inherent part of the American socialization process. We all, as Americans, have been culturally conditioned to accept these messages.

Lenhardt noted that "this means that the norms and rules about which categories of individuals will be valued or devalued are defined by society, even by the government, but not by nature. There is, after all, nothing inherently wrong with having dark skin or being a racial minority in society. Such a status does not itself lead to mistreatment or discrimination. An attribute that stigmatizes one type of possessor can confirm the usualness of another, and therefore is neither creditable nor discreditable as a thing in itself. An attribute becomes disfavored only because of the social information it carries."

This social information shapes "what we notice or overlook, what we regard positively, and what we regard negatively. Each society creates hierarchies of desirable and undesirable attributes." Regarding racial stigma, as Americans "we learn and are conditioned to expect racial minorities to conform to certain stereotypes about behavior, intellect, and morality." Being Black in America is stressful because "color, or more specifically, 'blackness,' has become synonymous with inferiority."

10

Moreover, racial stigma does not even have to be explicitly communicated (i.e., an explicit *stigmatizer* is unnecessary). Jennifer Crocker observed that "once it becomes widely known and shared in the culture, or among the stigmatized, it is not necessary for a prejudiced person to communicate the devaluation of the stigmatized for that devaluation to be felt." Stigma is then communicated and imposed implicitly via mainstream cultural practices and artifacts. Catherine Campbell concurred that "stigma is not something that *individuals* impose on others, but a complex social process linked to competition for power, tied into existing mechanisms of dominance and exclusion."

Society, explained Gregory Herek, "collectively identifies particular characteristics or groups, and assigns negative meaning and value to some of them, thereby 'constructing' stigma." Stigma isn't constructed organically, arbitrarily, or benignly. Whatever characteristic or social group that a society decides to negatively value is selected because it "consequently disadvantages, devalues, and disempowers those who have it."

Glenn Loury agreed that "awareness of the racial 'otherness' of blacks is embedded in the social consciousness of the American nation owing to the historical fact of slavery and its aftermath. This inherited stigma even today exerts an inhibiting effect on the extent to which African-Americans can realize their full human potential. Fundamental to the processes of race-making in the United States have been the institution of chattel slavery and the associated rituals and customs that supported the master-slave hierarchy and dishonored the slave. In the experience of the United States, slavery was a thoroughly racial institution. Therefore, the social meaning of race that emerged in American political culture was closely connected with the dishonorable status of enslavement."

"More than any other institution," added Matthew Desmond and Mustafa Emirbayer, "slavery would dictate" the specifics of racial stigma in America: "Blackness became associated with bondage, inferiority...Whiteness with freedom, superiority." For

11

centuries, slavery intentionally and brutally made "cheap and coercible labor" the exclusive social identity (and value) of Black people in America.

Consequently, *Blackness* in America gradually became culturally and cognitively associated with *slave*. The social definition of what it meant to be Black in America soon featured traits and expectations otherwise ascribable to being a slave. To be Black in America indicated being someone that is "completely subservient to," who will "work excessively hard" for, and is "forced to obey" a "dominating influence."

The social value of Black people in America insidiously became (and remains) associated with the efficiency in which they fulfilled their social definition (or role), which stigmatically was (being a) slave (i.e., cheap and coercible labor). The existential worth of Black lives in America has been and continues to be terribly vulnerable to the demand for our cheap and coercible labor. America's greatest dilemma is identifying what happens to this social value when slave (or slave-like) labor is suddenly obsolete.

The stigmatic origins of Blackness may have begun in slavery, but the end of slavery didn't simultaneously end Blackness being socially viewed as "undesired differentness" that "conveys a negatively valued social identity." America, Bryan Stevenson argued, had become a "society where slavery was a proxy for caste, and value, and worth. So, when you ended slavery (and slavery-like situations like sharecropping), you didn't end the presumptions about black inferiority" or Black people's social value being associated with how good (i.e., docile, diligent) of a slave they can be. "All those things carried on" unresolved in the culture.

Racial stigma is both a catalyst for and a specific type of race-based experience. Consequently, racial stigma can trigger what's known as "stigma stress." J.V. Schibalski et al. described as stigma stress as occurring "when perceived harm due to stigma exceeds one's perceived coping resources and is associated with emotional reactions such as shame and anxiety as well as broader outcomes like reduced self-esteem and hopelessness."

Carol Miller and Cheryl Kaiser confirmed that not only can "stigma be a source of chronic stress for stigmatized people," but "the core feature of stigma is that a stigmatized person has an attribute that conveys a devalued social identity within a particular context. Compared to other types of stressors, stigma may be especially stressful because it poses some unique demands on the individual. Although stigma is defined as a devalued social identity in a particular context, for many stigmatized people the context in which they are devalued is pervasive. People with physically obvious stigmas, such as members of devalued racial groups, face potential prejudice and discrimination across a broad range of social contexts. Some stigmatized attributes are so powerful in the reactions they engender that they are 'master status' attributes that become the core, identifying attribute of the person who possesses them. Thus, stigma can increase the quantity of stressors stigmatized individuals experience."

Furthermore, stigma is "linked to the individual's social identity. This feature of stigma can increase the potential for stress because unfair treatment or judgments can be triggered simply by group membership and thus have implications for collective as well as personal identity. Threats to collective identity are multifaceted. Seeing other group members suffer from unfairness due to stigma may result in vicarious stress responses. Other people's devaluation of the group may reduce the comfort and sense of belonging that group membership normally provides. Stigmatized people also may be pressured to be 'a credit' to their group or to otherwise represent their group to the nonstigmatized world. These stressors arise precisely because stigmatized people have a devalued social identity."

Racial stigma remains a chronically negative psychosocial experience responsible for a variety of aversive reactions from those subjected to it. Research shows that recurring experiences of racial stigma, either directly or vicariously, may cause shame, anxiety, anger, aggression, apathy, inequality, injustice, illness, despair, docility, self-handicapping behavior, stereotypic behavior, learned helplessness, and chronic stress.

For Black people, who we think we are (self-concept) and how we feel about who we think we are (self-esteem) is profoundly negated (i.e., made negative) by stigma. Negative views and stereotypes come to largely define who we are expected to be, characterize us as somehow negatively different, and frequently prevent us from being seen distinctively (i.e., as an individual[6]). Being Black in this country oftentimes comes with a persistent feeling of somehow being flawed and inadequate, or to quote Marilyn Sorenson, "of *being* something wrong." This feeling can become so fixed and normal that we lose awareness of its existence and stigmatic origins. "Nobody ever tells you it's something wrong with being Black," noted Ras Kass, "you just start feeling it."

Mitchell Weiss et al. described stigma as a "social process, experienced or anticipated, characterized by exclusion, rejection, blame, or devaluation that results from experience, perception, or

---

[6]   Anderson Franklin explained how this invisibility evolves, oftentimes unconsciously, when stigmatized individuals feel that "they live in a depersonalized context in which who they are as a genuine person, including their individual talents and unique abilities, is overshadowed by stereotyped attitudes and prejudice that others hold about them." The "invisibility" comes from individuals not being seen as distinct human beings, only one's stigma is acknowledged along with all the negative notions and assumptions that are attached to it. "Invisibility is considered a psychological experience wherein the person feels that his or her personal identity and ability are undermined by stigma in a myriad of interpersonal circumstances. Invisibility is defined as an inner struggle with the feeling that one's talents, abilities, personality, and worth are not valued or even recognized because of prejudice and stigma."

In other words, noted Frederic Poag, "when you're white in America you're given the freedom to be an individual without the connotations and limitations of your race. In short, you're just a person, instead of a black person. That's an important distinction, and it's one that people who aren't white desperately want to get rid of."

reasonable anticipation of an adverse social judgment about a person or group." For the stigmatized, who we think we are (self-concept) and how we feel about who we think we are (self-esteem) are profoundly negated (i.e., made negative) by this social process and resultant social judgment. Experiencing the exclusion, rejection, blame, and devaluation of stigma regularly prompts a persistent feeling of somehow being flawed and inadequate, or to quote Marilyn Sorenson, "of *being* something wrong." *That's* shame.

"Shame is the feeling of *being* something wrong. When a person experiences shame, they feel 'there is something basically wrong with me.'" Whenever we experience stigma, noted Goffman, "shame becomes a central possibility," if not a chronic stressor.

Shame explicitly targets the self-esteem. Shame evokes a fundamental sense of inadequacy along with a constant anxiety of our inadequacy being exposed by (or to) others. Shame is most readily activated by personal or collective association with a socially constructed "perception of a negatively evaluated difference," or what we call stigma.

Blackness in America has long been what Caroline Howarth refers to as an "embodied stigma." The stigma of Blackness is "marked on the body and embodied in ways of being seen, being treated, being feared as different. Race reduces the identity and the potential of those seen as 'raced': they are spoiled or blemished by the racist gaze. Those who are positioned as 'racial others'—those with black and brown skin—are seen as less than, different from, unequal to the racializing, normatively white, others. In this way, race invades the self as racialized expectations and stereotypes mark one's sense of self, one's own expectations, ambitions, and fears."

"For the most part," wrote Lenhardt, "racially stigmatized individuals have relatively few places where they can go and be assured of not being exposed to racist or racialized conduct or remarks. This reality may leave stigmatized individuals feeling

15

that they must be constantly 'on' and vigilant against racialized conduct."

"Part of the strength of the 'societal devaluations' associated with race in this country is that 'they cannot be dismissed as the ravings of some idiosyncratic bigot.' They are shared and consensual, which means that they cannot easily be ignored. This, perhaps even more than the precise character of the messages conveyed about race, is what makes racial stigma such a powerful social force."

Stigma creates a "hierarchical separation of human worth," explained Joe Pettit. "Stigma creates an 'Us vs. Them' sorting of human beings" that implies the inferior status, negative regard, displaced blame, and relative social powerlessness of members of the "them" group. Stigma enables the aforementioned negative outcomes associated with racial inequality to be "blamed either exclusively or primarily on the life choices of individual black people."

Stigma has such a profound impact on our self-concept and, consequently, self-esteem because stigma is a social construct directly indicative of how our social others see us (primarily negatively via our stigma). The existence of stigma implies that others in our society tend to see us as negatively different or possessing some negatively evaluated difference. Much of how we see ourselves originates from how we believe others see us and our typical interpersonal interactions in society (i.e., the looking-glass self). If how we believe others see us and our interpersonal interactions are largely tainted by stigma, then how we most likely see ourselves—and feel about what we see—will be correspondingly tainted. This is explicitly true whenever we are highly conscious of being stigmatized.

Stigma is not always promoted or perceived consciously. In fact, it's usually *not* consciously promoted or perceived. According to Sunyoung Hwang, "people differ in their experiences of stigmatization. Whereas some people do not allow a stigma to affect their experiences, others are constantly aware of, and therefore affected by, this stigma. The chronic awareness of one's stigmatized status is known as stigma consciousness." On a scale of 1 to 10 with 10 being really high, I'd roughly estimate my personal level of racial stigma consciousness at 138, which honestly isn't great. Not quite sure if this qualifies as one of those "it is what it is" moments...

"Stigma consciousness is not simply being aware of a stigma, as it is possible for a person to be aware of one's stigmatized status and not be affected by it. Rather, stigma consciousness describes a fixation on one's stigmatized status," or having a chronic awareness of *being something wrong*. People "high in stigma consciousness interpret interactions and experiences" and how (social) others see them "from a perspective that emphasizes their stigma." In other words, we are more vulnerable to experiencing race-based stress because we are more likely to perceive certain negative life experiences as race-based experiences.

People low in stigma consciousness are also, if not more so, vulnerable to the impact of stigma on our self-esteem, specifically our *implicit* self-esteem, or stigma as a chronic stressor. Our implicit self-esteem consists of our hidden or subconscious beliefs about who we are and how others see us along with how we feel about those beliefs. Our implicit self-esteem is symptomatic of the extent to which we automatically and absolutely consider ourselves to be adequate, competent, and valuable, perceptions that are all susceptible to negation by stigma regardless of our level of stigma consciousness.

Sabrina Zirkel wrote that most "stigmatized individuals are certainly aware of the negative stereotypes held about them. For some, the awareness of these negative stereotypes becomes a defining feature of how they perceive the world, and they become highly sensitive to race-based rejection or develop a strong stigma consciousness. The awareness of stigma and the everyday experiences of it remain a stressful and exhausting aspect of life for the stigmatized."

"Situations that evoke negative stereotypes are stressful." And this is exactly what stigma repeatedly does, constantly create interpersonal and institutional situations that evoke negative stereotypes. Stigma creates a unique "anxiety with which the stigmatized individual approaches interactions in society," explained Ilan Meyer. Stigmatized people "may perceive, usually quite correctly, that whatever others profess, they do not really 'accept' him and are not ready to make contact with him on 'equal grounds.'" Much of the chronic stress of being Black comes from the continuous anticipation of adverse stigma-influenced circumstances or experiences in our future.

To be Black in this country and relatively stigma conscious, is to most likely experience the stress of being Black almost all the time, (with a stigma consciousness score of 138) I *know* I do.

By the time American children are in kindergarten, noted by Sylvia Law, most are fairly aware of racial stigma, and, consequently, "both White and Black children attach positive value to Whiteness and negative value to Blackness." So, the first problem is figuring out how to control or cope with that stress so that it won't destroy us. I once read that the "stress of being Black," according to Steven Kniffley, "is literally killing us," which terrified me because I knew, deep down, that I still wasn't handling that stress strategically. Subsequently, I decided to write this book to help more of us understand just what the "stress of being Black is literally killing us" fundamentally means and how to survive it.

"A chronically stressed brain tends to reprogram itself and reinforce the behaviors responsible for the stress," concluded Nuno Sousa et al. Surviving the chronic stress of being Black in this country and experiencing contemporary racism requires intentionally rewiring those neural pathways in our brains previously reinforced by a lifetime of reacting recklessly. A different level of thinking is needed to end this terribly harmful cycle. Accordingly, the goal of this book is to provide an actionable, strategy-based approach to positively recognizing and responding to race-based and racism-related stress.

I wrote this book so more people could know that the stress they're dealing with and possibly being overwhelmed by is not unique to them or somehow indicative of their own individual weakness or inadequacy or insanity. There are so many of us going through this simultaneously just trying to survive it. We need to know that we're neither crazy nor alone and that we can all eventually be better in our response to the stress precipitated merely by the color of our skin.

I also wrote this book as a transparent, candid[7] account of my own life-long struggle to adequately cope with and heal from several life-threatening health issues directly and indirectly related to my experience with this specific, constant stress.

Being Black in America is typically experienced by Black people, myself included, as a chronic *stressor* starting in childhood, yet most of us are neither adequately familiar with this term nor equipped to minimize its impact on our well-being. Joseph Kaholokula et al. described a stressor as the "external circumstances that challenge the ordinary capacity of an individual or obstruct the individual from obtaining desired ends. Stress is the resulting internal state of arousal that occurs when our capacity to effectively deal with" (i.e., reduce, minimize, stop, or tolerate) the "stressor is taxed beyond our available resources."

In other words, a stressor is the stimulus (i.e., the actual or perceived threat) that causes stress. A stressor is basically anything (e.g., events, experiences, emotions, perceptions, or circumstances) that instigates stress (i.e., the stress response) once we are exposed to it. These events, experiences, emotions, etc. are perceived negatively as either physical (i.e., potential bodily harm) or psychosocial (i.e., damage to our self-concept, self-esteem, or social self[8]) threats to the individual.

---

[7]   And, to quote Khalil Gibran, "if indeed you must be candid, be candid beautifully."
[8]   Threats to our social self, observed Tara Gruenewald et al., feature "situations that contain the potential to devalue one's social self by calling into

19

The human brain, when faced with a real or imagined threat to our physical or psychosocial well-being, readies the human being to confront the threat or promptly get as far away (physically or psychosocially) from the threat as possible. Whether the threat is ultimately real or just imagined is irrelevant; it's the perception of threat that triggers the stress response. This "fight or flight" response is a reflexive reaction by our brain to rapidly provide our body with those resources (e.g., increases in the release of certain hormones and neurotransmitters to enhance pro-survival functioning) required for either resisting or running from a threat. Whether this threat is physical or psychosocial, the same brain responses to threat occur, and because they have become automatic (or hardwired due to past utility), these responses typically supersede critical thought or active choice for the sake of rapidity (and ensured survival).

Stress can be experienced as acute, chronic, or even traumatic. Acute (i.e., temporary or intermittent) stress doesn't kill us; it's actually good for us. The human brain is designed to recover quickly from acute stress. Moreover, explained Daniela Kaufer, acute stress is "good to push us just to the level of optimal alertness, behavioral and cognitive performance." Experiencing short-term stress "keeps the brain more alert, more attuned to the environment and to what actually is a threat or not a threat."

Unfortunately, the stress of being Black is *chronic* stress as opposed to acute stress. Chronic stress is stress resulting from repeated or constant exposure to circumstances and experiences perceived as threatening enough to trigger the stress response and the subsequent release of stress hormones, primarily cortisol, in the brain.

---

question abilities, competencies, or traits on which a positive social image is based, or situations characterized by potential or explicit rejection" or inequity. "Such situations are provocative because they contain social information pertinent to a primary human goal: that of achieving and maintaining a positive 'social self.'"

When repeatedly activated due to chronic stress, our stress response can evolve into a constant state of hypervigilance and hyperarousal. The neural circuitry and structures responsible for producing the stress response are altered to become the dominant areas of the chronically stressed individual's brain. Chronic stress, according to Machiko Matsumoto and Hiroko Togashi, changes the human brain by creating long-lasting negative "alterations in the neural circuits underlying emotional regulation and increase the subsequent reactivity to stress later in life." Consequently, negative emotional reactions (e.g., anxiety, anger, frustration, shame, hopelessness, helplessness) are easier to generate and harder to regulate.

Most importantly, chronic stress "over time, can cause damage that leads to premature death," noted Patricia Celan. Any type of stress causes the release of cortisol, a hormone designed to enable the brain to elevate blood sugar and pressure levels in order to enhance our ability to respond to danger. However, with chronic stress there is so much cortisol constantly being produced that it becomes toxic and creates a significantly higher risk of serious health issues including stroke, heart attack, diabetes, and cancer.

"Inflammation is partly regulated by the hormone cortisol and when cortisol is not allowed to serve this function, inflammation can get out of control." Chronic stress "alters the effectiveness of cortisol to regulate the inflammatory response because it decreases tissue sensitivity to the hormone. Specifically, immune cells become insensitive to cortisol's regulatory effect, and consequently, produce levels of inflammation that promote disease. The evidence is compelling and growing," wrote Camara Harrell et al., "that racism is pathogenic with respect to a variety of physical and mental health outcomes."

Generally, according to Sheldon Cohen et al., "stressful events are thought to influence the pathogenesis of physical disease by causing negative affective states (e.g., feelings of anxiety and depression), which in turn exert direct effects on biological processes or behavioral patterns that influence disease risk.

Exposures to chronic stress are considered the most toxic because they are most likely to result in long-term or permanent changes in the emotional, physiological, and behavioral responses that influence susceptibility to disease."

David Williams and Selina Mohammed realized that "for most of the 15 leading causes of death including heart disease, cancer, stroke, diabetes, kidney disease, and hypertension, African Americans have much higher death rates than Whites." Perhaps not at all coincidentally, a recent study led by Bruce McEwen and Teresa Seeman revealed that chronic stress increases our susceptibility to heart disease, cancer, stroke, diabetes, kidney disease, and hypertension. The logical conclusion: Black people in America are experiencing significantly more chronic stress than White Americans and disproportionately dying prematurely because of it.

Apparently, Kniffley was terribly accurate in concluding that the "stress of being Black is literally killing us." However, it doesn't have to *continue* killing us. We could live healthier, longer if we had less of this stress in our lives. That's why practicing proactive stress-reducing interventions and evidence-informed coping strategies is so important, as opposed to simply maintaining a victim mentality in which we choose tolerating over preventing our own demise.

The chronic stress of being Black in America features the recurrent stress of *race-based experiences* (or race-based stress).

"There are few advantages associated with being Black in America," noted Kathy Russell. And it's the constant, cumulative disadvantages associated with being Black that oftentimes spawn stressful race-based experiences (i.e., negative, uncontrollable things we experience as stressors primarily, but oftentimes ambiguously, because we are Black).

Robert Entman and Andrew Rojeck identified "a large difference in social status, economic resources, cultural influence, and political power between White Americans as a whole and Black Americans as a whole. Material conditions for African

22

Americans have undoubtedly improved since the major legal and political reforms in the 1960s. Yet racial identity remains an important component of social appraisal, and this continues to disadvantage Blacks while benefiting Whites."

Available statistical evidence, according to Richard Majors and Janet Billson, show a "clear disadvantage to being born Black in America: Black people have higher rates than White people of mental disorders, unemployment, poverty, injuries, accidents, infant mortality, morbidity, AIDS, homicide and suicide, drug and alcohol abuse, imprisonment, and criminality; we have poorer incomes, life expectancy, access to health care, and education."

These inequities and inequalities are largely rooted in local, state, and federal policies, regulations, and laws (along with enduring cultural messages and social norms) designed to efficiently maintain race-based social boundaries (see Richard Rothstein's *The Color of Law*).

Amos N. Wilson described how when we look at major American institutions relative to Black people, "we observe the following: the economic system keeps them poor; the criminal justice system mediates injustice; the educational establishment creates ignorance and intellectual incompetence; the family institution breeds broken homes and 'illegitimate' children; and the health and welfare system catalyzes sickness and administers health-care neglect (the lifespan of African-Americans is actually decreasing)."

Christopher Bracey detailed how "African-Americans with the same level of education as whites continue to earn substantially less. Blacks continue to occupy proportionally fewer managerial positions and proportionally greater service and unskilled labor positions. Median family income for African Americans is roughly two-thirds that of whites. Black youth continue to lag behind whites in performance on standardized tests for mathematics and reading comprehension. The percentage of African-American children under the age of eighteen who live in poverty is almost double that of whites. The same is true for the

23

number of births to unwed mothers. Homicide victimization rates for blacks are nearly double the rates for whites. Incarceration rates for black men are seven times those of white men. African-American adult men and women have a shorter life expectancy than their white counterparts; with black infant mortality rates approximately double those for whites."

"Each of us is perhaps familiar with one or two of these points of comparison, and it is easy to remain relatively unfazed by evidence of disparity in an isolated aspect of social life. Yet it is more difficult to remain unmoved when confronted by the totality of racial disparity presented here. The collected data create a mosaic image of a racial caste, and as such demand our full attention. It immediately calls into question banalities such as 'the civil rights era ended racial discrimination' or 'we live in a color-blind society.' More importantly, it gives force to the claim that nearly every aspect of our lives is mediated by race" and that it's highly doubtful Black people will ever be able to expect justice or gain full equality in this country, which can all be continuously stressful.

Yet, public perception and "policies tend to treat this racial inequality as a product of poor personal decision-making" or relative inferiority and incompetence on the part of Black people as a whole, observed Shuster, "rather than acknowledging it as the result of racialized systems and structures that restrict choice and limit opportunity."

There will never be an America in which being Black is no longer stigmatized or automatically disadvantageous as long as the racial (i.e., Black-White) wealth gap persists. This wealth gap, explained Derrick Hamilton, "is the most acute indicator of racial inequality. Regardless of age, household structure, education, occupation, or income, black households typically have less than a quarter of the wealth of otherwise comparable white households." This wealth gap is tangibly, terribly experienced by almost every Black people in America not only personally, but also as the ongoing, uncontrollable consequence of targeted, anti-Black social exclusion and structural inequality.

Undeniable racial disparities in inherited wealth, residential, educational, and, consequently, career and income *opportunities* perpetuate this intergenerational wealth gap. In America, explained Douglas Massey, "labor markets did not arise out of neutral institutional matrices that guaranteed equal opportunity to all; instead, they were embedded in a social structure that was itself riddled with categorical inequalities based on race and class." America remains "the most unequal society in the developed world" largely because it was inherently created to never provide equal opportunity, even when earned, to all Americans.

Opportunity inequity is currently based less on overt racism and more on certain systemic circumstances (e.g., an inherited wealth gap, targeted joblessness/labor obsolescence, corporate automation, corporate globalization, corporate suburbanization, residential segregation, imposed welfare dependency, educational inequity, implicit White privilege) that conspire to sustain certain social groups' distinct vulnerability to poverty. This group-based vulnerability typically trumps personal attributes and behavioral choices with regard to preventing Black wealth accumulation, which ultimately intensifies its perceived ambiguity, negativity, and uncontrollability as a stressful race-based experience.

The "configuration of both opportunities and barriers in workplaces, schools, and communities reinforce deeply entrenched racial dynamics in how wealth is accumulated," concluded Thomas Shapiro. "Due to the unearned advantages it transmits across generations, inheritance widens inequality." These advantages include the inevitability, according to Thomas Piketty, "that inheritance (of fortunes accumulated in the past) predominates over saving (wealth accumulated in the present). Wealth originating in the past automatically grows more rapidly, even without labor, than wealth stemming from work, which can be saved."

Wealth significantly determines an individual's life chances, yet African-Americans on average are five times less likely to inherit money than White Americans, White Americans' inheritances are ten times bigger, and, consequently, their familial wealth is about eight times that of ours. And while it's true that many among the contemporary affluent in America have amassed their impressive wealth via unprecedented opportunities in information technology, mass retail (including e-commerce), and finance, most of them (which excludes newly wealthy professional athletes and entertainers) still had direct access to significant intergenerational wealth for start-up capital. This reflects the sobering truth, to quote Shannon Moriarty, that Black people in America "have never had an equal opportunity to become wealthy."

"Wealth is a measure of cumulative advantage or disadvantage," explained Roderick Harrison. "The fact that black and Hispanic wealth is a fraction of white wealth also reflects a history of discrimination in which Whites have had more opportunities to accumulate wealth." Or as Dalton Conley recently phrased it, contemporary wealth reveals "the cumulative disadvantage of race for minorities or cumulative advantage of race for Whites," which originated during the American slavery era.

To reiterate, beyond being sad and regrettable, all these lived statistical realities are also chronically stressful for most Black folk. Experiencing them is oftentimes the way we begin tacitly feeling like it's something wrong with being Black.

Being Black in America, explained W.E.B. DuBois, "doesn't mean that some act of terror, brutality," exclusion, inequality, or injustice "has to be committed against us every day." Being Black "simply means that such an act 'can always occur' any day—it means never being out of danger" for no other reason than being Black.

As aforementioned, stress is the brain's reaction to any information from our external circumstances that reveal or imply threat, especially threat that we feel we don't have the capacity or resources to cope with. Accordingly, arguably the *most* stressful aspect of being Black is that Black life in America has obviously never been equally valued and, hence, is not equally *physically* protected (relative to White life). On any given day I can be killed because I'm Black and, because I'm Black, my family can't ever have a genuine expectation of assured safety for me or justice for my prospective killer. And this stress has been similarly felt by each and every generation of American deemed "Black."

In fact, it's simultaneously perplexing, embarrassing, and infuriating to ponder just how normalized the disproportionate murder of Black people has been throughout the history of this country—and continues to be. Or how historically whenever a White person (e.g., enslaver, slave patroller, Klan member, lynch mobber, race rioter, COINTELPRO agent, cop, civilian just "standing his ground," etc.) "kills an unarmed black person in America," noted Daniel Lathrop and Anna Flagg, "the killer often faces no legal consequences." Or how over the past decade, African-Americans are, on average, 3.5 times as likely as White Americans to be killed by a police officer. Police officers are rarely ever criminally charged for killing/murdering Black people, and in those rare cases that they are charged, a conviction is even rarer (despite repeatedly incriminating video evidence, conflicting accounts, the victim typically being unarmed, etc.). Or how for every year of the 21st century the rate of *intraracial* homicidal violence among Black people in America's ten largest cities has increased exponentially.

Intraracial homicidal violence among African-Americans (I refuse to use the malign misnomer "Black-on-Black violence"[9])

---

[9]   Even though the American media tends not to present it as such, over 90% of all homicidal violence is intraracial largely because homicide tends to be a crime of opportunity and proximity. In America, explained D. Amari Jackson, "more frequently than any other race of people, white people kill white people. As is customarily the case, white-on-white crime—murder, in particular—dominates federal statistics every year. Given this relatively small difference, and the consistent recognition that people victimize and murder those closest to

has gotten so common in recent decades that, according to Joshua Gillin et al., "some researchers say the single strongest predictor of gun homicide rates is the proportion of an area's population that is black." And as long as there is tangible inequity with regard to intergroup access to wealth, power, resources, and opportunity—in other words, as long as there is White privilege—many Black people exist within an imposed reality that fosters intense levels of stress, frustration, disappointment, underdevelopment, impulsivity, and aggression that oftentimes become an implicit catalyst for intraracial homicidal violence.

Although it never could or should justify the ridiculously high rate at which Black people kill other Black people at the most benign events and locales[10], systemic White privilege, according to

---

them both racially and residentially, it begs the question why so much attention has been paid to the issue of 'Black-on-Black crime.'"

"The term, Black-on-Black violence, comes from a sunken place," explained Paul Butler. "It is a way of pathologizing Black people and making it seem like we're different from everybody else. White people don't go around being afraid of other white people, yet they're afraid of Black men or 'thugs' when they are much more likely to be victimized by other white folks. But we don't have an expression called 'white on white crime.'" This definitely doesn't somehow excuse White-on-Black violence nor am I attempting to justify so-called Black-on-Black violence. The preventable death of Black people is wrong regardless of its perpetuator. "The lives of blacks killed by blacks are no less precious than those of blacks killed by whites," noted Stephen Carter.

[10] Most Black intraracial homicides occur "at neighborhood barbecues, family reunions, music festivals, basketball tournaments, movie theaters, housing project courtyards, Sweet 16 parties, and public parks," as reported by Sharon LaFraniere et al. "Where motives could be gleaned, roughly half involved or suggested crime or gang activity. Arguments that spun out of control accounted for most other shootings. About a third were provoked by arguments, typically drug- or alcohol-fueled, often over petty grievance."

Most of these arguments were not even "directly linked to criminal activity, such as a dispute over a drug deal. More often, a minor dust-up—a boast, an insult, a decision to play basketball on another gang's favorite court—was taken as a sign of disrespect and answered with a bullet" or social media evolved "minor disputes into deadly standoffs." None of which, at first glance, seems symptomatic of frustrated Black people merely reacting to racial inequality and domination.

Wilson, "by its very nature and intent requires the continuing oppression and subordination of Black people and, in time, may require their very lives. Subordination of a people requires that that people in some way or ways be violated, dehumanized, humiliated, and that some type of violence be perpetrated against them. The violently oppressed react violently to their oppression. When their reactionary violence, their retaliatory or defensive violence, cannot be effectively directed at their oppressors or effectively applied to their self-liberation, it then will be directed at and applied destructively to themselves."

People of all races and ethnicities die every day, but in America there's something terrifyingly *normalized* (i.e., made normal, natural, orderly, routine, typical, predictable, unexceptional, allowable, tolerable) about the disproportionate killing of Black people. The normalization of our slaughter seems to somehow echo the invisibility[11] imposed on our lives primarily for being Black.

There's been a persistent inequity with regard to the protection of Black versus White life implied by the inequality of consequence and public outcry for taking it. Accordingly, there's

---

[11] According to Anderson J. Franklin, many African-Americans experience an invisibility syndrome that evolves, oftentimes subconsciously, as we begin to feel that we "live in a racialized or depersonalized context in which who we are as a genuine person, including our individual talents and unique abilities, is overshadowed by stereotyped attitudes and prejudice that others hold about us." The "invisibility" comes from individual Black people not being seen as distinct human beings, only or primarily our Blackness is acknowledged along with all the racially stigmatic notions and expectations that are attached to it.

"Invisibility is considered a psychological experience wherein the person feels that his or her personal identity and ability are undermined by racism in a myriad of interpersonal circumstances. Invisibility is defined as an inner struggle with the feeling that one's talents, abilities, personality, and worth are not valued or even recognized because of prejudice and stigma, particularly in cross-racial circumstances. The negative meanings associated with race operate to obscure actual identity and promote inherent stress" that generally becomes chronic. This chronic stress has been common among African-Americans for generations and remains just as impactful.

29

never been an adequate level of dread associated with the intention of killing Black people, which if adequate may have prevented this intention from being actualized far too often. African-American lives—our physical and social existence—have long been treated as relatively valueless, disposable, nonessential, obsolete, unnecessary, *removable* as evident by the consistent impunity (relative or literal) and tolerance (apparent or actual) associated with the killing of Black people in America.

An impunity and tolerance so consistent that—although it oftentimes remains unexpressed—Black people in America exceedingly have an evolved, evidence-based expectation of untimely, unwarranted, and unpunished death. An expectation aggravated by what can no longer be an actually surprising conclusion: Black lives *matter* (i.e., are valued) comparatively little here (oftentimes, even to other Black people).

As the world knows, Ahmaud Arbery, Breonna Taylor, George Floyd, and Rayshard Brooks were all unnecessarily murdered during the writing of this book and, if we're being honest with ourselves, there is no expectation of adequate consequences or convictions for their murderers. And this is in spite of the horrifying viral videos and voice recordings, ambiguously anti-racism social media statements from various celebrities and corporate entities, aggregate weeks of popular interracial protests around the world, abolishment of various explicitly racist public artifacts, as well as subtle pro-status quo acts of micro-defiance mostly from various groups of White people.

I know now that I have never experienced an *expectation* of normalized racial equality, fairness, or justice (or the prerequisite end of racial stigma) and, if social inertia[12] is a legitimate phenomenon, and I believe it is, neither will my son or your children. Individual instances of racial justice currently seem rare, unusual, unintentional, surprising, abnormal, which would suggest

---

[12]   Social inertia is the natural tendency of societies or social groups to resist significant change, especially to its status quo; social inertia can be described as the opposite of social change.

that there is no such thing as coincidental racial justice—a society is either characteristically just or unjust. Consequently, there is a far more consistent expectation of injustice for us than justice for all.

There remain "important signs of continued White resistance to full equality of Black Americans," observed Gerald Jaynes and Robin Williams. "Despite improvements in various aspects of American life, racial stratification has not changed in any fundamental sense" because of this resistance and Black people's lack of adequate social power. According to Moss and Reed, "white Americans can hold egalitarian general racial attitudes at the same time as they disapprove or oppose policies that seek to operationalize equality."

Much of this resistance and apparent impotence is rooted in who Black people in this country are erroneously yet fundamentally understood to be.

Originating in slavery, the Black image in the White mind has generally remained a compilation of dehumanizing stereotypes largely associated with negativity, violence, stupidity, docility, and inferiority. And, to quote Donald Kinder and Lynn Sanders, "Whites' attitudes are powerfully influenced by their mental images of Blacks," whether they are conscious of them are not. Because America remains such a racialized society, Black folks are constantly vulnerable to internalizing the "racist stereotypes, values, images, and ideologies perpetuated by the White dominant society" about us, noted Karen Pyke, unconsciously triggering profound "feelings of self-doubt, disgust, and disrespect" and an implied belief in our own inferiority.

Michael Omi and Howard Winant asserted that "the presence of a system of racial meanings and stereotypes, of racial ideology, seems to be a permanent feature of U.S. culture." While "no presumption of inferiority attaches to whiteness in our culture," as noted by Lenhardt, it has long been normative American behavior to believe that "innate inferiority correlates with dark skin color." Although now it's hardly ever displayed publicly or spoken aloud,

31

it's constantly implied in microaggressive interpersonal interactions, consistent race-based injustices, and stubborn institutional inequities that in America, wrote James Baldwin, "being Black is a terrible thing to be."

Accordingly, life stress for Black people "must also include consideration of experiences that are related to the unique person-environment transactions involving race." A type of chronic stress is typically sustained "when one perceives that the racial group with which they identify is generally not treated fairly," concluded Shelly Harrell.

Because daily events, experiences, and "social situations in the United States are often tinged with race" and racial stigma, explained Evangeline Wheeler et al., "Blacks in the Unites States are more likely to engage in cognitive appraisal of racism," and are thus more likely to feel this chronic stress. It's difficult for Black people to completely deny or avoid the stressful significance of race in our daily lives (even if and when we want to). And simply acknowledging the significance of race (i.e., the stigma and disadvantages of being Black) in our daily lives (even when we're not conscious of doing so) can constantly trigger a stress response.

Just being Black in America makes us uniquely, highly, and constantly vulnerable to experiencing *race-based stress*. And we don't necessarily need to experience some form of racism in order to experience race-based stress; merely *being Black* is enough.

Carter described stress as "an emotional, physical, and behavioral response to an event(s) that is appraised as negative or unwanted. The initial appraisal is followed by a secondary assessment that is focused on action to cope and adapt to the event. If coping or adaptation fails, stress reactions intensify."

Accordingly, race-based stress describes a particular response to personally relevant encounters, events, evaluations, expectations, and experiences most likely to be negative and/or negating (i.e., dangerous, difficult, dehumanizing, or disappointing) primarily, but oftentimes ambiguously, because we are Black in America. Our response typically lacks the resources and capacity to effectively deal with (i.e., reduce, minimize, stop, or tolerate) the negativity and/or negation caused by these race-based encounters, events, evaluations, expectations, or experiences, which makes it stressful.

Race-based stress, noted Leonard Pearlin, should be understood as a "product of identifiable social conditions and threatening circumstances shared by large numbers of people possessing similar social attributes and not simply as a result of randomly occurring circumstances."

Race-based stress is caused by *race-based experiences*, which for Black people in America can occur at any time on any given day because we currently lack the individual and collective capacity and resources to stop the stigma and disadvantages of being Black in America.

Inherently negative, race-based experiences "may be severe or moderate, daily slights or microaggressions that can produce" physical or, most likely, psychosocial harm immediately or "when they have memorable impact or lasting effect or through cumulative or chronic exposure" to the stigma and various disadvantages of being Black in this country. "The most severe forms may not be physical attacks, but rather more subtle acts. The severity of a race-based experience should be determined by the strength and intensity of the person's reaction and the symptom cluster that emerges."

Because many aspects of *being raced* (i.e., made into and seen/treated as the "racial other") can "occur throughout one's life, severity may be a consequence of the cumulative effects of numerous experiences. For example, one seemingly innocuous or minor event could be the last straw in a series of accumulated racial incidents," causing us to consciously or implicitly feel that we can no longer manage the negative emotions of race-based experiences. The cumulative stress of a lifetime of race-based experiences tends to cause "psychological harm, such as depression, anxiety and feelings of powerlessness and worthlessness."

America's pervasive, normalized *anti-Blackness* fundamentally motivates these race-based experiences, and as long as it exists, these experiences will continue to be a chronic stressor to Black people.

In this sense, to be "anti-Black" is to somehow be intrinsically, yet also possibly unconsciously and/or subtly, opposed or hostile to Black people as a whole. Anti-Blackness features automatically perceiving Black people negatively or in opposition to, as "racial others." Loury recognized that anti-Blackness and this "profound awareness of the racial 'otherness' of Black people" has been "deeply ingrained in the American cultural consciousness"—an "otherness" that keeps in mind a plethora of negative characteristics and suspicions shared by or applicable to all Black people that collectively makes us who we are, at least supposedly.

Lawrence Bobo noted that contemporary anti-Blackness involves persistent, but not necessarily conscious, "negative stereotyping of Black Americans, a tendency to blame Blacks themselves for the Black-White gap in socioeconomic standing," an underlying antagonism and aggressiveness oftentimes subtly acted out interpersonally against Black people, along with rationalized collective "resistance to meaningful policy efforts to ameliorate America's racist social conditions and practices, with the latter views substantially rooted in perceptions of threat[13] and the protection of collective group privileges."

I have experienced directly and vicariously far too many unwarranted and undeserved instances of anti-Blackness; you probably have as well. It's not that I, and presumably most Black people, actively seek White favor, acceptance, or approval (although some of us do and will believe or do appalling things to

---

[13] According to Feagin, "central to all White concerns is a fear Whites have of losing status and power because of Black attempts to bring change." This specific fear sustains, largely subconsciously, "White resistance to substantial changes in the racial status quo," which itself is somehow justified by being at least implicitly anti-Black.

34

get it). But when we encounter White people in a variety of contemporary settings, too often we are unnecessarily confronted with their negative or negating beliefs about our differences, abilities, values, and intentions. Not sure if I have a choice in the matter, but I never wanted to be their enemy. That's what anti-Blackness feels like—like unwillingly being made an enemy[14].

"Racial barriers persist today," noted Feagin, "because a substantial majority of whites harbor anti-black sentiments, images, and beliefs and because a large minority are very negative in their perspectives. When most whites interact with black Americans at work, in restaurants, on the street, at school, or in the media they tend to think of the latter, either consciously or unconsciously, in terms of racist stereotypes inherited from the past and constantly reiterated and reinforced in the present."

Kihana Ross described anti-Blackness as the "inability to recognize black humanity." It captures the reality that the kind of physical, psychological, political, and economic violence that generally "saturates black life is not based on any specific thing a black person—better described as 'a person who has been racialized black'—did. The violence we experience isn't tied to any particular transgression. It's gratuitous and unrelenting."

Anti-blackness covers the fact that America's "hatred of blackness, and also its gratuitous violence against black people, is complicated by its need for our existence. For example, for white

---

[14]   Realistic conflict theory argues that people from unjustly privileged groups oftentimes feel that their privilege is being threatened by disadvantaged others. As a result, they become inclined to protect their privilege while developing hostility towards those they believe are threatening it. This threat, which is typically more imagined than factual, becomes perceived as a competition for scarce resources. This competition incites intergroup hostility as the threatened group becomes more convinced of a *zero-sum game*, in which because these resources are (erroneously) believed to be so scarce, only one group can possess them and the other cannot. Social boundaries are maintained by the privileged group to restrict or repress the perceived source of competition and sustain their position of advantage. Stigma against the disadvantaged others is then used to justify the hostility, social boundaries, and constant perception of threat.

people—again, better described as those who have been racialized white—the abject inhumanity of the black reinforces their whiteness, their humanness, their power, and their privilege, whether they're aware of it or not. Black people are at once despised and also a useful counterpoint for others to measure their humanness against. In other words, while one may experience numerous compounding disadvantages, at least they're not black."

Anti-Black attitudes and actions "persist in a climate of constant denial," observed Peggy Davis. "The denial and the persistence are related. It is difficult to change an attitude that is unacknowledged." While most would concede that anti-Blackness and its definitive dehumanization and delegitimization[15] of Black people existed history, too many cannot (or refuse to) see the continuation of anti-Blackness currently, but it certainly has continued.

When many Whites are made aware of their behavior, they tend to "deny that they intended to offend, believe the person of color raising the issue is 'oversensitive,' 'paranoid,' or has simply misinterpreted the situation." Even when acknowledging their unintentional (and usually habitual) anti-Blackness, offenders (oftentimes impulsively seeking self-defense) are more likely to trivialize, exceptionalize, or rationalize than adequately problematize it.

To *problematize*, by definition, is to make some thing or situation into (or begin to regard it as) a problem *requiring* a solution or end. Anti-Blackness has never been adequately made into something *requiring* a solution. Anti-Blackness is absolutely

---

[15] Delegitimization, explained Daniel Bar-Tal and Phillip Hammack, "naturalizes and rationalizes the nature of relations between the delegitimized and delegitimizing groups and the aggressive behaviors that the delegitimizing group is performing in this relationship. In the context of conflict, delegitimization provides justification for individuals and for the social system as a whole to intentionally harm the rival, and for continuing to institutionalize aggression toward the enemy. By providing moral justification for dominance, defense, or prevention, delegitimization operates to fulfill larger political goals related to exclusion."

problematic, but publicly and even personally it's never really *felt* problematic. It feels far too normal and, consequently, unemotional—and somehow even justified.

Sometimes a negative situation is not looked at as a problem because the onlookers can't yet see any potential for resolution (i.e., in the action of solving a problem). A lack of optimism distorts their perception of the situation and, most importantly, its causes. Oftentimes a tendency is developed to think about the situation's causes in a way that eventually encourages powerlessness. The inadequacy and irrelevance of any effort towards resolution are anticipated; a pointlessness evolves in merely identifying a situation now perceived as immutable as a problem (the accuracy of this perception notwithstanding).

That's how something that should be problematic becomes normalized (i.e., made normal, natural, orderly, routine, typical, predictable, unexceptional, allowable, tolerable)—even among the people most negatively impacted by it.

Please note that the stress of being Black in America doesn't require some act of anti-Blackness having to be committed against us every day. The stress of being Black in America means *always* having to prioritize being physically and psychologically prepared to survive anti-Black actions by anybody. It means that such an action can always occur—it means never being confidently out of danger. This feeling of "never being out of danger" can become a distinct, chronic stressor for Black people.

Regardless of how conscious of it we ever become, living with this constant threat of anti-Blackness has uniquely and profoundly changed how Black people in America learn, perceive, plan, problematize, problem solve, rationalize, emote, act, interact, react, overreact, remember, repress, rebel, internalize, fear, doubt, acquiesce, evaluate ourselves, and all things in between.

Race-based experiences occur because of our cultural and cognitive understanding of *race*, which "in America, is fundamentally a white-black issue," explained Michael Adams.

37

"Most Americans still believe in the traditional concept of race as a biological fact the way they believe in the law of gravity," wrote Joseph Graves. "They believe in it without even knowing what it is they believe in." According to Bernard Whitley and Mary Kite, race is one of the "primary categories for organizing information about other people, making it likely to be the first piece of information people take in about another." Neuroscientific research has revealed that we can identify another person's apparent race in less time than a blink of an eye, and with this cognitive transaction, "a complex network of stereotypes, emotional prejudices, and behavioral impulses" strengthened over a lifetime are automatically activated. The emotion-driven amygdala is particularly active in interracial situations. Consequently, humans don't perceive all other humans the same; race (still) matters.

However, it is important to remember that "*race* is a social category, not a biological one." For example, "genetic studies find more differences within traditionally defined racial groups than between them. In statistical terms, the differences between races that do exist are trivial relative to the genetic factors common to all people." However, "its social nature does not diminish the psychological importance of race. It remains a fundamental basis for how people think about and interact with each other."

Desmond and Emirbayer described race as a social fabrication, "a symbolic category based on phenotype or ancestry and constructed according to specific social and historical contexts, that is misrecognized as a natural category." Naturalization is when "something created by humans is mistaken as something dictated by nature. Racial categories are naturalized when these symbolic groupings—the products of specific historical contexts—are wrongly conceived as natural and unchangeable. We misrecognize race as natural when we begin to think that racial cleavages and inequalities can be explained by pointing to attributes somehow inherent in the race itself (as if they were biological) instead of understanding how social powers, economic forces, political institutions, and cultural practices have brought about these divisions."

Race is used to maintain functional, hierarchal distinctions between "us" and "them." Rita Kohli et al. described race as a "socially constructed and fluid measure of phenotype" that has historically been utilized by Whites to "differentiate themselves from the 'Other.' Race is used to include and exclude specific groups from equal participation, resources, and opportunity in U.S. society."

This understanding of race and the racial otherness of Black people has become profoundly hardwired in the collective brain of this nation. Nora Hyland wrote that "the construction of racial categories has played a fundamental role in American history, and Whiteness developed in relationship to particular political and economic forces as a way to create an ingroup. The construction of an ingroup, or dominant group, necessitates the construction of one or more subordinate outgroups which have been configured in different ways throughout history but have always included people of African descent. Therefore, Whiteness is intimately linked to the subordination and oppression of people of color." Consequently, it has become quite difficult for most Americans to genuinely aspire to or confidently anticipate any kind of racial coexistence beyond the master-slave situation that has existed historically. Sad, ain't it? It's also stressful.

So, "instead of being some remnant from the past, the social hierarchy based on race is a critical component in the organization of modern American society." David Wellman wrote that "subordination because of the color of one's skin is a primary determinant of people's position in the social structure. Racism is the structural relationship based on the subordination of one racial group by another. Given this perspective, the determining feature of race relations is not overt prejudice towards blacks, but rather the superior position of whites and the institutions—ideological as well as structural—which maintain it." All of this forms the foundation of race-based stress.

Experiences in which a goal that matters to us is at stake—such as efficacy, equity, or survival—and the disadvantages or demands of the experience outweigh our apparent capacity or resources for coping with it can trigger the stress response. For too many Black people, these stressful experiences are oftentimes race-based (i.e., because we are Black).

The more our brain responds to these race-based experiences by repeatedly activating the stress response, the more of a stimulus-reinforcement association is established. These associations are patterned neuronal activity in which certain emotions (or even thoughts) are paired with specific external stimuli (e.g., race-based experiences) in order to increases the probability of a specific response (e.g., stress). Patterned neuronal activity changes the neural structure and functioning of the brain; thus, stimulus-reinforcement associations are in effect consequences of maladaptive *neuroplasticity*.[16]

The more we employ the stress response, the more hyperactive it (along with the neural structures and pathways associated with it, e.g., the amygdala) becomes until we find ourselves constantly hypervigilant to race-based experiences. In other words, the more

---

[16] "The human brain can change itself. Nature has given us a brain that survives in a changing world by changing itself," noted Norman Doidge. Neuroplasticity—also known as brain plasticity, neuronal plasticity, cerebral plasticity, cortical remapping, or cortical plasticity—is "the property of the brain that enables it to change its own structure and functioning in response to activity and mental experience." Chronic experiences, especially those that are highly emotional, are most likely to produce lasting brain changes.

Neuroplasticity is possible because of the capacity of neurons to extend and create connections between brain regions and structures in order to facilitate efficient recall of past experiences along with reflexive instigation of a response. Recurring cognitive, emotional, and behavioral responses become patterned neuronal activity that can cause us to begin responding to the circumstances of our lives habitually based on these (re)established neural activation patterns (i.e., brain changes). Maladaptive neuroplasticity are those brain changes that somehow instigate negative outcomes (e.g., diminished ability to regulate negative emotions and impulsivity, chronic hypervigilance, weakened capacity to regulate the inflammatory response, etc.).

we experience race-based stress, the more our brain changes to continue to experience race-based experiences as stressors. Race-based stress can become a catalyst for significant negative brain plasticity.

Most people underestimate the validity or gravity of stress. "Stress is real," explained Eric Jensen. It's the brain's cognitive, emotional, and behavioral reaction to actual or anticipated threats to our personal (i.e., physical or psychological) or social integrity and the fear of not having the capacity or resources to effectively respond to or survive these threats.

Even while enduring it, most Black people are either not adequately familiar with or underestimate the validity or gravity of race-based stress. Race-based stress is real. It's our brain's reaction to the constant threat of race-based experiences and the fear of not having the capacity or resources to effectively respond to or survive it.

A stressor is basically something (e.g., race-based experiences) that instigates the stress response once we are exposed to it. In even nerdier neuroscientific terms, a stressor is any circumstance that threatens human homeostasis. For arguably the nerdiest description of a stressor, I turn to the originator of the term Hans Selye, who proposed that physical and "psychosocial stressors are defined principally by cognitive or affective components and reflect an anticipation of a looming challenge to homeostasis."

New key term here: *homeostasis*. Homeostasis, as I have come to understand it, is a regulatory process by which humans (and living things in general) sustain the relative internal stability (i.e., optimal functioning of all internal systems) necessary for survival while concurrently responding to adverse and/or altering external stimuli. Stressors, by definition, are adverse and/or altering external stimuli that disrupt homeostasis. Stressors are anything that interrupts the relatively balanced functioning of the brain. The survival-oriented human brain is designed to maintain a state of homeostasis. Stress disturbs homeostasis as the stressor is

41

dealt with. Chronic stress makes homeostasis virtually impossible (and *allostasis* potentially devastating).

Allostasis (or next new key term) is the reactionary process by which the human brain automatically compensates for stressful environmental or external stimuli (e.g., race-based experiences) in order to reestablish relative internal stability (i.e., homeostasis). While stress disrupts homeostasis, allostasis attempts to restore it. However, this attempt at restoring stability requires change (i.e., neuroplasticity).

Bruce McEwen and Peter Gianaros acknowledged that "the brain determines what is threatening, and hence stressful, to the individual; regulates the physiological, behavioral, cognitive, and emotional responses that an individual will deploy in order to cope with a given stressor via dynamic and plastic neural circuitry; and changes in its plasticity both adaptively and maladaptively as a result of coping with stressful experiences."

Allostasis is the process of attaining the relative internal stability (i.e., homeostasis) required for survival through physiological, behavioral, cognitive, emotional, and/or brain changes. According to David Borsook et al., "the brain responds to potential and actual stressful events by activating hormonal and neural mediators and modifying behaviors to adapt. Such responses help maintain physiological stability (allostasis). When behavioral or physiological stressors are frequent and/or severe, allostatic responses can become dysregulated and maladaptive (allostatic load). Allostatic load may alter brain networks both functionally and structurally. As a result, the brain's responses to continued/subsequent stressors are abnormal, and behavior and systemic physiology are altered in ways that can, in a vicious cycle, lead to further allostatic load."

Oftentimes a psychosocial stressor, in order to be sufficiently alleviated (and allostasis achieved), requires a coping response that is beyond what we are currently capable of generating. This is particularly true when the stressor is ambiguously negative, unpredictable, chronic, and uncontrollable (race-based experiences typically feature these characteristics); the stress it produces is actually aggravated.

Whenever we're not capable of coping effectively with certain stressors and cannot accomplish allostasis, the consequence is a cumulative effect known as *allostatic load*. With allostatic load, instead of achieving relative internal stability, especially with regard to emotional regulation, overutilization of the stress response (and oversaturation of neural structures and circuitry by stress hormones, especially cortisol) is *normalized* as patterned neuronal activity.

Our survival-oriented brain somehow becomes convinced that constantly being stressed is necessary for survival. Eventually, constantly being stressed (i.e., overactivation of the stress response) can lead to an enduring inability to achieve homeostasis because the brain becomes stuck in perpetual allostasis. Allostatic load (or overload) is the neuroplastic result of our brain's chronic exposure to an exaggerated neural response due to continuous stress and allostasis. Neural pathways and structures (e.g., prefrontal cortex, hippocampus, and amygdala) are maladaptively changed as the brain is burdened by being constantly forced to adapt to abnormally recurrent adverse physical or psychosocial situations.

Javier Gilabert-Juan et al. asserted that chronic "aversive experiences, such as stress, can induce neuronal structural and functional plasticity" as a "neuroprotective mechanism." In other words, chronic stress compels the brain to change in an attempt to preserve relatively normal neuronal structure and/or functioning (i.e., achieve homeostasis via allostasis). However, if these experiences and subsequent changes are too prolonged it makes returning to *normal* much more difficult. A new normal is established that may not provide adequate or appropriate adjustment to past experiences and may promote increased vulnerability to comparable experiences in the future.

For instance, when functioning properly (i.e., without the burden of chronic stress), the amygdala directs incoming emotional information to the prefrontal cortex (or PFC) where it is logically evaluated for response or repression. The primary functions of the highly plastic PFC are the regulation of emotional behavior and the processing of external information in order to decide reasonable cognitive, behavioral, and emotional responses to the information. However, the altered neural circuitry of a chronically stressed or anxious amygdala experiencing allostatic load blocks the flow of information to the PFC. Instead, the amygdala's function is modified to now include the processing of external information in order to decide cognitive, behavioral, and emotional responses to the information (in lieu of the PFC).

This is particularly maladaptive considering how inherently irrational any decisions led by the emotion-based amygdala must be. This functional change inevitably limits most cognitive, behavioral, and emotional responses to incoming emotional information—especially negative emotional information—to the repeated activation of the stress response, which only aggravates the cumulative impact of additional stress on allostatic load.

I'd be remiss if I failed to emphasize that certain Black people constantly exposed to the possible stress of race-based experiences can adapt appropriately and cope effectively. Our response to race-based stressors is not monolithic. Some of us can somehow prevent or reduce the maladaptive neuroplasticity described above. We (or more specifically, our brains) are exceptional, but only because we are informed and intentional in our response to race-based experiences. More often than not, Black people exposed to the chronic stress of race-based experiences endure lasting adverse brain changes, but only because too many of us are uninformed and, consequently, can't be intentional in our response. Hopefully, this book can help change that.

Race-based stress, specifically the stress associated with the lived psychosocial experience of being Black in America, is a type of *minority stress*.

Minority stress, according to Meyer, "describes the chronically high levels of psychosocial stress faced by members of stigmatized minority groups as a result of their social position" and "sociocultural stigmatization and discrimination." Minority stress is generated by "stigma, prejudice, and discrimination" combining to "create a hostile and stressful social environment."

Minority stress is "(a) unique—that is, minority stress is additive to general stressors that are experienced by all people, and therefore, stigmatized people are required an adaptation effort above that required of similar others who are not stigmatized; (b) chronic—that is, minority stress is related to relatively stable underlying social and cultural structures such as racism, ableism, sexism, and heterosexism; and (c) socially based—that is, it is not produced solely from interpersonal interaction with members of dominant social groups. It stems from social processes, institutions, and structures beyond the individual rather than individual events or conditions that characterize general stressors or biological, genetic, or other nonsocial characteristics of the person or the group."

Aggravating the impact of minority stress is the fact that, as reported by Kelly McGonigal, "minority stress relates to something that is unchangeable—some aspect of the self, like race, gender identity, or sexual orientation—that is essential to who you are." And because the "source" of this stress (e.g., being Black, race-based experiences) is essentially unchangeable, our brain's stress response becomes fixed and ultimately maladaptive.

"The human stress response is designed to help us survive emergencies, fix solvable problems, or navigate temporary social circumstances. It focuses our attention and floods us with energy, but in a way that is not sustainable as a default way of functioning. So, when the source of stress is related to something we do not want to 'fix' (ourselves), is pervasive rather than occasional (e.g., living or working in a place where you experience stigma), or is unlikely to change in the short-term (e.g., society's perspective), our brain's usual ways of responding to stress is unlikely to be helpful. It may motivate us to try to change the world," but it's more likely to merely cause chronic stress. And unfortunately, of all the forms of chronic psychosocial stress, "stress related to the 'self' and related to social status/belonging seems to have the largest consequences on our well-being" as well as the intensity of stress-related neuroplasticity.

Minority stress (and, consequently, race-based stress) is a specific form of *social stress*. Meyer explained that social stress "extends the concept of stress to elements of the social environment which act as stressors and force individuals to adapt to new conditions." Social stress stems from problematic relationships and interactions with social others or from a hierarchical, highly stigmatized societal structure (and low social ingroup status within that structure). Most of the modern-day "threats" our brains are responding to (with stress) are social (versus the physical threats common to earlier humanity).

Social stress is the probably the most subtly pervasive, everyday stressor. The redundancy of social stress makes its cumulative impact far more intense than other types of stressors. According to David Almeida, "although daily stressors may be unpredictable, more often they arise out of the routine circumstances of everyday life. Major life events may be associated with prolonged physiological arousal, whereas daily hassles may be associated with spikes in arousal or psychological distress confined to a single day. Yet minor daily stressors affect well-being not only by having separate, immediate, and direct effects on emotional and physical functioning, but also by piling up over time to create persistent irritations, frustrations, and overloads that may result in more serious stress reactions such as anxiety and helplessness."

Race-based stress is also, even more specifically, a *psychosocial stressor*. Psychosocial stressors are those circumstances or experiences that generate an ominous cognitive appraisal (i.e., we believe there's a threat) in which what's apparently at stake in terms of socioeconomic status, self-esteem, or ingroup valuation is greater than what the individual can do anything about or adequately cope with. These types of circumstances or experiences tend to be consistent (and individually uncontrollable), which makes psychosocial stress typically a chronic (and oftentimes traumatic) from of stress.

Race-based stress is a unique type of psychosocial stress where one's membership in a highly stigmatized racial outgroup exists in perpetual conflict with a social environment that systemically favors the privileged racial ingroup. It features chronic distal and proximal stressors.

Distal stressors are external, inclusive of interracial social experiences such as avoidance, rejection, segregation, bias, inequality, injustice, and discrimination.

Oftentimes the consequence of our reaction to distal stressors, proximal stressors are internal. Race-based proximal stressors include constant hypervigilance, anticipation, anxiety, and learned helplessness with regard to the aforementioned interracial social experiences along with an overall negative evaluation of our racial ingroup (and internalization of that evaluation). These consequences and reactions are emotionally and cognitively taxing and, ultimately, chronically stressful.

Stress is the brain's reaction to any information from our external circumstances that reveal or imply threat, especially threat that we feel we don't have the capacity or resources to cope with. The stress response is also referred to as the "fight or flight" response because it effectively prepares us to either fight or flee from this implied threat. Carter recognized that stress increases if an experience is "ambiguous, negative, unpredictable, and uncontrollable."

The perpetual implicit burden of being Black in America typically prompts chronic, brain changing race-based stress. The human brain, explained Jensen, is "designed by nature to reflect its environment, not to 'automatically' rise above it." According to various studies, most Black people repeatedly experience or anticipate race-based experiences that White people in this country "never have to confront, and our brains have adapted to suboptimal

47

conditions. Each stressor builds on and exacerbates other stressors and slowly changes the brain."

The lived and social experience of race in America, to cite Brian Smedley et al., still "influences how people are treated, what resources and jobs are available to them, where they are likely to live, how they perceive the world, what environmental exposures they face, and what chances they have to reach their full potential. Educational, housing and wealth-accumulating opportunities have been shaped by a long history of racism that continues to confer socioeconomic advantage to some groups while disadvantaging others. Segregation and social isolation, the cumulative impact of everyday discrimination on chronic stress levels, the degree of hope and optimism people have" are all significantly racially determined.

Because being Black in America is generally perceived as something ambiguously, unpredictably, uncontrollably, and oftentimes overwhelmingly negative, largely due to racial stigma, simply being Black is oftentimes experienced as a chronic stressor in our daily lives. Moreover, being Black in America involves the continuous perception of threat (i.e., being physically or psychologically threatened by race-based experiences or being perceived as a threat because of racial stigma or White privilege).

The negative perception and experiences associated with being Black are partly consequences of being socioculturally "raced" (i.e., made into and seen/treated as the racial other). "Race reduces the identity and the potential of those seen as 'raced,'" observed Howarth. "They are spoiled or blemished by the racist gaze. Those who are positioned as 'racial others'—those with black and brown skin—are seen as less than, different from, unequal to the racializing, normatively white, others. In this way race invades the self as racialized expectations and stereotypes mark one's sense of self, one's own expectations, ambitions and fears."

Conversely, being White, according to Henry Giroux, is "unquestioningly seen as the human norm, and race is something applied to non-white peoples. In other words, people whose skin is not White are members of a race, Whites are just people, and there is no position more powerful than that of being 'just people.'"

White people in America, explained Allan Johnson, "have the privilege of being able to assume acceptance as 'normal' members of society…living in a world full of cultural images that confer a sense of legitimacy and social desirability." Nia Addy noted that the "assumption that whiteness is the norm creates an automatic classification of 'otherness' and confers a sense of racial dominance and superiority. This dominant position affords white people numerous unearned privileges and advantages that, for the most part, are so ingrained in white culture that they are virtually invisible to and unfelt by those who benefit from them."

Frederic Poag agreed that "when you're white in America you're given the freedom to be an individual without the connotations and limitations of your race. In short, you're just a person, instead of a black person. That's an important distinction, and it's one that people who aren't white desperately want" to *get rid of* (e.g., in an individual capacity socially integrate away/escape from their own Blackness) because it is a common stressor.

"What the privilege of being White in America "gives you is freedom to be who you are. It might not seem special if you have it. It's subtle and you won't notice it until it's pointed out to you. You still have bills. You still deal with bullshit. You still have a shit job. You might be held down by other forces, especially if you're poor, but you don't have to worry about how your race affects the perception of your actions. You don't have to try extra hard to overcome the biases someone might have about you because you're not white."

Being raced or "racially othered" is highly stressful because the racial other is seen "first and foremost as a racial group member," observed Loscocco. Our "humanity and individuality are oftentimes ignored" and replaced by stereotype-based assumptions and expectations. Moreover, there's little we can do to effectively deal with (i.e., reduce, minimize, stop, or tolerate) being seen this way. White people collectively possess the "power and resources to create" and maintain a "race hierarchy that reflects its preeminence, ordering groups from best to worst, from valued to devalued, from human to 'other.'"

"Research shows that the problem with our society is that the levels of negative stereotypes against blacks are very high. Not only are blacks viewed negatively, they're viewed markedly more negatively than whites view themselves. The common stereotypes that black people are unintelligent, lazy, poor, and dangerous are deeply embedded in American culture." By contrast, David Williams identified that "what's associated with 'white' in American culture is completely different. Wealthy, intelligent, hardworking, normal, safe, successful—these are the stereotypes that we have been fed, and then they've become a part of who we are and shape our behavior in powerful ways."

If stereotypes didn't exist, being Black would be *a lot* less stressful. But they do, so maybe being more informed about why they exist would enable us more to have more control over our (stress) response to them being used against us.

We automatically perceive stereotypes as something negative, which is somewhat understandable for Black folk, but a stereotype is how the human mind naturally arranges other people into recognizable groups. A stereotype is a specific type of schema.

Schemas are cognitive shortcuts used by humans to process information and make judgments quickly, although sometimes inaccurately. Schemas are heuristics, which are described by Gerd Gigerenzer as "efficient cognitive processes, conscious or unconscious, that ignore part of the information" for the sake of speed and expediency.

Stereotypes are group schemas consisting of a predetermined collection of characteristics that are attributed to all or the majority of the members of a particular social (e.g., racial) group; these associations are accessed so routinely they become practically automatic. Jean Moule defined stereotypes as "simplistic images or distorted truths about a person or group based on a prejudgment of habits, traits, abilities, or expectations."

50

Kristin Henkel et al. added that "a stereotype is a generalization of beliefs about a group or its members that is unjustified because it reflects faulty thought processes or overgeneralization, factual incorrectness, inordinate rigidity, an inappropriate pattern of attribution, or a rationalization for a prejudiced attitude or discriminatory behavior."

Research in neuroscience has revealed that most anti-Black stereotypes activate "inaccurate beliefs" about Black people as a "social group that ascribe predominantly negative qualities to the group and its members," concluded Gordon Moskowitz et al. The negative components of these stereotypes are "the more dominant association to the group, causing a person's overall reaction to a member of the group to be infused—unintentionally—with negative qualities."

"These triggered negative components of the stereotype exert a well-established influence on perception, judgment, evaluation, and behavior. The effect is a dissociation between a person's conscious experience of being unbiased and a person's actual response, which is often guided by unconscious negative stereotypes. The influence of such unconsciously triggered negative and inaccurate components of a stereotype has been shown to bias judges' sentencing decisions, employers' hiring decisions, teachers' evaluations of students, police officers' decisions to respond with shows of force, and people's judgments about one another's personality during everyday encounters." In other words, racial stereotypes motivate race-based experiences (and race-based stress).

Jack Roviere asserted that "racial stereotyping might be based on a kernel of truth, and many people justify stereotyping by pointing to statistics. However, what people fail to realize is that in most cases, the statistics don't conclude anything" about a *specific* person (i.e., you or I as an individual). The "associations and expectations of a particularly stereotype may be flat-out wrong and unsubstantiated…there are no concrete genetic imperatives that stress" or validate the "common stereotypes of any race."

In other words, there is nothing biologically or genetically that would *automatically* or innately make me (or any other Black person) more likely to be lazy, violent, unintelligent, criminal, irresponsible, incompetent, dangerous, degenerate, disrespectful, apathetic, hostile, unqualified, problematic, self-destructive, excuse-dependent, complaint-oriented, diabolical, flawed, incorrigible, and/or generally inferior simply because I am Black. However, there is something culturally, cognitively, and affectively in this country that tends to make White people (and occasionally even other Black people) consistently presume and expect that I am any combination of these stereotypes due to the stigma America has socioculturally attached to Blackness. And there's not much I (or any other individual Black person) can do to stop these people from probably applying these negative presumptions and expectations to me, which can be both terrifically and routinely stressful.

Racial stereotypes are only accurate in that they tend to accurately represent our society's established cultural perception and expectations of the racially stigmatized. Racial stereotypes (much like racial stigma or the concept of "race" itself) are socially fabricated, not naturally authentic. Yet, as explained by Jaakko Lehtonen, stereotypes are designed to bias us to "favor information that is consistent with existing expectations and to ignore or reject information that is inconsistent with the stereotypes. Expectations drive our attention as observers" in ways so pervasive that stereotypes seem, in fact, innate and precise.

Behaviors that confirm these expectations are acknowledged exaggeratedly and those that don't are discounted as exceptional. However, experiences at variance with stereotypes are not indicative of exceptions among the stigmatized, but are more accurately revealing of the innate flaw (or imprecision) of stereotyping as well as the full humanness of the stigmatized in spite of the social conspiracy to restrict it.

A recent study led by Eaaron Henderson-King and Richard Nisbett verified that "it took observing only one negative action by a single Black person to activate negative stereotypes and attitudes toward Black people in general." This "person-to-group generalization" occurs because people usually "perceive outgroups as less variable and therefore see individual outgroup members as prototypic of the larger group."

Annie Paul agreed that while "we tend to see members of our own group as individuals, we view those in outgroups as an undifferentiated—stereotyped—mass." Our perception of individual outgroup members (e.g., a Black person) can be automatically negated, explained Teun van Dijk, "primarily because they are thought to belong to another group, that is, as group members and not as individuals. Negative properties attributed to the group as a whole are thus applied to its individual members, who therefore are seen as essentially alike and interchangeable."

Many oft-cited studies on stereotyping have argued that humans tend to stereotype others (i.e., generate stereotypical inferences and responses) largely in response to having insufficient information about them; or to cite Ziva Kunda and Bonnie Sherman-Williams, "in the absence of other information, expectations about an individual will be guided by stereotypical beliefs." However, recent (and less popular) research has consistently confirmed that stereotyping doesn't necessarily occur only when a stereotyper is unfamiliar with the stereotyped—an overused logic probably intended to excuse or normalize even specific stereotyping (e.g., anti-Black stereotyping) as simply *human* behavior.

"Stereotypes affect impressions even in the presence of individuating information, by affecting the construal of that information." Research conducted by David Dunning and David Sherman confirmed that possessing "specific information about individuals does not reduce the impact of stereotypes, as stereotypes often lead people to make tacit inferences about that information. These inferences alter the meaning of the information to affirm the implicit stereotypes people possess, even in the absence of conscious endorsement." In effect, stereotypes create an "inferential prison" in which "people's inferences and impressions of other people never escape far from the confines of the stereotype even as knowledge of the other increases."

Stress is essentially an interaction between an external, negative stimulus and our brain's response, a response largely determined by the magnitude of the stimulus as compared to our personal or collective competence or resources for dealing with the stimulus. Whenever we perceive (consciously or unconsciously, accurately or inaccurately) a negative discrepancy between the magnitude of the stimulus and our competence or resources to cope, we experience acute stress; if we perceive this discrepancy recurrently, then we experience chronic stress.

Smedley et al. detailed how new research suggests that anti-Black stereotypes may be damaging to Black people "because they can trigger the stress response—over and over again." On their own, these stereotypes can be perceived as an unpredictable and uncontrollable psychosocial threat (i.e., danger to our self-concept, self-esteem, or social self[17]). And, as aforementioned, racial stereotypes motivate stressful race-based experiences.

When we perceive a physical or psychosocial threat that is difficult to manage or control, our brain's alarm bells go off. The brain goes on alert and initiates a stress response by releasing cortisol and other stress hormones that trigger a physiological cascade: our senses are heightened, blood pressure and heart rate increase, glucose levels rise, our immune system is primed, all to help us hit harder (fight) or run faster (flight). When the threat passes, our brain returns to its normal state. But when stressors are always present and stress is experienced constantly, even if

---

[17] Threats to our social self, observed Gruenewald et al., feature "situations that contain the potential to devalue one's social self by calling into question abilities, competencies, or traits on which a positive social image is based, or situations characterized by potential or explicit rejection" or inequity. "Such situations are provocative because they contain social information pertinent to a primary human goal: that of achieving and maintaining a positive 'social self.'"

unnoticed, the brain can't return to normal. The stress response remains activated, structurally and functionally changing the brain over time.

Chronic stress, according to Matsumoto and Togashi, changes our brain by creating "long-lasting alterations in the neural circuits underlying emotional regulation and increase the subsequent reactivity to stress later in life." The chronic stress of race-based experiences, for instance, weakens our brain's ability to maintain neural circuits that enable *stress resilience*[18]. This brain change, explained Smedley et al., "can even carry over to the next generation, with the pregnant mother's stress hormones affecting fetal development in the womb." We a born into this world already primed to experience our Blackness as a stressor.

The persistent negative stereotyping of Black people in America can be a chronic stressor because racial stereotypes motivate recurrent race-based experiences (i.e., negative, uncontrollable things we experience as stressors primarily, but oftentimes ambiguously, because we are Black). For the most part, wrote Lenhardt, "racially stigmatized individuals have relatively few places where they can go and be assured of not being exposed to racialized" (i.e., anti-Black) conduct or stereotype-based assumptions and expectations. "This reality may leave stigmatized individuals feeling that they must be constantly 'on' and vigilant against racialized conduct" and stereotype-based thinking. It may also have additional psychological consequences, including constant vulnerability to a unique feeling of race-based invisibility.

According to Anderson J. Franklin, many of us experience an invisibility syndrome that evolves, oftentimes subconsciously, as we begin to sense that we "live in a racialized or depersonalized

---

[18] Stress resilience is the ability to cope with stress successfully with only minimal allostasis and concurrent maladaptive neuroplasticity. According to Faith Ozbay et al., "stress resilience seems to be associated with an ability to keep the hypothalamic-pituitary axis (HPA) and noradrenergic activity within an optimal range during stress exposure and terminate the stress response once the stressor is no longer present."

context in which who we are as a genuine person, including our individual talents and unique abilities, is overshadowed by stereotyped attitudes and prejudice that others hold about us." The "invisibility" comes from Black people individually not being seen as distinct human beings, only or primarily the negativity of our Blackness is acknowledged along with all the racially stigmatic notions and stereotype-based expectations that are attached to it. The constant anxiety and anticipation of imposed invisibility could become "part of the individual's intrapsychic structure…which makes membership in the target group" (i.e., being Black) undesirable and potentially stressful.

Stress is the brain's reaction to any information from our external circumstances that reveal or imply threat, especially threat that we feel we don't have the capacity or resources to cope with. Invisibility can be considered both a perpetual psychosocial threat (i.e., danger to our self-concept, self-esteem, or social self) and unavoidable race-based experience wherein a Black person "feels that his or her personal identity and ability are undermined by racism in a myriad of interpersonal circumstances. Invisibility is defined as an inner struggle with the feeling that one's talents, abilities, personality, and worth are not valued or even recognized because of prejudice and stigma, particularly in cross-racial circumstances. The negative meanings associated with race operate to obscure actual identity and promote an inherent stress" that generally becomes chronic. This chronic stress has been common among African-Americans for generations and remains just as impactful.

"Invisibility evolves out of society's racism as a mechanism for achieving its comfort with people considered unacceptable. People and places embracing racism generate a climate of disregard for African Americans by denying appropriate recognition and other elements essential to a positive identity. It evolves from superficial rather than authentic and intimate social contact with the African American community. Use of stereotypes and racial slights promotes a unifying, subjective experience of invisibility," even when used unconsciously or implicitly.

"Encountering repeated racial slights can create within the individual a feeling of not being seen as a person of worth. Accumulated experiences of racial slights reinforce the perception that perpetrators of these acts are truly blind to the 'personhood' of the individual they have encountered. This subjective sense of psychological invisibility takes the form of a struggle with inner feelings and beliefs that personal talents, abilities, and character are not acknowledged or valued by others, nor by the larger society, because of racial prejudice. Feelings of being victimized are nurtured in African Americans who connect their present experiences to the collective unconscious about the legacy of depersonalization and dehumanization poignantly associated with African-American history. Achieving visibility" within a racialized society, while sustaining our self-determination, self-worth, and self-confidence, is "a stressful psychological process for many African Americans."

This concept of being "not seen" originated in Ralph Ellison's classic novel *Invisible Man*, in which he wrote that as a Black person in America he is "an invisible man...I am invisible, understand, simply because people refuse to see me...When they approach me, they see only my surroundings, themselves, or figments of their imagination—indeed, everything and anything except me. I am what they think I am."

As aforementioned, being raced or "racially othered" is highly stressful because the racial other (e.g., a Black person in America) is seen "first and foremost as a racial group member," observed Loscocco. Our "humanity and individuality are oftentimes ignored" and replaced by negative stereotype-based assumptions and expectations. In other words, the root of racial invisibility is being racially othered; it's the reason why we are "not seen." And there's little we can do to effectively deal with (i.e., reduce, minimize, stop, or tolerate) not being seen. White people collectively possess the "power and resources to create" and maintain a "race hierarchy that reflects its preeminence, ordering groups from best to worst, from valued to devalued, from human to 'other.'"

Pyke declared that "the *creation* of a dominant, 'superior' group depends upon the existence of groups of exploitable 'others' distinguished by their *alleged* inferiority" (emphasis added). This creative process is specifically known as "othering" (or racial othering).

Michelle Fine explained othering as "the process whereby a dominant group defines into existence an inferior group" and justifies their own privileged social position via stigmatizing or labeling the "other" as inferior. "Othering is a form of collective identity work aimed at creating and/or reproducing inequality," wrote Michael Schwalbe et al. "Meanings are created that shape consciousness and behavior, such that inequality is directly or indirectly reproduced."

In the othering process, explained Jeff Gagnon, "the group that has been designated as other does not reflect an *actual* group as it exists in reality, but is instead a fiction created to solidify the identity and superiority of the in-group and to justify its existence," (re)actions, and privilege. "Groups that are designated as being other are portrayed as being both inferior and threatening. All members of the group being *othered* are believed to share a set of intrinsic negative characteristics that make them what they are."

Othering, according to James Jones, features the indiscriminate and deliberate "ways in which people devalue, disadvantage, demean, and in general, unfairly regard" those people deemed the "other." It also includes the "ways in which people value, advantage, esteem, and, in general, prefer and positively regard people who are like themselves or belong to their own group."

Othering, while typically done implicitly or unconsciously, is extremely strategic and oppressive. Othering becomes psychologically advantageous in social situations where intergroup inequality (and guilt for benefiting from this inequality) becomes ubiquitous and, therefore, undeniable. The threat involved with group-based privilege (privilege, by its existence, perpetuates the possibility of rebellion by the disprivileged and subsequent loss of privilege) prompts othering as a cognitive strategy for resolving this guilt-based anxiety. By creating psychological distance from the disadvantaged other, by *dehumanizing* them collectively as a social entity (and social threat[19]), both the guilt and the anxiety is considerably diminished.

Because of the existence of stigmatic social boundaries, social justice *cannot* be "applied equally to different social groups," noted Susan Opotow. As Americans (especially White Americans), we tend to assume "an equal inclusion of all the social groups within the sphere of justice, but this assumption is called into question by the processes of moral exclusion," which include dehumanization.

To dehumanize is to exclude members of a targeted, typically stigmatized outgroup from one's own "moral community," which is the recognized, typically privileged/dominant social ingroup to which a "psychological boundary for fairness" applies and "concerns with justice govern our conduct." The dehumanized are *morally excluded*, which "rationalizes and justifies harm" to them—commonly based upon the belief that they are somehow a social threat—and subsequently "viewing them as expendable, undeserving, exploitable, or irrelevant."

The morally excluded are then socially "perceived as nonentities, expendable, or undeserving." Consequently, society will somehow accept the perpetuation of inherently unjust, harmful, and/or antagonistic race-based experiences against the morally excluded (as a chronic stressor) as "appropriate, acceptable, or just." They will "be ignored or condoned as normal, inevitable, and deserved."

Oftentimes "subtle and difficult to detect when it is socially condoned," moral exclusion is rooted in the human "tendency to

---

[19]   Specifically, the "perception of threat of outgroup members who may reduce the dominant group's share of resources and power," explained Martin Schönteich.

see the world in two categories, *us* and *them*." And then exacerbated by the constant use of social boundaries to instigate and sustain fabricated differences across social groups "in order to keep greater resources at the dominant group's disposal." Accordingly, it's stressful always being *them*, the threat, the morally excluded, the *othered*. Nevertheless, the "signal of dark skin color," explained Entman and Rojeck, has become enough to prompt the majority of White Americans to morally exclude Black people *automatically*.

"The human mind tends to make distinctions between one's own group and the other. These distinctions, when adequately reinforced by cultural norms, experiential data, and/or various schemas (e.g., stereotypes), can become 'meta-schemas,' which are overarching associations between sets of schemas that link concepts of the good and the valued and distinguish them from the bad and feared. Thus, in many Whites' minds, a meta-schema that registers the concept of 'other' or 'them' loosely links ideas like 'Black,' 'poverty,' 'crime' and so forth, and clearly distinguishes from the more valued traits connected with 'us.'"

"Individuals seem inclined to attribute a higher degree of humanity to the ingroup than the outgroup," observed Dora Capozza et al. "The ingroup is perceived as 'fully human,' while the outgroup is dehumanized, namely perceived as less human than the ingroup."

Stigmatized outgroups are "denied unique human characteristics and attributes such as intelligence, language, politeness, cognitive abilities and more unique human emotions," explained Dalskleva and Kunst. "Emotions such as hope, love, guilt and contempt are seen as more complex emotions, and are generally perceived as exclusive to humans and are called secondary emotions. Secondary emotions are contrasted to the more universal primary emotions such as happiness and anger, which are more easily associated with both humans and animals than secondary emotions. Prejudice involving the denial of uniquely human emotions to outgroups is therefore a form of dehumanization. Consequently, one way to assess dehumanization tendencies is to measure the extent to which people deny the outgroup secondary emotions, indicating a view of the outgroup as less human than the ingroup."

People tend to "attribute more secondary emotions to their ingroup relative to the outgroup, regardless of the emotional valence (i.e., whether emotions were positive or negative). Consequently, secondary emotions seem more likely to be attributed to the ingroup, even if they have a negative valence. Disgust has been found to be a predictor of prejudice and dehumanization toward outgroups. Feelings of disgust are often accompanied with animalistic dehumanization of outgroups, where the people are likened to animals."

Further aggravating the situation is that Black people in America are generally referred to, according to the Stereotype Content Model (or SCM), as an "extreme outgroup," a social group that is both "stereotypically hostile and stereotypically incompetent." African-Americans are generally perceived as being low in warmth and competence. Our extreme outgroup status makes us uniquely vulnerable to dehumanization and disgust by other social groups (as well as ourselves to a different extent).

According to Lasana Harris and Susan Fiske, "the SCM proposes that societal groups are appraised as intending either help or harm (warmth) and as either capable or not of enacting those intentions (competence). Only the most extreme out-groups, the low-low, receive unabashed disliking and disrespect: Groups stereotyped as neither warm nor competent elicit the worst kind of prejudice—disgust and contempt—based on perceived moral violations and subsequent negative outcomes that these groups allegedly caused themselves. Disgust is unique among the emotions predicted by the SCM because it can target either humans or nonhumans, making people functionally equivalent to objects."

"Outgroups perceived as low in both warmth and competence elicit disgust, an emotion that is not exclusively social, being directed both at people and objects that seem repellant. Perceiving low–low outgroups as 'disgusting' suggests that people perceive these groups as so strikingly different (as less than people) that they do not evoke an exclusively social emotion. From the perceiver's own experience of emotion, SCM studies suggest that extreme outgroups also do not elicit these complex, exclusively social emotions *in the perceiver.*"

Social neuroscientific studies featuring functional MRI (fMRI) have produced visual evidence of the human brain experiencing disgust and dehumanization with regard to considering African-Americans, as an "extreme outgroup." The evidence revealed that the brain regions associated with the emotion of disgust, particularly the insula (along with the amygdala), was overactivated by mere images of Black people. On the other hand, those brain areas associated with social cognition, particularly the medial prefrontal cortex (or mPFC), were significantly deactivated, which suggests that someone like me, because I'm a member of an extreme outgroup (i.e., Black people in America), will typically be perceived as somehow *less human.*

Social cognition is how the human brain processes, retains, and utilizes information about other people. Documented patterns of mPFC deactivations among White Americans viewing African-Americans visually indicate that the former tends to perceive the latter, to quote Darren Schreiber and Marco Iacoboni, "as an 'it' rather than another human of equal social cognitive status."

Harris and Fiske realized that stigmatized "social groups that elicit disgust are differentially processed in mPFC. Social neuroscience suggests the medial prefrontal cortex (mPFC) is necessary for social cognition. However, the mPFC activates less to members of extreme outgroups that elicit disgust, an emotion directed toward both people and objects. Because of its role in social cognition, reduced mPFC activity may suggest that people belonging to extreme outgroups" may be perceived by the human brain differently, *more like objects than human beings.*

People dehumanize members of these outgroups, "not perceiving them as human to the same extent that they perceive in-groups or moderate out-groups as fully human. Compared with the in-group and other out-groups, extreme out-groups may not promote significant mPFC activation if they are not processed primarily as human beings. Their mPFC activation might even be equivalent to that for objects."

Research conclusively identified diminished mPFC and increased insula activation among White American participants looking at African-Americans; we tend to automatically *disgust* White people who accordingly look at us more as *things* than fellow humans. Or, to quote William Jones, "it's like we are seen as animals."

I've seen this *look* up close far too often in my lifetime. It's such a creepy, insidiously stressful feeling—to recognize someone looking at you like you're an "it" versus a "he." Oftentimes the look is accompanied emotionally by annoyance, avoidance, apprehension, disdain, and, of course, disgust. They're usually expressed very subtly and possibly even unconsciously, but my spirit still can't help but cumulatively experience these emotions. "These people," to quote Baldwin, "have deluded themselves for so long that they really don't think I'm human. I base this on their conduct, not what they say."

How exactly am I supposed to react to *that* look? How exactly am I supposed to (psychologically) survive all this (stress)? Am I supposed to somehow prove my *full humanity* to every White person I encounter, be angry and "anti-White," rationalize it with my newfound understanding of social neuroscience, become indifferent, or just internalize it (and then imitate it with other Black "people")?

For humans, "disgust is a voice in our heads," wrote Valerie Curtis, "it is the voice of our ancestors telling us to avoid infectious disease and social parasites." Sadly, racial stigma has labeled Black people as a group "social parasites," our presumed inferiority (and retaliatory potential) a plague detrimental to normal society (i.e., White privilege).

Disgust, described Daniel Kelly, is "not just a physical sensation, it's a powerful emotional warning sign. Although disgust initially evolved to keep us away from rotting food and contagious disease, the defense mechanism changed over time to effect the distance we keep from one another."

Disgust and fear are closely related; they are some of the most basic emotions expressed by the human brain for the explicit purpose of survival. We react to perceived threats with either fear or disgust; disgust is a fundamental feature of the fight or flight response. Whereas fear encourages us to flee from threat, disgust influences us to avoid (contact with) it. Since members of certain outgroups (e.g., Black people) tend to automatically be perceived as threats to an ingroup's (e.g., White people's) social advantage, it's only *logical* that the former prompt disgust (as well as fear) among the latter.

To justify White privilege, African-Americans continue to be dehumanized collectively. Even if they're not fully aware of the role racial othering plays in creating them, White people are certainly aware of the socioeconomic and psychological advantages that they enjoy. They are perhaps equally aware of the many disadvantages that come with darker skin in this country. Dehumanization, especially when stigma-based, thwarts the guilt that may accompany such awareness. "When you think people are less than human," wrote Anderson, "you tolerate their mistreatment" and disadvantage, at least unconsciously. Dehumanization is a moral disengagement mechanism, which, in this situation, has enabled Whites to cognitively disengage from such alleged moral standards as racial equality.

"Empirical studies find support for people's tendency to dehumanize outgroups. One significant way of erasing a person's humanity is to assume that the person does not feel the full range of human emotions that others do. Research on dehumanization and emotion examines attributions about primary emotions, those emotions experienced by all humans and most primates, such as joy, anger, fear, and sadness—and secondary emotions, those emotions that are thought to be uniquely human and not experienced by non-human animals, such as pride, guilt, shame, and embarrassment. People tend to attribute fewer secondary emotions to outgroups. What does it mean that people attribute fewer secondary emotions to members of the outgroup? It implies outgroup members do not share the same humanity as ingroup members, that people different from us do not feel the same range of emotions as fully human individuals feel. It puts outgroup members closer in our minds to how we might think about and treat animals."

When it comes to limited emotional experiences and Black humanity, there is a sad and often unacknowledged irony. Obviously, the issue isn't our inability to experience certain emotions, but the racial disproportionality that exists with regard to access or probability of experiencing certain emotions. As a Black person living in an anti-Black racialized society, it's hard consistently feeling optimistic, excited, safe, seen[20], special, successful, supported, desired, beautiful, potent, competent, considered, adequate, equivalent, or unrestricted primarily *because of* our Blackness.

Conversely, it's far too easy to feel chronically angry, afraid, attacked, frustrated, pessimistic, endangered, prejudged, unseen, disappointed, devalued, disregarded, dehumanized, disadvantaged, powerless, inadequate, indifferent, hypervigilant, vulnerable, or excluded primarily because of our Blackness. Moreover, we are typically aware of just how little if any control over or capacity to effectively cope with (i.e., reduce, minimize, stop, or tolerate) the disproportionality of these feelings we have because of what it means to be Black in America, who we think we are, how we feel about who we think we are, how others see us, and who we are expected to be.

To quote Derrick Bell, "Black people will never gain full equality in this country," and most of us understand this

---

[20] Even though, to quote Michelle Obama, "we can't afford to wait for the world to be equal to start feeling seen."

cognitively and emotionally. Race[21], according to Glenn Harris, is "still the leading indicator of whether or not one succeeds" in America, and most of us understand this cognitively and emotionally. Because of race, Black people "do not have the ultimate decision-making power over the decisions that control our lives and resources," noted Donna Bivens, and most of us understand this cognitively and, possibly more conclusively, emotionally.

This may sound like naïvely being stuck in "Black victimhood," but it's really *so much* bigger than that. Black people in this country have both uniquely normalized and been constantly overwhelmed by negative emotions and experiences primarily because of our Blackness. And for most Black people, all of this triggers, oftentimes unconsciously, chronic race-based stress.

Stress is the brain's reaction to any information from our external circumstances that reveal or imply threat, especially threat that we feel we don't have the capacity or resources to cope with. Being Black in America involves the perpetual perception of threat, especially implicitly *being perceived as a threat* on account of racial stigma or White privilege that must somehow be neutralized, which implies a constant possibility of experiencing race-based stress.

The stigma of Blackness is "marked on the body and embodied in ways of being seen, being treated," and perhaps most decisively, *"being feared* as different," observed Howarth. According to Biernat and Dovidio, recent studies reveal that White Americans "tend to interpret ambiguously aggressive behaviors as more threatening and violent when they are performed by a Black person than by a White person. Such results strongly suggest the

---

[21] "Millions of Americans still think and talk about race in terms of fixed biological or genetic categories," explained Manning Marable. "A strikingly different way to view the concept of 'race' is as an unequal relationship between social groups based on the privileged access to power and resources by one group over another. Race is historically and socially constructed, created (and recreated) by how people are perceived and treated in the normal actions of everyday life."

presence of a cognitive schema fixing the meaning of Blackness as dangerous."

"Whiteness carries with it the luxury of invisibility. The white presence is deemed benign and eternally welcome. In contrast," explained Joy-Ann Reid, "the black presence (the brown presence, too, but particularly the black presence) is rarely viewed as benign. It is by default deemed suspect."

White America's contemporary physical and psychological fear of Black people, particularly Black males, is also based on their historically "dominant fear of someday living without the privilege that comes with whiteness," noted Robert Jensen.

"White people's fear of losing what we have—literally the fear of losing things we own if at some point the economic, political, and social systems in which we live become more just and equitable. That fear is not completely irrational; if white privilege were to evaporate, the distribution of resources in the United States would change, and we would have less. That redistribution of wealth would be fairer and more just. But in a world in which people have become used to affluence and material comfort, that possibility can be scary."

But more importantly, this fear is actually race-based. "Central to all White concerns," according to Feagin, is a historical "fear Whites have of losing status and power because of Black attempts to bring change," which may fundamentally explain why almost any emotional response we reveal other than smiling and grinning is interpreted by them as aggressive. "Any time a Black man attempts to change the slave image," concluded Huey P. Newton, "he will scare White people."

Always *actually*[22] being big for my age and conspicuously intelligent (not intended to be boastful), I, like Baldwin, have spent

---

[22] A series of seven studies newly published by the American Psychological Association determined that White people are generally more likely to perceive Black men as larger, more muscular, stronger, and, consequently, more threatening and potentially more harmful in a confrontation than White men, even when they were the exact same size and weight.

too much of my life instinctively "watching white people and outwitting them so that I might survive" potentially being recognized as threatening. Not *ever* in the "house slave" kind of way, but more like Nat Turner or Denmark Vesey probably did. I even realized one day, it was so long ago I can't remember exactly when, *what* I was doing and *why* I was doing it. And continued doing it. There were a few significant concessions, however, as I matured.

During my senior year of high school, I stopped smiling and grinning *automatically*[23] around White people. At first, I stopped organically and unconsciously, but later I recognized my subtle act of defiance for what it was and consciously decided to continue it, indefinitely.

Growing up in the South, I guess subconsciously I had noticed what I apparently deemed as too many Black people unnaturally smiling and grinning during interracial interactions, even some in my own family, and abruptly refused to do the same. To me reacting that way seemed to somehow simultaneously imply docility, fear, and programmed deference, but I had no intentions of being docile or afraid or in any underserved way deferential. I knew early on that this would always be a risk, because my docility, fear, and deference was *expected*, but it is a risk I continue to take as efficiently and strategically as possible.

In fact, as I aged, traveled the world, and outgrew my Southern upbringing, I began to enjoy noticing the exact moment that various White people I encountered, mostly professionally, oftentimes in "White spaces," realized that I had no intentions of being docile or afraid or in any underserved way deferential because they were White. It typically shook them up quite a bit because it was *still* expected, even if only implicitly, oftentimes creating an otherwise preventable enemy and consequences sometimes too significant for me to just deal with.

---

[23] Unless there is genuine humor involved, then I have no problem responding appropriately.

Being Black in America features the secondary burden of constantly deploying cognitive and socioemotional resources in order to somehow depict yourself as *unthreatening* to White people in spite of their implicit, intergenerational fear of Blackness. It means instinctively representing some type of evidence that adequately contradicts the assumption that because I am Black, I am somehow a threat. Not doing so has always resulted in some type of consequence, usually unfair, sometimes fatal. Continuing to do so resulting in chronic, race-based stress because we inherently lack the capacity or resources needed to reliably control our threateningness relative to White people or their privilege.

Most Black people instinctively continue to "wear the mask that grins and lies," as once described poetically by Paul Laurence Dunbar, because it "hides our cheeks and shades our eyes. With torn and bleeding hearts we smile" because smiling around White people seems *safer* than not smiling. Even though it ensures nothing, too many of us still don this mask in hopes of either surviving the constant physical or psychological aggression of an anti-Black society or securing some of the scarce scraps of resource and opportunity inconsistently spilling out of the boundary cracks of White privilege. I know this for certain from decades of having witnessed, studied, and done it myself.[24]

This semiconscious defensive reaction has long roots stretching all the way back to slavery, specifically since November 11, 1831. It was on that day[25] that Nat Turner was very publicly

---

[24]   One day I stopped after becoming more terrified of someday forgetting that I was, in fact, wearing a mask than I was of the consequences of refusing to continue wearing it. I *do* remember that day. It was a difficult, but necessary, day. I was forever changed, for the better I believe, after that day.

[25]   Weeks before and after that day, White mobs frantically took their revenge on enslaved (and even many free) Blacks across the state of Virginia and neighboring areas. An estimated 500 African-Americans were murdered shortly after Turner's rebellion for no other reason than being Black and Blackness—because of Turner's own liberatory spree of homicidal violence—now urgently being perceived as a threat to White people and their systemic privilege.

hanged from a tree, emasculated, decapitated, quartered, dissected, and *flayed* (or, if you prefer, skinned). Eyewitnesses to his death bragged about it for decades, as if simply being in Courtland, Virginia on that day was some kind of life achievement. The luckiest among them received parts of his professionally butchered body. And according to John Cromwell, "Turner was also skinned to supply such souvenirs as purses, his flesh made into grease, and his bones divided as trophies to be handed down as heirlooms."

Most evident in this exact period of American history was the widespread suspicion and apprehension among White people "eternally attached to the slave himself, the suspicion that a Nat Turner might be in every Black family, that the same bloody deed could be acted over at any time and in any place, that the materials for it were spread through the land and always ready for a like explosion," described John Blassingame.

Being Black in America forever changed (or perhaps evolved) since that November day. Being Black in America, explained DuBois, would now mean that some White fear-based act of terror, brutality, exclusion, inequality, or injustice (i.e., an anti-Black action) would *probably* be "committed against us every day." Being Black would now enduringly mean that "such an act 'can always occur' any day—it means never being out of danger" and possibly seen as physically or socially threatening[26].

The social construction of threat (to racial hierarchy and privilege) leads to the social construction of boundaries to somehow minimize that threat. The social group currently with the most social power creates boundaries to reject or contain social groups with less power (yet perceived as threatening) in order to maintain intergroup inequalities. Scott Harris explained that the "differences between groups, in terms of resources and privileges, are not always self-sustaining even after they are in place." Social

---

[26] Specifically, the "perception of threat of outgroup members who may reduce the dominant group's share of resources and power," explained Martin Schönteich.

boundaries require some type of persistent boundary maintenance. Accordingly, "in a racist society built on white domination, black submission, and black invisibility," concluded Vincent Harding, "the unsupervised black presence itself, especially in the aggregate, is a threat."

Some sort of social boundary maintenance employed against Black people has been constant throughout our American existence. As the slavery era matured, boundary maintenance began to be seen as much more of a priority as more and more enslaved Blacks "refused or were perceived by Whites as refusing to accept a subordinate or oppressed status," explained Allen Grimshaw. For the next several generations of Americans that immediately succeeded the national threat of Nat Turner, White privilege was maintained (and White fear of some sort of Black retaliation was suppressed) systematically via Slave Codes, Black Codes, the de jure and de facto practices of Jim Crow, and America's contemporary racialized caste system.

Albert Cleage added that privilege "depends upon power for its existence, but rarely possesses more than the illusion of power and depends in large measure upon passive acceptance." Accordingly, since "the first heroic handful of ragged, hungry, hopeless Black men banded together and struck out killing white people, white people have not had one night of fearless sleep. Not one day have they lived without a consciousness of the constant threat that Black people represent," perhaps now more so to their privileged social existence than actual physical survival. "This is a basic part of the American social structure and the conscious intent to keep Black people powerless" and negated by racial stigma.

If you really want to, you can still see this fear. I see it all the time. I have seen and been uniquely burdened by their fear of *me* for my entire life. Whether communicated verbally, nonverbally, or even environmentally, this fear tends to reveal itself in interracial situations in the form of subtle snubs, looks, gestures, tones, and disclosed expectations, all indicative of some degree of fear-based annoyance, avoidance, apprehension, disdain, or disgust.

I have directly and vicariously experienced their fear far too often in "brief and commonplace daily verbal, behavioral, or environmental slights, insults, indignities and denigrating messages, whether intentional or unintentional," that communicate fear-based "hostile, derogatory, or negative racial slights and insults towards people of color." Racial microaggressions, according to Derald Sue, are enveloped by a *semiconscious* fear of the racial other.

(I'd be remiss in failing to note that not all White people express this fear monolithically; many even seem to somehow genuinely overcome it. Regrettably, they represent the exceptional response.)

You can still literally see it in the brains of most White Americans. Recent research has confirmed that when White people see Black people, even if only subliminally, the part of the brain called the amygdala becomes more active than when they see other White people. This is significant considering that the amygdala is the part of the brain that processes social cognition as well as specific emotional reactions such as fear, guilt, shame, anger, and hate. The amygdala works faster than our conscious awareness, so it reveals our most instinctive emotions.

Chris and Uta Frith described how "irrational feelings reveal their strength in autonomic and brain imaging measures. When white Americans were shown the faces of unknown black Americans, activity was elicited in the amygdala. The magnitude of the activity in the amygdala correlated with an implicit measure of race prejudice (the Implicit Association Test), an important tool for investigating the presence of unconscious prejudices. In this example, black faces have become conditioned stimuli for fear responses largely through cultural transmission rather than direct experience." In other words, their more afraid of what they think I am than who I really am.

Harris and Fiske also observed how "faces of Black men can evoke a stronger amygdala and insula response in White participants than ingroup faces. This increased activation correlates with greater implicit measures of fear and prejudice."

According to fMRI studies conducted by Jennifer Kubota et al., the amygdala appears to be directly involved in the detection and processing of interracial stimuli (as emotionally relevant stimuli); the application of stigma-based evaluations of racial others; as well as the acquisition, storage, and expression of conditioned fear of and compensatory emotional reactions toward racial others.

The amygdala, according to Elizabeth Phelps et al., is "involved in grasping that something is emotionally significant." In an experiment led by Phelps, neuroimaging identified that the amygdala of White test subjects "lit up" more when it saw a Black face than when it saw of a White face, an indication of increased amygdala activity. White test subjects showed lower amounts of amygdala activity when viewing White faces and Black test subjects showed lower amounts of amygdala activity when viewing Black or White faces.

Neuroimaging has confirmed a neural correlation emanating from the amygdala between fear or anticipated fear (i.e., anxiety), stress, and racial stigma and the brain's response to racial outgroups, primarily due to the amygdala's role in the stress response and fear conditioning. "White subjects generally showed significantly greater amygdala activation when exposed to unfamiliar Black faces compared to unfamiliar White faces...The amygdala's involvement in perceiving emotional faces is demonstrated by its preferential response to fearful faces as measured by fMRI, even if such faces are presented subliminally." This response was regardless of their *explicit* measure of racial bias (i.e., how racially biased they *believed* they were).

This fear is terribly logical. Consistent inequity and increasingly declining opportunity often result in violent rebellion, primarily because frustration and hopelessness often lead to violence. Ted Gurr explained the basic frustration-aggression proposition as "the greater the frustration, the greater the quantity of aggression against the source of frustration. This postulate provides the motivational base for an initial proposition about political violence: the greater the intensity of deprivation, the greater the magnitude of violence." But I don't think White people currently fear us literally killing them so much as they fear Black people in America somehow becoming socioeconomically competitive with or equal to them or aggressively rebelling against perpetual White privilege, which may be subconsciously distorted and fantasized as Black people literally killing them.

Ever since slavery, Black people in America have been perceived as violent, dangerous, criminal, and threatening primarily because my ancestors had the audacity to frequently reject enslavement. Herbert Aptheker noted that "there were over two hundred and fifty documented cases of organized slave rebellions in the United States," which maintained a "justifiable paranoia" among Whites that they could eventually fall victim to the violence of Black rebellion. These rebellions and their incalculable undocumented counterparts constantly confirmed White America's collective fear of "someday living without the privilege that comes with Whiteness because of Black attempts to bring change."

Only because "they were more numerous, better organized, armed, educated, and more mobile than slaves," White Americans of that era were "able to crush every slave rebellion with relative ease, and more importantly, to prevent the development of a tradition of successful revolt in America." Blassingame added that "unless he was totally blind, a slave could not fail to perceive how hopeless revolt was, given the size and undeniably superior firepower of the whites."

Nevertheless, "from an analysis of the constantly recurring rumors of insurrections, it is obvious that many whites considered black slaves dangerous, insubordinate, bold, evil, restless, turbulent, vengeful, barbarous, and malicious. The white man's fear and his anxiety about the slave was so deep and pervasive that it was something pathological. An epidemic of runaways, a group of whispering slaves, mysterious fires, or almost any suspicious event caused alarm, apprehension, and a deepening state of paranoia among whites," especially after that November day in 1831.

Just "thinking about Nat kept whites 'in a state of perpetual anxiety and apprehension.'" The mere recollection of Nat Turner's revolt "forced some whites to conclude that to live among black slaves was 'really a dreadful situation to be in.' The persistent fear of the slave even in the absence of revolts may indicate that there was overwhelming circumstantial evidence and hundreds of individual acts which convinced whites that slaves were ungovernable and potentially dangerous. Many of them slept behind doors with pistols under their pillows."

"Often the slaves had to mask their feelings in their relations with their masters because of their attitudes toward whites. Most slaves hated and were suspicious of all whites. The treatment the slave received verified this suspicion and left him angry." Frequently slaves were heard "talking about wreaking vengeance on their masters, killing them, and appropriating their homes, food, clothes, and women." And although the abovementioned 250 acknowledged slave revolts were considered unsuccessful because they did not directly lead to the permanent emancipation of all slaves, as explained by David Pilgrim, they "did send this message to slaveholders: for years you have degraded and killed us, now there is the real possibility that we will kill you."

"Whites, including non-enslavers, fearing rebellion among the slaves, used many strategies to ensure that angry slaves did not rebel: slaves were routinely searched for weapons; rebellious slaves were punished, publicly and harshly—including cropping ears, castrating, hanging, burning, and mutilating; the all-white army and militias were constantly on guard; and, anyone, black or white advocating rebellion among the slaves could be lynched.

Despite these measures and others, slavers lived with the constant fear that slaves would rise up and kill whites."

Beginning formally in the late 17th century, most Southern states eventually enacted "Slave Codes" as an early form of social boundary maintenance. Employed in conjunction with the constant use or threat of oftentimes barbaric violence, Slave Codes were basically a succession of common laws designed to prevent circumstances in which Whites could be killed by or somehow appear equal or inferior to any Black person in this country. According to Alan Lamm, "Virginia was the first of the 13 colonies to adopt such regulations, using earlier Caribbean slave codes as models. Other colonies quickly followed suit, patterning their codes after the Virginia laws."

Slave Codes effectively contained the unsupervised Black presence by systemically enforcing several strategic expectations, including that slaves could not possess weapons; leave their owner's estate without permission; or commit any type of violence against Whites, even if self-defense from an unjust attack. In fact, there were Codes that actually encouraged the murder of any slave with the audacity to assault a White person, regardless of their reason and despite the "property loss" ultimately incurred for doing so.

Because slaves *were* property, they had no defensible rights to own property or accumulate wealth. Slaves could not assemble en masse unless a White person was present and in a clear supervisory role. Slaves could not be taught to read or write or even possess "inflammatory" literature. Slaves could not vote in any type of government election. Slaves could not sue or testify against White people. Legal marriage among the enslaved was not permitted (which eased any White guilt that could have been felt for the notoriously frequent transregional, transactional separation of enslaved families).

Any slave caught while attempting to escape could be killed without penalty for refusing to surrender nonviolently. In times of actual or perceived unrest, Whites "rigorously enforced the slave codes both through the courts and by establishing slave patrols. Composed of white men who took turns covering a particular area of their county, slave patrols watched for runaways or assisted owners in enforcing the slave codes on their plantations." These patrols would become the precursor to the American police force.

Slave Codes made "bondage a lifelong condition and ensured that all descendants of slaves would be slaves as well. Slave codes also gave white masters nearly total control over the lives of slaves, permitting owners to use such corporal punishments as whipping, branding, maiming, and torture" to induce docility.

Whites apparently felt that their relationship with enslaved Black people in America was "one of continual war requiring eternal vigilance in order for the master to maintain the upper hand," described Blassingame. "It is obvious that many whites did not believe the slaves were innately docile. Too many governors received requests for arms and troops from thousands of whites, the U.S. Army marched and countermarched too often, too many panic-stricken whites spent their nights guarding their neighborhoods. In a sense, this is indicated by the constant changes in the slave codes."

"Every effort was made to keep the slaves in awe of the power of whiteness and ignorant of their own potential power. The idea of the superiority of whites was etched into the slave's consciousness by the lash and the ritual respect he was forced to give to every white man. The lash, frequently applied, was an awesomely successful fear-inducing instrument. Added to the slave's fear of the lash was the dread of being separated from loved ones. The congregation of crowds of slaves, their independent movement, possession of arms, and degree of literacy, were all strictly regulated. The rebellious slave was punished swiftly and cruelly to discourage others. The oppressive acts consisted of cropping ears, castrating, hanging, burning, and mutilating. The army, the militia, and the entire white community stood ready to aid any embattled region. In all of these actions, the whites demonstrated that, even if slaves did not revolt, they were considered rebellious."

Manfred Berg added that Slave Codes "singled blacks for extremely cruel punishment, thus marking black bodies as innately inferior" and "legitimate objects of excessive violence." These codes "allowed for horrible corporal punishment short of death, including savage whipping, branding, castration, nose slitting, and the amputation of toes, fingers, feet, or hands." This excessive interracial violence could be "carried out not only by the authorities" (e.g., slave patrols), "but rather by all white men in the country, who not only felt, but actually were privileged and entitled to do so." In this way, Slave Codes "set clear patterns for future racial violence in America" and intergenerational race-based stress.

Alvin Poussaint wrote that "when slavery was abolished, the Negro had been stripped of his culture and left with this heritage: an oppressed black man in a hostile white man's world. In the late 1800's and early 1900's the systematized racist and sometimes psychotic propaganda of the white man, haranguing about the inferiority of the Negro, increased in intensity. He was disenfranchised, terrorized, mutilated and lynched. The Negro became every unacceptable, negative idea and impulse that the white man's psyche wished to project, i.e., the black man was an animal with a tendency for violence, ravaging sexual impulses, etc. The intensity of the white man's psychological need that the Negro be shaped in the image of this projected mental sickness was such as to inspire a whole system of organized discrimination, segregation and exclusion of Negroes from society"—it was called Jim Crow.

Jim Crow was exclusively established formally in the Southern part of the United States only because at that time most Black people in America resided in this region. The North had its own subtle forms of segregation appropriate for a smaller—and supposedly less threatening—Black population. Jim Crow consisted of laws that required public schools, services (e.g., hotels, restaurants, hospitals), and transportation have separate, segregated facilities for Whites and Blacks, with those of the latter being grossly inferior to the formers. Socioeconomically, this separation was intended to keep African-Americans in a subordinate political, social, and economic position. Psychologically, it served a double purpose: convince Blacks of their own inferiority and inability to compete with Whites (which should make us more docile) as well as allow Whites a systematic way to avoid their innate fear of Blacks by avoiding Black people all together (or secluding them to situations of interracial contact where they were always in explicit control).

Jerrold Packard realized that "many whites in the South had grown more physically fearful of blacks. Part of the reason was that by the turn of the century the majority of African-Americans no longer bore any personal experience of slavery, and as some younger and better-educated blacks began to press for greater opportunities, and even for equality, many whites considered such efforts a dangerous challenge to the sine qua non of their existence, which was, of course, the unequivocal supremacy of their race. In many of those minds, 'custom' had become insufficient to guarantee this outcome, and accordingly it was time to make sure the African-American's place in the Southern order of things was spelled out, clearly and beyond challenge, in law."

Perhaps more so than being physically afraid, "perceived social equality...aroused white fears." Black people could "not be allowed for a moment to forget that they were in every way subordinate and inferior to whites."

Accordingly, Jim Crow sought and achieved in effect the total disenfranchisement of Black men regardless of Reconstruction and the Fifteenth Amendment, which gave the right to vote to all men despite race. Voting meant socioeconomic control, at least locally, and Blacks couldn't be allowed any. "Near-total disfranchisement of blacks—meaning the virtual elimination of African-Americans from the South's politics and exclusion from the ballot and from the democratic process—was not going to be corrected by

79

'guarantees' related to the Fifteenth Amendment, the Supreme Court having already let it be known that the region's exclusionary techniques—poll taxes, understanding clauses, and whites-only primaries and nominating conventions—would withstand any assault on their legality or constitutionality. When in 1915 the court did reverse itself and ruled some of these disbarments unconstitutional, Southern registrars and voting officials merely switched to well-established tools of intimidation to keep blacks from the polls. Less spectacular but more ubiquitous than actual physical terror, such methods included firing recalcitrant blacks or depriving them of the credit to obtain farm implements or destroying their property up to and including the burning of African-American homes. In the end, of course, there remained the almost always effective threat, and even delivery, of beatings and torture should a black ignore Jim Crow."

"All these measures, including lynching, the ultimate terror and the weapon of choice of the Ku Klux Klan, met with nearly universal official and public approval in the South—and most often, nearly universal official and public indifference in the North."

"Legalized Jim Crow infiltrated Southern life almost faster than could be comprehended…Besides the comprehensive drive to remove African-Americans from each community's political functioning, much of Jim Crow was enacted to forestall the possibility of a social breaching of the barriers that held back contacts between the races. Where members of the two races unavoidably met daily and informally—in common transportation carriers, on the streets, or in shops or places of business—whites strove to ensure that the caste rules separating whites and blacks were never and nowhere infringed, one of the purposes of which was to ensure blacks not be allowed for a moment to forget that they were in every way subordinate and inferior to whites. Importantly, this applied to *every* black man, woman, or child in relationship to *every* white man, woman, or child."

"Fundamental to Jim Crow was the principle that any white person was superior to every black person, and conversely, that any black person was inferior to every white person. There could be no exceptions if the system was to retain its operating logic."

Explicit racial segregation demonstrated just how afraid White people actually remained of Black people. This fear, even as it continued to evolve into hatred, was demonstrably neurotic. Neurotic fear, as described by Rutledge, is "a persistent, irrational fear of a specific object [or persons], activity, or situation that leads to a compelling desire to avoid it." Much of Jim Crow was based on explicit segregation, with White people avoiding Black people outside of situations where they were clearly in control and thus had less to "fear." Jim Crow and contemporary residential segregation are evidently an outward expression of neurotic fear. Yet, to quote Lerner, "avoidance will make you feel less vulnerable in the short run, but it will never make you less afraid."

Consequently, as recognized by Moss and Reed, "not much change in racial attitudes is expected among white citizens in the near future because whites still do not indicate a willingness to choose interracial contact. Contemporary surveys of whites indicate a reluctance to live with black neighbors, a desire to insulate themselves from contact with black people, and a desire to maintain a social distance from black Americans even while agreeing to formal legal and civil rights for black citizens. This suggests an insularity at the core of white Americans racial attitudes that may persist for some time."

White people's collective, implicit fear of Black people—and Black males in particular—has never actually been adequately alleviated, and in many ways has been aggravated. Part of the reason for the perpetuation of this fear into the 21st century has been the media's consistently biased, criminalized depiction of Black people, which has maintained White people's adoption of the many negative stereotypes of Black people as dangerous, violent, criminal, and threatening. Fear, noted Ian Loft, is "one common reason that people will stereotype." Entman and Rojecki

81

reported that "media stereotypes consist of recurring messages that associate persons of color with traits, behaviors, and values generally considered undesirable, inferior, or dangerous. In the context of crime coverage, there is considerable evidence that media portray blacks and Latinos as criminal and violent."

As a Reaction to White Presence[27]
Recognizing Racism as a Chronic Psychosocial Stressor

"The racism I have experienced since a child as a normal part of life contributed enormously to never feeling safe, never feeling enough, constantly being on guard."

-Louisa Parker

"The details and symbols of Negro life in this country have been deliberately constructed to make you believe what white people say about you. Please try to remember that what they believe, as well as what they do and cause you to endure, does not testify to your inferiority but to their inhumanity and fear."

-James Baldwin, The Fire Next Time

Mari Matsuda et al. emphatically described racism as being "endemic to American life." I have never forgotten reading their study in graduate school (almost twenty years ago), that rather unique (at least to me) statement especially. Actually, that one word, in particular: endemic. *Endemic* is a somewhat uncommonly used, but highly compelling word. Endemic is oftentimes confused with epidemic or incorrectly used interchangeably. I have even heard several so-called pundits erroneously refer to racism in America as an epidemic. As its primary targets and victims, Black people in America wish racism was *just* an epidemic.

---

[27] Excerpted from the following Toni Morrison quote: "Racism's hoped-for consequence is to define Black people as a reaction to White presence."

According to Elliot Currie, "there is a basic distinction between 'epidemic' and 'endemic' phases of a disease" or some other problematic situation. Epidemics "move swiftly and devastatingly through vulnerable populations and then subside, while an affliction which has become deeply entrenched in a population and stubbornly resists eradication is said to be endemic." Consequently, an endemic is a problematic situation that a large portion of a particular population *is expected to encounter* at some point in their lifetime.

"African-Americans in the United States are exposed regularly to racism, which could represent a continuous stressor," concluded Ma'at Lewis-Coles and Madonna Constantine.

If racism was actually an epidemic as opposed to endemic, it would have been much less of a chronic stressor for Black people in America than it continues to be. Racism in this country may have evolved and, as a result, is now less explicit, but it certainly has never *subsided.* Epidemics stop. Racism hasn't (and apparently won't). I, like most Black people in America, have already encountered and expect to continue to encounter racism, in various forms, at numerous points in my lifetime. Racism, as an experience, *is endemic* to my/our life and, as such, remains a chronic stressor.

"Racism is a sensitive word," noted Clarence Page. "How you define it reveals something about you, how you see the world and your place in it." Too many people, regardless of their race, prefer believing that racism hardly ever still happens or, when it does, is only caused by "a few bad apples." These same people tend to share a very simplistic definition of racism that focuses almost exclusively on individual acts of explicit racial bias or hostility as opposed to racism now being a more multifaceted phenomenon.

Racism in America is currently so much "more than a matter of individual scattered episodes of discrimination," to quote Joe Feagin and Hernan Vera. Or whether or not White people (appear to) *like us* (i.e., express interpersonal favor or fondness for people of color). Marimba Ani recognized that racism was never "attitude alone" (i.e., what White people tend to feel and believe about people of color in this country), but "the power to control the lives of those who are despised."

Camara Harrell et al. described racism as a comprehensive "system where power is unevenly distributed along racial lines resulting in the oppression and exclusion of non-White groups" and collective privileging of White people.

According to Charmaine Wijeyesinghe et al., racism is the "systemic subordination of members of targeted racial groups who have relatively little social power in the United States (Blacks, Latino/as, Native Americans, and Asians), by the members of the agent racial group who have relatively more social power (Whites). This subordination is supported by the actions of individuals, cultural norms and values, and the institutional structures and practices of society."

Shelly Harrell further defined racism as a "system of dominance, power, and privilege based on racial-group designations; rooted in the historical oppression of a group defined or perceived by dominant-group members as inferior, deviant, or undesirable; and occurring in circumstances where members of the dominant group create or accept their societal privilege by maintaining structures, ideology, values, and behavior that have the intent or effect of leaving nondominant-group members relatively excluded from power, esteem, status, and/or equal access to societal resources."

Consequently, concluded Robert Carter, "racism is stressful," especially for members of the social groups most targeted and harmed by racism. An event or experience is clearly stressful if it is concurrently "ambiguous, negative, unpredictable, and uncontrollable." Racism creates events and experiences that are uniquely negative, ambiguous, unpredictable, and uncontrollable for its victims. Hence, "racism is stressful."

Moreover, to quote Nia Heard-Garris, "racism is a pervasive stressor." Racism is a normative experience for people in color in this country and, therefore, a pervasive (or *endemic*) stressor.

85

Contemporary racism can be experienced as systemic, individual, institutional, cultural, unconscious, aversive, everyday, anticipated, perceived, internalized, or microevents, which radically increases the probability and regularity of experiencing it in some form as a stressor (i.e., causes racism-related stress).

Racism-related stress is different than race-based stress. Comparable, *correlative*, but distinctive. And if we are to survive either, we must know these differences well enough to feel them almost instinctively.

So, just to recap. "Being Black in a racist society is stressful," noted Danielle Williams. Existing in a "social environment in which Black Americans bear the stigma burden of their racial group while White Americans are allowed to view themselves as individuals" is stressful, explained Margaret Hicken et al. Having to deal with, possibly to some degree on a daily basis, the negative assumptions and expectations now associated with being Black in America is stressful. Enduring "unequal life experiences and chances based on the socially constructed racial group membership categories" being "woven into our social structure and institutions" is stressful.

Being Black in America makes us uniquely, highly, and constantly vulnerable to experiencing race-based stress. And we don't necessarily need to experience some form of racism in order to experience race-based stress; merely *being Black* is enough.

Race-based stress describes a particular response to personally relevant encounters, events, evaluations, expectations, and experiences most likely to be negative and/or negating (i.e., dangerous, difficult, dehumanizing, or disappointing) primarily, but oftentimes ambiguously, because we are Black in America. Our response typically lacks the resources and capacity to effectively deal with (i.e., reduce, minimize, stop, or tolerate) the negativity and/or negation caused by these race-based encounters, events, evaluations, or experiences, which makes it stressful.

"There are few advantages associated with being Black in America," noted Kathy Russell. And it's the constant, cumulative disadvantages associated with being Black that oftentimes spawn stressful race-based experiences (i.e., negative, uncontrollable things we experience as stressors primarily, but oftentimes ambiguously, because we are Black). Race-based stress is caused by race-based experiences, which for Black people in America can occur at any time on any given day because we currently lack the individual and collective capacity and resources to stop the stigma and disadvantages of being Black in America.

Conversely, *racism-related stress* is stress specifically triggered by experiencing some form of racism[28] or racist behavior, inclusive of any act of racial discrimination, hostility, violence, exclusion, inequality, or injustice perceived or experienced as somehow threatening. "Racism embedded in American society and enacted by individuals, institutions, and systems can act as a chronic or life event stressor for Blacks," concluded Deidre Franklin-Jackson and Robert Carter.

Racism has the additional capacity, according to Amos N. Wilson, to produce and perpetuate conditions that increase our exposure to traditional life stressors—such as "inadequate family incomes, health care, education, job training, housing, employment, and economic development—which strain the Black community's coping mechanisms. The effects of these stressors are amplified by the relatively dependent and reactionary orientation of the Black community."

Because of the excessive likelihood of recurrently experiencing some form of racism, throughout our lives we tend to endure the double burden of general (or non-race specific) life stressors (e.g., death of a loved one, job loss, divorce, a major or chronic injury or illness, financial scarcity, parenting, etc.) *along with* racism-related stress.

"Unlike other general stressors," noted Ivy Hall, "the context in which racial discrimination occurs is pervasive, thus worsening

---

[28] Including systemic, individual, institutional, cultural, unconscious, aversive, everyday, anticipated, perceived, or internalized racism as well as racial microevents.

the chronic nature of the stress" Black people in this country attempt to withstand collectively.

Numerous new studies have revealed the continuation of widespread racial discrimination nationwide. Such studies confirm that Black people from all socioeconomic backgrounds, along with other people of color, continue to encounter subtle and flagrant interpersonal (i.e., face-to-face) as well as institutional (or systemic) discrimination in housing, employment, education, criminal justice, and healthcare.

According to one study conducted by Elizabeth Klonoff and Hope Landrine, an estimated 98% of African-Americans experience racial discrimination as a chronic stressor. Moreover, "experiencing some sort of racism was an extremely common experience."

Everybody experiences stress, especially acute stress, but members of certain social groups are more vulnerable to the type of chronic stress that induces maladaptive neuroplasticity[29] than others. Leonard Pearlin explained that "to understand stress and stress reactions, one must consider the role of social structures. Many stressful experiences occur within the context of social structures or systems of social stratification such as socioeconomic

---

[29] "The human brain can change itself. Nature has given us a brain that survives in a changing world by changing itself," noted Norman Doidge. "Neuroplasticity is the property of the brain that enables it to change its own structure and functioning in response to activity and mental experience." Chronic experiences, especially those that are highly emotional, are most likely to produce lasting brain changes.

Neuroplasticity is possible because of the capacity of neurons to extend and create connections between brain regions and structures in order to facilitate efficient recall of past experiences along with reflexive instigation of a response. Recurring cognitive, emotional, and behavioral responses become patterned neuronal activity that can cause us to begin responding to the circumstances of our lives habitually based on these (re)established neural activation patterns (i.e., brain changes). Maladaptive neuroplasticity are those brain changes that somehow instigate negative outcomes (e.g., diminished ability to regulate negative emotions and impulsivity, increased reliance on self-handicapping, chronic hypervigilance, etc.).

status, race, and gender and are often related to a person's place within that structure." In other words, as a result of racism in America, Black people tend to experience far more chronic stress (and chronic stress-induced neuroplasticity) than White people and other people of color.

Yet, as Eduardo Bonilla-Silva observed, most White people "insist that minorities (especially blacks) are the ones responsible for whatever 'race problem' we have in this country. They denounce blacks for 'playing the race card,' for demanding the maintenance of unnecessary and divisive race-based programs, such as affirmative action, and for crying 'racism' whenever they are criticized by whites. Most whites believe that if blacks and other minorities would just stop thinking about the past, work hard, and complain less (particularly about racial discrimination), then Americans of all hues could 'all get along.' But regardless of whites' 'sincere fictions,' racial considerations shade almost everything in America."

Shawn Utsey surmised that "in U.S. society, resources, opportunities (social, economic, and educational), and self-regard are unequally distributed and members of lower status groups are likely to experience their devalued social status as a source of chronic stress." By "lower status groups," he meant people of color, *primarily* Black people.

Rodney Clark et al. described how an "emerging body of research indicates that racism (whether or not it is perceived) is a potential source of acute and chronic stress for many ethnic group members, including Caucasians." However, in a society in which experiencing racism and stress are daily possibilities, racism appears to target, endanger, harm, and, as a result, trigger a stress response among Black people the most. This is largely because historical and contemporary racism, racial inequality, exclusion, violence, and injustice in America has mainly and most severely been *anti-Black*.

"In the United States, Blacks are disproportionately exposed to environmental stimuli that may be sources of chronic stress. The historical basis for many of these exposures has been experienced by few, if any, other ethnic groups to the extent it has by African-Americans. A myriad of these stimuli could be perceived as involving racism. Although members of other ethnic groups report experiences of racism in the United States, the sociopolitical history of racism in the United States as it relates to Blacks has been more pervasive" and has contributed to acute and chronic experiences that have been especially stressful to us. Feagin agreed that "'white-on-black' racism represents the 'archetype' of racial oppression in America."

So, in addition to the stress experienced merely by *being* Black in America and the stress of experiencing the disadvantages and negative assumptions and expectations now associated with being Black in America (i.e., race-based stress), Black people disproportionately suffer from racism-related stress. Lewis-Coles and Constantine identified a number of studies that confirm "African-Americans perceive greater amounts of racism-related stress than do other people of color."

Racism-related stress, according to Shelly Harrell, results from "race-related transactions between individuals or groups and their environment that emerge from the dynamics of racism, and that are perceived to tax or exceed existing individual and collective resources or threaten well-being." Much of this stress comes from living with the almost constant "threat of racism," which for us requires, noted Philomena Essed, "planning, almost every day of one's life, how to avoid or defend oneself against racial discrimination," hostility, violence, exclusion, inequality, or injustice.

Further exacerbating the potential (neuroplastic) impact of racism-related stress is that Black people in America tend to experience racism *cumulatively*, "whereby new encounters are interpreted on the basis of past experiences with racism, knowledge of others' experience with racism, and knowledge about the systemic nature of racism," observed Utsey.

Because we can experience racism in one form or another "almost every day" of our lives, the actual (neuroplastic) impact of racism-related stress is oftentimes a "consequence of the cumulative effects of numerous events," explained Carter. "One seemingly innocuous or minor event could be the last straw in a series of accumulated racial incidents, causing a person to feel that he or she can no longer manage the stress and pain of encounters with racism. One may be stressed, but the level of stress may not reach the threshold for being traumatic until the trigger or last straw."

At some point in their lives, too many Black people have begun to perceive, usually implicitly, their cumulative experiences of racial discrimination, hostility, violence, exclusion, inequality, and injustice as "traumatic or outside of their ability to cope. Some racial and ethnic minority individuals may experience racial discrimination as a psychological trauma as it may elicit a response comparable to posttraumatic stress" (i.e., trauma-based maladaptive neuroplasticity).

"Trauma is a form of stress; it is distinct in that it is a more severe form of stress." Largely because it is felt cumulatively, racism, as opposed to being a benign negative experience, is "a potential source for traumatic stress," noted Lillian Polanco-Roman et al. Chalsa Loo et al. concurred that "the stressful effects of racism could be additive and that cumulative racism can be experienced as traumatic."

A *traumatic* stressor is anything (e.g., events, experiences, perceptions, or circumstances) that communicates a threat so powerful and dangerous that it could overwhelm an "individual's capacity to regulate their emotions" and "ability to cope with what they have experienced" (i.e., physically or psychologically survive the experience). Trauma is not necessarily "an event in itself," noted Lenore Terr, "but is instead the reaction to extremely stressful life circumstances." Trauma is oftentimes an overwhelmingly stressful experience that forever changes our natural belief that the world is just and safe and our world is controllable.

Racism as a traumatic stressor, or the psychological (and sometimes physical) "trauma of racism, refers to the cumulative negative impact of racism on the lives of people of color," observed Dottie Lebron et al. "Racial trauma is experiencing psychological symptoms such as anxiety, low self-esteem, feelings of humiliation, hypervigilance to threat, sense of a foreshortened future, or lack of hopefulness for your future as a result of repeated exposure to racism or discrimination," explained Erlanger Turner. "There is so much continued racism either directly or indirectly that it's hard to recover from one incident before another occurs. Sometimes the brain cannot quite heal the trauma, and there are long-term changes in the brain." This inability to recover due to chronicity and uncontrollability is largely responsible for racism-related stress becoming traumatic, even though "not every incident of racism will result in racial trauma."

Being traumatized implies that the traumatic stress-inducing experience (e.g., act of racism) was somehow able to instigate distinct, negative (or maladaptive), and enduring changes in our psychological capacity to regulate our emotional reactions to highly stressful situations or experiences subsequently. Neuroimaging has confirmed that being traumatized in any way can structurally and functionally change the brain of the traumatized. "The organ being plastic," observed Philip Perry, "trauma fundamentally changes how the brain operates."

Traumatic stress is defined by the American Academy of Experts in Traumatic Stress (AAETS) as the "emotional, cognitive, behavioral, physiological experience of individuals who are exposed to, or who witness, events that overwhelm their coping and problem-solving abilities." Whenever traumatic stress is "prolonged, extreme, or repetitive, the neuron pathways in the amygdala lose their 'elasticity' or ability to recover." As a result, "the brain keeps sensing danger, sending out stress response signals," and releasing neurotransmitters and hormones such as cortisol. When certain neural structures and pathways (e.g., prefrontal cortex, amygdala, hippocampus) are chronically awash with these brain chemicals and hormones, these neural structures and pathways can be significantly changed structurally or functionally.

Kimberley Shilson acknowledged that "psychological trauma impacts such brain areas as the amygdala (involved in emotion management) and the hippocampus (involved in memory and memory consolidation). If traumatic stress is experienced repeatedly or over a prolonged period, cortisol (a hormone released during times of stress) is released too much, subsequently activating the amygdala and causing even more cortisol to be released."

An almond-shaped neural structure centrally located in the medial anterior temporal lobe, the amygdala (which is actually Greek for "almond") processes external stimuli and reflexively determines an emotional significance and response to that stimuli (particularly when deemed threatening), which is then sent out to other regions of the brain. The amygdala is directly associated with learned emotional responses (e.g., fear, anger, affection, disgust) and is *proportionately plastic*, which means chronic overactivation of neurons in the amygdala enlarges and hypersensitizes the amygdala (by strengthening its internal and outbound neural circuitry) which causes excessive, conditioned emotional reactions to recurrent (and potentially threatening) stimuli.

In other words, the more we repeatedly overreact emotionally to certain (e.g., racism-related) life circumstances and experiences, the more likely we are to overreact equally emotionally to those same (or similar) circumstances and experiences in the future because of changes to our amygdala. These overreactions tend to become maladaptive since overreacting emotionally subdues rational thought, active coping, and authentic problem solving.

Constant cortisol saturation significantly changes neural structures like the hippocampus and prefrontal cortex (PFC), both of which are gradually reduced in size and activity as cortisol annihilates hippocampus and PFC neurons via prolonged overactivation. Conversely, continuous cortisol production increases the size and activity of the amygdala. According to research by Christopher Pittenger and Ronald Duman, chronic stress "enhances synaptic plasticity and the function of amygdala neurons, an effect quite distinct from the atrophy it induces in the hippocampus and PFC. This could both result from and contribute to overactivation of neuronal circuits that control fear, anxiety, and emotion."

The now hyperactive and hypertrophied amygdala promotes persistent states of hypervigilance and heightened emotional reactivity, even our stress response is exacerbated. The hypervigilant amygdala is constantly activating the stress response, and every activation makes a future activation much more likely (as it becomes patterned neuronal activity).

Chronic racism-related stress strengthens the neural pathway between the amygdala and hippocampus and weakens the neural pathway between the hippocampus and prefrontal cortex. Consequently, our fight or flight response to perceived threats is drastically quickened because our ability to moderate this response is linked to the functional efficiency of the hippocampus and prefrontal cortex, both of which are neuronally atrophied by continuous cortisol saturation. In other words, an exaggerated stress response is a consequence of the brain changes brought about by experiencing chronic racism-related stress.

Additionally, our cumulative experience with racism-related stress tend to prompt anticipation of racism and additional racism-related stress in our future. After a certain level of cumulative experience, most Black people in America begin, usually unconsciously, to "anticipate racism in their contacts with members of the dominant group regardless of whether they are actually discriminated against on each occasion." This, according to Essed, is an intuitive "strategy of self-protection." However,

94

this constant anticipation of experiencing racism becomes, in itself, a source of chronic stress.

Somehow, we seem to "learn to anticipate—indeed, expect—negative regard from members of the dominant culture," explained Ilan Meyer. "To ward off potential negative regard, discrimination, and violence [we] must maintain vigilance. The greater one's perceived stigma, the greater the need for vigilance in interactions with dominant group members. By definition such vigilance is chronic in that it is repeatedly and continually evoked in the everyday life" of Black people in this country, who must "be constantly on guard, alert, or mindful of the possibility that the other person is prejudiced."

Once we anticipate experiencing racism often enough, our hippocampus and amygdala can begin to condition our brain to believe that this experience is inevitable and records/repeats how we react to it. In other words, whenever we constantly anticipate a racism-related experience as threatening and typically react with the stress response, our amygdala begins to categorize this anticipation as a stressor. The next time we begin to anticipate, we will reflexively recall the stress we repeatedly felt before and feel it again. We will automatically feel the stress, and once we accept the stress (or refuse to not accept it), the neural association between the anticipation of racism and this reaction (i.e., racism-related stress) is reinforced. And because this happens so quickly, we have very little conscious control over it. Oftentimes, even the stress—which almost inevitably becomes chronic—is unconscious.

Racism in America, according to Frances Cress Welsing, is "the imposition, from birth to death, of a stressful, negative and non-supportive social/environmental experience upon" people of color (Black people especially). This "negative and stressful social experience, which is structured to affect every aspect of life activity, leads to the development of a negative self-concept, a loss of self-respect and the development of self- and group-destructive behavioral patterns."

95

Many of the unseemly, detrimental behaviors we tend to practice disproportionately as a group can be directly linked to the neuroplastic impact of chronic racism-related stress on our capacity to regulate negative emotional reactions.

Repeatedly experiencing some form of racism can trigger chronic stress and chronic stress changes the human brain.

Chronic racism-related stress "increases the complexity of neurons in the amygdala, the brain's emotion center" and "often results in a condition known as *allostatic load*. Allostatic load is 'carryover' stress. Instead of returning to a healthy baseline of homeostasis, the brain adapts to negative life experiences so that it becomes either hyper-responsive or hypo-responsive."

Constant allostasis inevitably produces allostatic load. Allostatic load causes neuronal atrophy in the hippocampus and PFC and neuronal hypertrophy in the amygdala. These are significant structural (i.e., neuronal size) and functional (i.e., neuronal excitability) changes in the brain. Rick Nauert recognized that the hippocampus and PFC are "necessary for processing information about the controllability of stressors as well as applying this information to regulate responses to subsequent stressors." Having an undersized hippocampus and PFC can make people more susceptible to stress and anxiety throughout their lives, essentially creating an inertia-like effect on their stress response.

The now enhanced connection between the amygdala and hippocampus makes us considerably more anxious (i.e., threats appear ubiquitous and overstated); thus, chronic anxiety is an additional consequence of the brain changes brought about by chronic stress. Constant cortisol saturation reinforces the neural circuitry connecting the amygdala and hippocampus, which effectively creates a brain predisposed to existing in a perpetual state of fight or flight (as well as allostasis).

Research led by Supriya Ghosh shows that chronic stress rewires our brain to "discount factual information and to rely heavily on emotional experiences." Our capacity for emotional self-regulation depends heavily on the functional efficiency of the neural circuitry connecting the prefrontal cortex and amygdala. This connectivity is compromised dramatically in the brains of people who have experienced chronic stress.

When we can efficiently regulate our negative emotions, we influence if, when, and how we experience and are affected by them. When we can't, negative emotions can negatively bias our thoughts and actions; they can control us rather than the other way around. Emotional self-regulation is the ability to react to negative emotional stimuli (including stress) without compromising our long-term best interest, which typically means inhibiting our reflexive response in favor of a more appropriate one. When this ability is intact, we can scrutinize and manage our own emotions, thoughts, and actions as well as constructively modify them when circumstances require it. Our brain's natural capacity for regulating its reaction to negative emotions is essential, not just for survival but for success in anything. Chronic stress-induced neuroplasticity terribly compromises this ability.

Consequently, negative emotional reactions (e.g., frustration, fear, anger, apathy, embarrassment, hopelessness, helplessness) are easier to generate and harder to regulate. Our underdeveloped capacity to regulate negative emotions can make us more vulnerable to displaying distasteful, damaging behaviors (e.g., a dysregulated chronic fear of scarcity could encourage money-oriented criminal behavior) that are hastily accepted by others as confirmation of stereotype-based expectations.

Despite America's general tendency to deny, minimize, and rationalize the existence of contemporary racism, various studies have confirmed that racism (i.e., racial discrimination, antagonism, exclusion, inequality, and injustice) is a specific type of chronic stressor that uniquely influences the overall physical and psychosocial well-being of Black people in America historically and currently. This isn't an ultra-radical suggestion with regard to the blatant atrocities associated with pre-Civil Rights Movement racism (e.g., enslavement, Jim Crow, lynchings, assassinations, etc.), which clearly disadvantaged Black people and this clear disadvantage undoubtedly contributed to their chronic stress. However, recent research asserts that modern forms of racism, even though more understated and implicit, may actually instigate more chronic stress than its explicit predecessor.

Much of the problem is that there are so many different forms of racism nowadays and this multiplicity can lead to ambiguity (i.e., difficulty being certain whether an experience was, in fact, racist) and anticipation (i.e., expect an experience to be racist even if it's not), in addition to actually racist experiences.

Binna and Pearn Kandola likened racism to "a virus that mutates, taking on different forms as it adapts to a changing environment." Contemporary racism in America can be systemic, individual, institutional, cultural, unconscious, aversive, everyday, anticipated, perceived, or internalized, which radically increases the probability and regularity of experiencing it. Since the various contexts of racism may be experienced simultaneously as well as repeatedly (which creates chronicity), this will increase the probability of developing chronic racism-related stress. However, "just as racism does not affect dominant and dominated racialized groups in the same manner," explained Kwame McKenzie, "it does not affect the dominated in a uniform manner either." True. But there are some disturbing, discernible trends that must be discussed.

When studying racism, there is a tendency to focus only on major or overt acts of racial discrimination. I believe that this is a mistake. It's the mundane and micro[30] experiences that are most

---

[30] Racial microaggressions, explained Kimberly Griffin, can occur as "everyday interactions that signal that a person's identity or social group is less valued or perceived negatively." Derald Sue et al. defined racial microaggressions as "brief and commonplace daily verbal, behavioral, or environmental slights, insults, indignities and denigrating messages, whether intentional or unintentional, that communicate hostile, derogatory, or negative racial slights and insults towards people of color." Studies support the fact that people of color "frequently experience microaggressions, that they are a continuing reality in their day-to-day interactions." Racial microaggressions

pervasive, least resolved, and impactful to so many aspects of everyday life. It's the routine experiences with racism that ultimately produce the greatest burden of chronic stress, particularly among African-Americans. The chronic stress of racism as an unending series of stressful life experiences impacting practically every aspect of our existence is thought to accumulate over time. It is this cumulative effect that appears to make chronic racism-related stress so remarkably consequential.

When asked for scholarly studies and whatnot, most African-Americans admit that racism has been stressful to them personally. But few of us ever really contemplate just how stressful experiencing racism can be and how all of that stress impacts us or how to stop it from impacting us so damagingly.

Contemporary racism in America, acknowledged Teun van Dijk, "does not consist of only white supremacist ideologies of race, or only of aggressive overt or blatant discriminatory acts. The Civil Rights Movement, antidiscrimination laws, policies of equal opportunities, and modest forms of Affirmative Action have today curtailed the more blatant and overt manifestations of racism against minorities." However, too many White Americans still seem to anticipate (perhaps unconsciously) some degree of Black subservience in interracial situations and are genuinely shocked when it is not demonstrated. It's subtle, but noticeable (especially by Black people). At least I notice it, far too often, and it's stressful. Whether communicated verbally, nonverbally, or even environmentally, anti-Black racial biases tend to reveal themselves

---

usually feature actions or reactions by White people rooted in hostility or lowered expectations and result "in a negative racial climate and emotions of self-doubt, frustration, and isolation on the part of victims."

These subtle, recurring actions and interactions signal that the target individual or group's social identity is perceived negatively and merits less valued treatment than "normal" people. Racial microaggressions are "often unconsciously delivered in the form of subtle snubs or dismissive looks, gestures, and tones. These exchanges are so pervasive and automatic in daily interactions that they are often dismissed and glossed over as being innocent and innocuous."

in interracial situations in the form of subtle snubs, looks, gestures, tones, and disclosed expectations, all indicative of some degree of racist annoyance, avoidance, apprehension, disdain, or disgust.

For its targets and victims, racism is oftentimes an omnipresent stressor. Essed described present-day racism as a "coherent complex of oppression continuously present and systematically activated personally through encounters, vicariously through the experiences of other Blacks (or people of color), through the media and through the daily awareness of racial injustice in society. From racism there is almost no relief."

Racism has evolved into a constant system of oppression in which the potential of members of particular racial groups to become fully human is deliberately and fundamentally reduced for the undeniable benefit of members of another racial group, the latter somehow already being deemed more human. The various tangible, social mechanisms, noted Harrell et al., "that have made the privileges associated with being White and the disadvantages associated with being a person of color relatively permanent characteristics of Western societies" are still in full effect.

"Many of the contours of opportunity for individuals and groups in the United States," as explained by Keith Lawrence et al., continue to be "defined—or 'structured'—by race and racism." Contemporary racism features "a system in which public policies, institutional practices, cultural representations, and other norms work in various, often reinforcing ways to perpetuate racial group inequity. It identifies dimensions of our history and culture that have allowed privileges associated with 'whiteness' and disadvantages associated with 'color' to endure and adapt over time."

Within systems of oppression such as racism, explained Rita Hardiman et al., "differences are used as an indicator that demarcates those who will benefit from oppression and those who will be targeted by it. An individual will have more or less power, privilege, and access to resources within a system of oppression, depending on whether the group to which she or he is perceived to

100

belong to." This systemic inequity is inherently stressful for those excluded and disadvantaged by it.

However, the overtness of historical, violent White supremacy has been mostly replaced by the sustainable subtleness of contemporary *White privilege*. It is so subtle most White people consistently dare to claim not to see or benefit from it. Many, however, do see it—and bear witness to benefiting from it. Because I'm not White and, consequently, am incapable of truly appreciating White privilege first-hand, I'll quote extensively their understanding of this unique set of positive, stress-reducing (for White people) life circumstances.

"White people live in a social environment that protects and insulates them from race-based stress," noted Robin DiAngelo. "This insulated environment of racial protection builds white expectations for racial comfort while at the same time lowering the ability to tolerate racial stress. In the U.S., while individual whites might be against racism, they still benefit from their group's control. Yes, an individual person of color can sit at the tables of power, but the overwhelming majority of decision-makers will be white. Yes, white people can have problems and face barriers, but systematic racism won't be one of them."

Francis Kendall alleged that White privilege is "hard to see for those of us who were born with access to power and resources. It is very visible for those to whom privilege was not granted." (It sure is Mrs. Kendall. It sure is.)

Furthermore, "the subject is extremely difficult to talk about because many white people don't feel powerful or as if they have privileges others do not. It is sort of like asking fish to notice water or birds to discuss air. For those who have privileges based on race...it just is—it's normal. All of us who are white, by race, have white privileges, although the extent to which we have them varies. For those of us who are white, one of our privileges is that we see ourselves as individuals, 'just people,' part of the human race. Most of us are clear, however, that people whose skin is not white are members of a race."

101

White privilege, to quote Peggy McIntosh, is basically "unearned power conferred systematically" to White people. "Privilege exists when one group has something of value that is denied to others simply because of the groups they belong to, rather than because of anything they've done or failed to do. Access to privilege doesn't determine one's outcomes, but it is definitely an asset that makes it more likely that whatever talent, ability, and aspirations a person with privilege has will result in something positive for them."

Maurianne Adams explained that "White privilege is about the concrete benefits of access to social resources and advantages and the power to shape the norms and values of society that whites receive, unconsciously or consciously, by virtue of their skin color in a racist society."

Allan Johnson added that "privilege is a feature of social systems, not individuals." Privilege is defined in relation to a social group or category. "Privilege exists when one group has something that is systematically denied to others not because of who they are or what they've done or not done, but because of the social category they belong to."

Unfortunately, these privileges advantage "some groups *at the expense of others.* Privilege creates a yawning divide in levels of income, wealth, education, housing, dignity, safety, health, and quality of life. It promotes fear, suspicion, discrimination, harassment, and violence. It's always at someone else's expense and always exacts a cost. Everything that's done to receive or maintain it, however passive and unconscious—results in suffering and deprivation" and stress for members of the disprivileged group.

However, "privilege doesn't necessarily lead to a 'good life,' which can prompt people in privileged groups to deny resentfully that they even have it. But privilege doesn't equate with being happy. It involves having what others don't have and the struggle to hang on to it at their expense."

Cory Collins confirmed that "White privilege is *not* the suggestion that white people have never struggled. Many white people do not enjoy the privileges that come with relative affluence, such as food security. Many do not experience the privileges that come with access, such as nearby hospitals. And white privilege is *not* the assumption that everything a white person has accomplished is unearned; most white people who have reached a high level of success worked extremely hard to get there. Instead, white privilege should be viewed as a built-in advantage, separate from one's level of income or effort."

Christopher Vang categorized "White privilege as a combination of exclusive standards and opinions that are supported by Whites in a way that continually reinforces social distance between groups on the basis of power, access, advantage, majority status, control, choice, autonomy, authority, possessions, wealth, opportunity, materialistic acquisition, connection, access, preferential treatment, entitlement, and social standing."

Joe Feagin and Eileen O'Brien wrote that "White privilege is ubiquitous and imbedded even where most whites cannot see it; it is the foundation of this society. It began in early white gains from slavery and has persisted under legal segregation and contemporary racism. Acceptance of this system of white privileges and black disadvantages as normal has conferred advantages for whites now across some fifteen generations. Most whites inherit significant social networks that are heavily or exclusively white and that provide access to important social contacts or capital. Once networking is in place, it tends to persist over the generations. Thus, whites' lives are shaped as much by the racialized system as the lives of those who are oppressed by it."

Kendall perceived "White privilege as an institutional (rather than personal) set of benefits granted to those of us who, by race, resemble the people who dominate the powerful positions in our institutions. One of the primary privileges is that of having greater access to power and resources than people of color do; in other words, purely on the basis of our skin color doors are open to us that are not open to other people."

"Often it is not our intent, as individual white people, to make use of the unearned benefits we have received on the basis of our skin color. Most of us go through our days unaware that we are white or that it matters. Regardless of personal intent, the impact is the same."

"On the other hand, the creation of a system in which race plays a central part—one that codifies the superiority of the white race over all others—has been in no way accidental or haphazard. Throughout American history white power-holders, acting on behalf of our entire race, have made decisions that have affected white people as a group very differently than groups of color. History is filled with examples of the purposeful construction of a systemic structure that grants privileges to white people and withholds them from others."

Again, to reiterate, "White privilege doesn't mean your life hasn't been hard," concluded Jimmy Kimmel. "It just means the color of your skin isn't one of the things that makes it harder."

Laura Pulido acknowledged that "White privilege is distinct from both white supremacy, a more blatant and acknowledged form of white dominance, as well as from more individual, discriminatory acts. Rather, it flourishes in relation to these other forms. Because most white people do not see themselves as having malicious intentions, and because racism is associated with malicious intent, whites can exonerate themselves of all racist tendencies, all the while ignoring their in-vestment in white privilege. It is this ability to sever intent from outcome that allows whites to acknowledge that racism exists, yet seldom identify themselves as racists."

"White privilege is a form of racism that both underlies and is distinct from institutional and overt racism. It underlies them in that both are predicated on preserving the privileges of white people (regardless of whether agents recognize this or not). But it is also distinct in terms of intentionality. It refers to the hegemonic structures, practices, and ideologies that reproduce whites' privileged status. In this scenario, whites do not necessarily *intend* to hurt people of color, but because they are unaware of their white-skin privilege, and because they accrue social and economic benefits by maintaining the status quo, they inevitably do."

Racial equality cannot coexist with White privilege. White privilege, wrote Wilson, requires the "subordination of other groups." Beginning with slavery, "the oppressive configuration White people have assumed in relation to Black people is in good part the result of the fact that we (Black people) have permitted ourselves to remain in a complementary subordinate configuration conducive to their oppressive designs." And that's on us (Black people). It's *also* a consequence of the neuroplastic impact of chronic racism-related stress on our capacity to regulate negative emotional reactions, like fear (i.e., we've been too afraid to be *completely* anti-racist[31]).

---

[31]   Welsing wrote in *The Isis Papers* that Black people in America "have been forced into passive and cooperative submission to white supremacy. The major strategy has been the installation of an overwhelming fear. Specific tactics range from actual physical castration and lynching, to other overt and more subtle forms of abuse, violence, and cruelty. The total Black collective in the U.S. has yet to confront consciously the 'mind-blowing' logic and thought-distorting shock and fear that set in following the assassinations of practically all courageous Black male leaders...who all were aware of the necessity to resist and destroy white supremacy. It has been demonstrated that the almost certain consequence of a pattern of consciously determined resistance to and destruction of white supremacy is death at the hands of white supremacy advocates—those who see and understand white supremacy as necessary to white survival. Since all of these deliberate deaths have occurred, there has been a profound disinclination by surviving Blacks to confront the awesome and murderous reality of white supremacy directly...Even young Black children are able to perceive and articulate that 'If you try to help Black people, you will be killed.'"

"This fear of death at the hands of the white supremacy system—because it cannot be admitted aloud by the adult Black population—has been repressed. Since the demise of these Black men, the remaining rhetoric coming from our Black collective is consistent with *submission to* and/or *cooperation with* the racist oppressive dynamic—albeit with an historical and continuing chorus of

105

Racism even as some awesome, omnipresent oppressive system has remarkably palpable, personal consequences for people of color (Black people especially). As brilliantly articulated by Marilyn Frye, the experience of racially "oppressed people is that the living of one's life is confined and shaped by forces and barriers which are not accidental or occasional and hence avoidable, but are systematically related to each other in such a way as to catch one between and among them and restrict or penalize motion in any direction. It is the experience of being caged in."

That distinct experience of being caged in, which can be both psychological and tangible, is inherently stressful. Chronically, profoundly, and sometimes traumatically stressful.

Racism-related stress is stress triggered by experiencing some form of racism or racist behavior, inclusive of any experience of racial discrimination, hostility, violence, exclusion, inequality, or injustice perceived or experienced as threatening, negative, and uncontrollable.

This chronic form of stress comes not only from repeated experiences of racism themselves, but our repetitive negative emotional responses to these experiences. "Exposure to racism," observed Clark et al., tends to make us feel ashamed, "anxious, paranoid, angry, helpless, hopeless, frustrated, resentful, and fearful" over and over again. We experience these racism-related feelings far longer and more often than we experience instances of racism. At some point, we get just tired of feeling this way so often, but we still lack the capacity or resources to control (i.e., stop) the experiences that cause these emotions. This dilemma, directly caused by racism, is fundamentally stressful, and can affect our "ability to function in school, work, and social settings." Moreover, the "perception of an environmental stimulus as racist results in exaggerated psychological and physiological stress

---

complaints. This behavior...is consistent with the illusion that there can be a complete *integration* of non-whites into the white supremacy system."

106

responses," which "over time, these stress responses influence health outcomes" far more than we typically fathom.

Experiencing any type of racism is still uniquely stressful for most Black people in America, all of which have come "to acquire negative emotional properties through direct association with an aversive stimulus," according to Elizabeth Phelps et al. Franklin-Jackson and Carter explained that "stress reactions depend on the individual's perception that the event or experience is negative and unwanted," which all instances of any type of racism are. Racism creates experiences that are often perceived as harmful, unexpected, ambiguous, repetitive, out of our control, and, consequently, stressful. Also, the "person's ability to cope with the stressful experience must be unsuccessful," which is too often the case.

While I doubt its probability, it's theoretically possible that a Black person in America never personally experiences an act of racism in any of its possible forms. However, to quote Harrell, "living in a society where the occurrence" of an act of racism in any of its possible forms "is at all times a distinct possibility can create stress above and beyond the generic stresses of life."

"Although the expression of outright racial discrimination has been greatly reduced in recent decades, more subtle and chronic forms of racial discrimination are still very real," observed Kenneth Ponds. Contemporary racism, according to Brian Smedley et al., is largely expressed as "a system of social structures that produces cumulative, durable, race-based inequalities" in nearly every meaningful facet of life against people of color. In other words, racism is now mostly *systemic*.

Racism, to quote Feagin, "is systemic because it infiltrates most aspects of life. In the United States, racism is structured into the rhythms of everyday life. It is lived, concrete, advantageous for whites, and painful for those who are not white."

It is "a diverse assortment of racist practices; the unjustly gained economic and political power of whites; the continuing resource inequalities; and the white-racist ideologies, attitudes, and institutions created to preserve white advantages and power. One can accurately describe the United States as a 'total racist society' in which every major aspect of life is shaped to some degree by the core racist realities."

Systemic racism, noted Annie Reneau, "goes beyond individual beliefs and feelings about people of other races. It means that the systems on which a society functions—the economic system, the education system, the healthcare system, the criminal justice system, etc.—are both infused with and impacted by the racism within which they were created and maintained."

Systemic racism also goes beyond the conscious intent of White people to *be racist* because "regardless of conscious intent," explained Ponds, "everybody in our society is conditioned, affected, and infected by racism. Racism extends beyond personal values and beliefs. The broader societal systems support the notion that whiteness represents superiority and non-whiteness signifies inferiority. Systemic racism disadvantages people of color and operates to the advantage of whites, whether or not they are aware of these privileges or even want them."

Systemic racism is particularly stressful because every major part of a Black person's life will most likely somehow be negatively impacted by racism at any time. Systemic racism features the almost constant "threat of racism," which for us requires, noted Essed, "planning, almost every day of one's life, how to avoid or defend oneself against racial discrimination," hostility, violence, exclusion, inequality, or injustice. Systematic racism, observed Feagin, "means always having to be prepared for anti-black actions," which, as a specific type of constant hypervigilance, can be a chronic stressor.

Chronic stress causes the brain to change its physical response to stress. Stress causes the release of cortisol, a hormone designed to enable the brain to elevate blood sugar and pressure levels in order to enhance our ability to respond to danger. Without cortisol, the survival-oriented brain couldn't be survival-oriented. However, with chronic stress there is so much cortisol constantly being produced, it basically becomes meaningless to the normal neural circuitry. The brain has to recalculate what it considers an abnormal amount of cortisol just to sustain its ability to respond reflexively to serious threat.

Constant cortisol saturation significantly changes neural structures like the hippocampus and PFC, both of which are gradually reduced in size and activity as cortisol annihilates hippocampus and PFC neurons via prolonged overactivation. Conversely, continuous cortisol production increases the size and activity of the amygdala. According to research by Pittenger and Duman, "chronic stress enhances synaptic plasticity and the function of amygdala neurons, an effect quite distinct from the atrophy it induces in the hippocampus and PFC. This could both result from and contribute to overactivation of neuronal circuits that control fear, anxiety, and emotion."

The now hyperactive and hypertrophied amygdala promotes persistent states of hypervigilance and heightened emotional reactivity, even our stress response is exacerbated. Chronic stress strengthens the neural pathway between the amygdala and hippocampus and weakens the neural pathway between the hippocampus and PFC. Consequently, our fight or flight response to perceived threats is drastically quickened because our ability to moderate it is linked to the functional efficiency of the hippocampus and PFC, both of which are neuronally atrophied by continuous cortisol saturation. In other words, an exaggerated (or anticipatory) stress response is a consequence of the brain changes brought about by the chronic stress of systemic racism.

Exacerbating systemic racism as a chronic stressor is the fact that it will continue so long as there is no counterpressure adequate enough to force change. And if White people inherently benefit from it and people of color (Black people especially) continue to lack the social capacity (i.e., power[32]) and social courage[33] to stop

---

[32] Maulana Karenga defined "power as the social capacity of a group to realize its will, even in opposition to others." Welsing boldly described how Black people continue to "live under the power of the white supremacy system

of total oppression and domination, implying the absence of any true power to determine ultimately what happens to their individual and collective lives. But because this is a frightening and painful reality upon which to focus our attention, we as Blacks, particularly in the U.S., succumb to circular thought. Likewise, there is not only a failure to approach problem solution, but there is a stubborn refusal even to look directly at the problem. Ultimately, there is a disturbance in problem perception. Therefore, Black people in the U.S. reject the conscious recognition of the global white supremacy system, its absolute necessity of non-white oppression and its very specific implications of a continuing powerlessness and potential destruction—as opposed to a natural death—for Blacks and other designated non-whites."

As a result, "there is no commitment by Blacks to analyze the problem of white supremacy comprehensively. Blacks are without a perception or analysis of racism, or of a scientific counter-racism. Every energy and psychological effort is expended, at both the individual and collective levels, to avoid focusing on the true problem of white supremacy. All Blacks realize, consciously and/or unconsciously, that to engage in such a realistic focus can mean certain death at the hands of white supremacists."

[33] Conditioned fear of White superiority is perhaps the most significant catalyst to the perpetual acceptance of systemic racism (i.e., Black docility) in America by Black people. Damn near every Black person who ever dared to tangibly (not just rhetorically) and publicly rebel against systemic racism has been killed, incarcerated, or discreetly co-opted. Inevitably, that's going to have an impact, implicitly or not, on how Black people as a group react to it now and moving forward.

Malcolm X admitted "that societies often have killed the people who have helped to change those societies," especially Black people competently threatening White privilege. Since the acknowledged murders of Jemmy Cato, Toussaint L'Ouverture, Gabriel Prosser, Denmark Vesey, David Walker, Nat Turner, Medgar Evers, Dedan Kimathi, Patrice Lumumba, Amilcar Cabral, Martin Luther King, Jr., Fred Hampton, Mark Clark, George Jackson, Steve Biko, Walter Rodney, Thomas Sankara, the 11 MOVE members bombed and burned to death in 1985 in Philadelphia, Kenule Beeson Saro-Wiwa, and Malcolm himself, Black people worldwide have internalized the terrifying inference that "if you try to help Black people, you will be killed." And there were so many others *not acknowledged*, but murdered nonetheless.

It's actually illogical to assume a stimulus-reinforcement association between Black rebellion and inevitable defeat (i.e., punishment) *would not* somehow be created and, consequently, change the brains of African-Americans collectively (via patterned neuronal activity). Our survival-oriented brains have been uniquely conditioned to automatically fear and avoid the punishments that

110

being collectively subjugated and diminished by systemic racism, then systemic racism will continue indefinitely.

Further intensifying systemic racism as a chronic stressor is that so many people, including some Black people[34], argue that it's not a *real issue* (or, consequently, a stressor), which can make experiencing it as a victim more ambiguous (and, as a result, even more stressful).

Racism is not *over*. "This system of Whites as dominant and people of color as subordinated" that we all, as Americans, live in "has become so ingrained in our society that it is virtually invisible," explained Sheri Schmidt," but it (systemic racism) certainly *exists*. Of course, I'd rather it didn't, but I know it does. You probably do too. Despite popular (White) opinion, I, like most Black people I'd suppose, don't need to allege racism merely to *self-handicap*[35]. We'd actually rather total racial equality, if it too was systemic (i.e., impacting every major aspect of life).

---

became associated with attempted rebellion. These associations became stronger and more automatic the more frequently we activated them. As a result of racism-related neuroplasticity and fear conditioning, docility has increasingly become our preferred (or learned) response to systemic (and most other forms of) racism.

[34]   ...who, at least to me, appear *overly desperate* to somehow get rid of the distinction noted by Frederic Poag: "When you're white in America you're given the freedom to be an individual without the connotations and limitations of your race. In short, you're just a person, instead of a black person. That's an important distinction, and it's one that people who aren't white desperately want to get rid of" (e.g., in an individual capacity socially integrate away/escape from their own Blackness). Perhaps denying or diminishing the continued significance of race in general (oftentimes while exaggerating the blame of Black people for "their" own disadvantage) is their arguably maladaptive way of coping personally with the chronic stress of being Black in America.

[35]   Self-handicapping, as originally defined by Steven Berglas and Edward Jones, is "any action that enhances the opportunity to externalize (or excuse) failure," especially in anticipation of failing, "thus enabling the individual to avoid or discount negative implications of a poor performance" on their self-worth. Self-handicapping, concluded Ted Thompson and Anna Richardson, "involves the strategic establishment of an impediment or obstacle to success," such as racism, "prior to a performance situation which thereby provides a

"The hegemonic acceptance of these dominant/subordinated relationships creates a commonsense reality where white supremacy is unconsciously seen as part of the natural order of things," which makes systemic racism even more stressful for those who are somehow conscious of what's really going on. "Both dominant and subordinate group members internalize the idea of the system as normal and correct and thus help to perpetuate it. White supremacy is thus supported by an invisible notion of white as the 'defined norm' that is backed up by access to both economic and institutional power."

"The shift from conceptualizing racism as an individual phenomenon to seeing it as a systemic problem is particularly challenging because the notion of racism as systemic is in direct contrast to many people's core values and assumptions that America is built on the principles of hard work and merit. White people in particular tend to believe that all Americans are seen and treated as individuals and that any individual who works hard will be rewarded through a fair and just society," while consciously or unconsciously holding the stereotype-based belief that Black people are lazy (and, consequently, use racism as an excuse for not succeeding).

"Most white Americans also do not see slavery, legal segregation, or contemporary racism as aspects of an American system of racism. They see them, instead, as brief incidents that unfortunately were 'tacked on to a great nation for a short time.' Racism is seen as a blemish on American history that, with the

---

convenient excuse for poor performance." By creating this impediment or obstacle to success, explained Roy Baumeister and Steven Scher, "the self-handicapper minimizes the implications of failure, because failure is discounted—that is, it is attributed to the obstacle rather than to low ability."

Most researchers, including Tim Urdan and Carol Midgley, believe that self-handicapping is "born out of a fear of failure and the motive to avoid the negative implications about ability that such failure represents." In other words, people who self-handicap fear giving their best effort and still failing, because failure would then be indicative of their own inherent inadequacy and incompetence.

exception of a few 'bad' individuals, has essentially been eradicated. Many people hold so tightly to a view of racism as an 'incident' in history and to beliefs in meritocracy that it is very hard for them to see that racism can be anything more than random acts of thoughtlessness and hatred."

Unique to systemic racism, realized Stephen Ostertag and William Armaline, is "its ideological component, sometimes called 'color-blind racism' or 'color-blind ideology,' which is crucial to its covertly institutionalized structural form. Color-blind ideology refers generally to the ideas or beliefs that (a) racism does not exist, or is no longer a problem; (b) inequalities along racial lines are not the result of racism, rather some other form of oppression (e.g., social class) or personal fault(s) of those racially oppressed; and (c) whites, particularly white elites and policymakers, no longer 'see' race, and are 'color-blind' in action and thought." What differentiates systemic racism "from the more open and obvious manifestations of past eras is that overt coercion is no longer the primary or singular mechanism for its persistence. Instead, contemporary racism endures because it now reflects more sophisticated, hegemonic mechanisms for the uneven distribution of power and resources despite resistance."

The built-in ambiguity of systemic racism increases its capacity as a chronic stressor for Black people in this country. To constantly question for ourselves or feel that we must prove to others the very existence of racism (or the validity of our experiences of racism), before we could even attempt to cope with whatever feelings experiencing racism may cause, only enhances this type of racism-related stress.

Contemporary racism being largely systemic doesn't entirely exclude or excuse (or eradicate the stress generally caused by) *individual racism*, which features individuals or a small group of individuals acting against other individuals (i.e., on an interpersonal level) because of negative attitudes held towards members of their race. This form of racism includes the conscious and unconscious individual expression of various types of anti-

113

Black (or people of color) biases, beliefs, insults, and behaviors ranging from public injustice to physical aggression. Kathryn Anderson noted that individual racism "may take the more overt forms of social avoidance and social exclusion, discrimination in the workplace, stigmatization, or harassment and threat, or it may take the less-perceptible forms such as attitudes and beliefs against minorities in the form of 'microaggressions.'"

Elizabeth Brondolo et al. observed that this form of racism "can take place in a number of different contexts, including work, public places, the criminal justice system, or social and personal venues." And it's particularly worth noting that "during episodes of interpersonal racism in each of these contexts, stereotypes held by the perpetrator are activated by the targeted individual's phenotypic or cultural characteristics. These stereotypes, and not the targeted individual's unique characteristics, influence the perpetrator's perceptions of and responses to the target."

Many White people still demonstrate a significant degree of individual (or interpersonal) racism which, to quote James M. Jones, suggests a persistent "belief in the superiority of one's own race over another" (e.g., Black people) and in the "behavioral enactments that maintain those superior and inferior positions." Research led by Callie Burt et al. confirmed that "interpersonal racial discrimination is a common experience for African American adults and youth alike."

According to Glenn Loury, underlying the interpersonal emotions of contemporary racism "is a profound awareness of the racial 'otherness' of blacks that is deeply ingrained in the American cultural consciousness—an 'otherness' that brings to mind a host of negative presumptions, taboos, and suspicions. When a group is stigmatized in this manner, to the point where social identity ascribed to group members by external observers essentially devalues their humanity," injustice, hostility, and avoidance may become endemic with regard to interacting with members of that group individually or interpersonally.

114

Individual racism is what most people think of when they consider the word "racism." It's the most obvious form of racism and consists of interpersonal acts of prejudice involving differential, negative assumptions about abilities, motives, and intentions; discrimination involving biased actions and behaviors; or stereotyping involving suspicion, devaluation, and dehumanization towards people of color. Individual racism, according to Hart Blanton and James Jaccard, is "characterized by explicitly racist attitudes regarding the inferiority of blacks or other minorities and overt tendencies to engage in unambiguously discriminatory behavior."

Individual racism is uniquely stressful for Black people in America. Brondolo et al. described how individual racism "may erode the quality of routine interpersonal exchanges and engender anxiety about interacting with cross-race peers," which can certainly trigger a stress response in anticipation of or after experiencing a negative racism-related experience.

Individual racism can also be so unambiguous, so flagrant, so obviously wrong, yet we still lack the social capacity and courage required to stop or adequately cope with it and are oftentimes directly harmed psychologically or physically by these biases, beliefs, insults, and behaviors. Furthermore, there's no genuine *expectation* of consistent justice or adequate consequences for the perpetuators of individual racism. In other words, not only is there nothing we can do to stop it, we shouldn't expect those with the social capacity to stop it to do anything to support or protect us.

In effect, other types of contemporary racism (e.g., institutional, unconscious, aversive) conveniently diminish this expectation by rationalizing, obscuring, or minimizing the intent of the racist as well as the harm done to us. This systemic response somehow takes away much of the aforementioned overtness of individual racism and creates an artificial ambiguity that ultimately exacerbates it as a racism-related stressor.

Institutionalized racism is another form of contemporary racism that creates circumstances and experiences that are uniquely negative, ambiguous, unpredictable, and uncontrollable for its victims. Hence, institutionalized racism is another chronic stressor for Black people in America. An institutional conception of present-day racism, according to Miguel Unzueta and Brian Lowery, "equates racism with institutional rules and procedures that (intentionally or not) have a disproportionately positive and negative effect on members of dominant and subordinate groups, respectively."

Institutionalized racism consists of the racist attitudes and actions that have been sustained by the governmental (or political), media, educational, legal, economic, and healthcare institutions in this country for centuries. According to ERASE Racism, "institutional racism is a term that describes the way government and other public and private institutions systematically afford White people an array of social, political and economic advantages, simply because they are White, while marginalizing and putting at a disadvantage African Americans and many other people of color. White people often cannot see and do not question the sources and legitimacy of their privilege and power, whereas people of color experience daily its consequences. Even without conscious, personal racial animosity, these institutional structures, policies, and practices generate and maintain racial discrimination, segregation, and inequalities of opportunity that keep African Americans and other people of color apart from the mainstream of American economic and political life."

"The institutional policies may never mention any racial group," noted Sally Leiderman et al., "but their effect is to create, maintain or fail to remedy accumulated advantages for white people and accumulated disadvantages for people from other racial groups."

"Institutional racism is more subtle, less visible, and less identifiable but no less destructive to human life and human dignity than individual acts of racism. Institutional racism deprives a racially identified group, usually defined as generally

116

inferior to the defining dominant group, equal access to and treatment in education, medical care, law, politics, housing, etc."

Louis Knowles explained that in order to fully understand institutional racism "it is best to consider first what institutions are and what they do in a society. Institutions are fairly stable social arrangements and practices through which collective actions are taken. Institutions have great power to reward and penalize. They reward by providing career opportunities for some people and foreclosing them for others. They reward as well by the way social goods and services are distributed—by deciding who receives training and skills, medical care, formal education, political influence, productive employment, fair treatment by the law, decent housing, self-confidence, and the promise of a secure future for self and children."

"No society will distribute social benefits in a perfectly equitable way. But no society need use race as a criterion to determine who will be rewarded and who punished. Any nation that permits race to affect the distribution of benefits from social policies is racist. To detect institutional racism, especially when it is unintentional or when it is disguised, is a very different task. And even when institutional racism is detected, it is seldom clear who is at fault."

Institutionalized racism, to quote Thomas Brown, reflects a sustained attempt to "keep power, control, and wealth under the auspices of the dominant culture in our society." Yet, "White Americans seldom critique what it means to be white and to recognize the unearned benefits that result therefrom. Consequently, they have created some rather ingenious methods to deny the existence of racism. This denial is based on a fear of losing the material and psychological advantages they enjoy." Institutionalized racism is one of those ingenious methods of denial because institutionalizing racism creates just enough ambiguity to enable at least personal denial of racism. Of course, this ambiguity exacerbates the stress felt by the victims of institutionalized racism.

In some way or another, ambiguity has been a common component in the abovementioned forms of contemporary racism. Most importantly, ambiguity causes or increases stress. Ambiguity occurs when numerous interpretations of an experience or situation (or the causes of an experience or situation) are plausible, creating uncertainty. In the case of racism, ambiguity occurs when the target or victim of a racist experience or situation can't identify with certainty that racism is the cause of the experience or situation (i.e., they are, in fact, experiencing racism). It doesn't help that so many people try to claim that racism is over and we're just using it as an excuse for our own presumed laziness, mediocrity, or incompetence.

When this differential access spread throughout into our institutions, it eventually becomes common practice, making it that much harder to recognize, much less rectify. Eventually, racism-based circumstances dominate our media, educational, legal, economic, and healthcare institutions and is unconsciously reinforced by the thoughts and actions of all within the institution. Another difficulty with recognizing or reducing institutionalized racism is that there is no truly identifiable perpetrator. When racism is built into an institution, it appears to be an act of the collective population. Once racism takes hold and is embedded within institutions it no longer requires racist intent or individual racists. It is a kind of racism without obvious racists. Rather, institutional racism can be perpetuated by seemingly benign policies, practices, behaviors, traditions, structures, etc., which is how it remains so ambiguous.

At the macro-level, added Feagin, "large-scale institutions—with their white-controlled normative structures—routinely perpetuate racial subordination and inequalities." However, "these institutions are created and recreated by routine actions at the everyday micro-level by particular individuals." In other words, there *is* a significant degree of individual culpability (i.e., individual racism) within institutional racism if you have the audacity to look hard enough for it (as opposed to deny, minimize, rationalize, or normalize it, which is the national tendency).

Institutional racism generally enables White people to continue to enjoy the tangible and psychological benefits of White privilege without the explicit guilt of doing so. I feel like I'd be remiss if I didn't repeat that while I am consciously being anti-racist, my goal here is not *in any way* to be anti-White. For some reason, possibly hypervigilance with regard to my own well-being[36] or perhaps just out of respect for the positive relationships I've established with many White people, at points like this I instinctively feel it suddenly necessary to clarify that I am not now nor have I ever intended to be anti-White as a person or a writer. Fully acknowledging racism and White privilege is neither anti-White nor synonymous with suggesting that all (or even most) White people are necessarily racist or that somehow racism or White privilege is necessarily (or explicitly) responsible for all (or most) things impacting Black people, including stress.

White privilege, wrote Wilson, requires the comprehensive subordination of non-White people. Accordingly, "American institutions operate in opposition to their publicized missions when dealing with the subordinated groups." While attempting to project an "image of objectivity and neutrality," these institutions "in actuality operate in the oppressive interests of the society's ruling groups and against the interests of its subordinate groups."

Hence, "when we look at major American institutions relative to African-Americans, we observe the following reversals: the

---

[36] Wilson also explained that "the White American community severely punishes through social ostracism, ridicule, mockery, employment discrimination, physical assault and denial of fundamental civil rights, those African-Americans who openly identify with and espouse African culture, history, values, autonomy and liberation," which may include any direct attack on White superiority or privilege. Conversely, "African-Americans who demonstrate an apparent rejection of their African identity, African culture, history and values, and acknowledge their subordination to European domination, are rewarded with increased opportunities, material and social compensation, although restricted relative to White Americans."

119

economic system keeps them poor, the criminal justice system mediates injustice; the educational establishment creates ignorance and intellectual incompetence; the family institution breeds broken homes and 'illegitimate' children; and the health and welfare system catalyzes sickness and administers health-care neglect (the lifespan of African-Americans is actually decreasing)." Institutional racism directly and deliberately creates constant experiences of disadvantage and discrimination for Black people in America that we lack the individual or collective capacity to control or stop, which clearly makes it a chronic stressor.

Institutional racism has the capacity to produce and perpetuate conditions that increase our exposure to traditional life stressors—such as "inadequate family incomes, health care, education, job training, housing, employment, and economic development—which strain the Black community's coping mechanisms. The effects of these stressors are amplified by the relatively dependent and reactionary orientation of the Black community."

In addition to enhancing the stress caused by institutional racism, the ambiguity of this type of racism enables White America to continue to promote "racism as a phenomenon rooted in individuals instead of institutions." Unzueta and Lowery realized that this is done, mostly unconsciously or implicitly, "because an institutional conception of racism, more so than an individual conception of racism, raises their awareness of White privilege, a concept threatening to Whites' self-image." White Americans may generally "be motivated to avoid conceiving of racism as an institutional phenomenon because this conception is associated with an increased awareness of the advantages associated with belonging to the dominant racial group. Therefore, accepting an institutional conception of racism may raise Whites' awareness of White privilege—a concept threatening to Whites' self-image because of the discomfort associated with the idea that their personal successes were facilitated by unearned group-based privileges."

120

"White privilege represents an external attribution for Whites' personal success that threatens to discount their internal attributions (e.g., talent and effort) for such success," which would actually be stressful for White people. "As such, for the benefit of their self-image, Whites may be motivated," again, mostly unconsciously or implicitly, "to downplay the existence of White privilege," which is easier to do due to the downplayed existence of institutional racism.

Another form of contemporary racism we commonly experience is *cultural racism*. Wijeyesinghe et al. defined cultural racism as those constant aspects of American "society that overtly and covertly attribute value and normality to white people and Whiteness, and devalue, stereotype, and label People of Color as 'other,' different, less than, or render them invisible."

Black people in America encounter and tend to internalize mostly negative and depreciating portrayals of who we are expected to be and what it means to be Black because of cultural racism. What or who is seen and treated as physically beautiful, artistically valuable, culturally appropriate, naturally inventive, or historically accurate are all based on the false notion of White superiority (i.e., whatever is most associated with Whiteness or White people is automatically "better than").

To be so consistently and comprehensively negated (i.e., made negative) by the cultural prioritizing of Whiteness and lack the social capacity to control or adequate cope with being negated is inherently stressful. "Situations that evoke negative stereotypes are stressful," noted Sabrina Zirkel. And this is exactly what cultural racism does, constantly create interpersonal and institutional situations that ultimately evoke negative stereotypes in the evaluation of people of color.

Anti-Black cultural racism, concluded Hicken et al., specifically results in a constant misrecognition of Black people via the "attachment of crude, stigmatizing stereotypes that mischaracterize their humanity and obscure within-group variation." This form of racism makes it easier for non-Black people (and, once internalized, even Black people ourselves) to assign a set of negative characteristics to all Black people (as similarly seen members of a specific, highly stigmatized social outgroup).

Various studies have confirmed that within American culture specifically there is a terribly high concentration and extensive history of anti-Black stereotypes and stigma. Not only are Black people consequently viewed negatively, we are viewed markedly more negatively more quickly (or automatically) than any other social or racial group in this country.

The norms, images, and messages within American culture have consistently affirmed the "assumed superiority of white people and the assumed inferiority of people of color," noted Beverly Tatum. Patricia Devine wrote that "during socialization, a culture's beliefs about various social groups are frequently activated and become well-learned." In other words, these cultural beliefs are internalized—even a thought repeated unconsciously can develop into patterned neuronal activity that changes or rewires the brain in order to repeat it constantly. As a result, "these deep-rooted stereotypes and evaluative biases are automatically activated, without conscious awareness or intention, in the presence of members of stereotyped groups."

Highly negative stereotypes tend to minimize perceived variation within outgroups. They allow encourage the erroneous, automatic perception that members of an outgroup targeted by cultural racism are all the same (i.e., share the same negative characteristics promoted culturally) as opposed to being diverse, complex individuals. For Black people, who we think we are (self-concept) and how we feel about who we think we are (self-esteem), at least implicitly, is profoundly negated as a result of cultural racism. Negative views and stereotypes come to largely define who we are expected to be, characterize us as somehow negatively different, and frequently prevent us from being seen distinctively (i.e., as an individual[37]).

A recent study led by Eaaron Henderson-King and Richard Nisbett verified that "it took observing only one negative action by a single Black person to activate negative stereotypes and attitudes toward Black people in general." This "person-to-group generalization" occurs because people usually "perceive outgroups as less variable and therefore see individual outgroup members as prototypic of the larger group."

Annie Paul agreed that while "we tend to see members of our own group as individuals, we view those in outgroups as an undifferentiated—stereotyped—mass." Our perception of individual outgroup members (e.g., a Black person) can be automatically negated, explained Teun van Dijk, "primarily because they are thought to belong to another group, that is, as group members and not as individuals. Negative properties attributed to the group as a whole are thus applied to its individual members, who therefore are seen as essentially alike and interchangeable."

As a result of cultural racism in America, all Black people are generally expected to be lazy, violent, unintelligent, criminal, irresponsible, incompetent, dangerous, degenerate, disrespectful, apathetic, hostile, unqualified, problematic, self-destructive, excuse-dependent, complaint-oriented, diabolical, flawed,

---

[37] Anderson J. Franklin explained how this invisibility evolves, oftentimes unconsciously, when stigmatized individuals feel that "they live in a depersonalized context in which who they are as a genuine person, including their individual talents and unique abilities, is overshadowed by stereotyped attitudes and prejudice that others hold about them." For Black people, this "invisibility" comes from individuals not being seen as distinct human beings, only the stereotypes associated with being Black in America is acknowledged along with all the negative notions and assumptions that are attached to Blackness. "Invisibility is considered a psychological experience wherein the person feels that his or her personal identity and ability are undermined by stigma in a myriad of interpersonal circumstances. Invisibility is defined as an inner struggle with the feeling that one's talents, abilities, personality, and worth are not valued or even recognized" as a result of cultural racism.

incorrigible, and/or generally inferior because we are Black. I need more White people to somehow *feel* just how awful and infuriating and discouraging this can be; most of us already know. I have known for what seems like forever. And there's not much I (or any other individual Black person) can do to stop these people from probably applying these negative presumptions and expectations to me, which can be both terrifically and routinely stressful.

Jack Roviere asserted that "racial stereotyping might be based on a kernel of truth, and many people justify stereotyping by pointing to statistics. However, what people fail to realize is that in most cases, the statistics don't conclude anything" about a *specific* person (i.e., you or I as an individual). The "associations and expectations of a particularly stereotype may be flat-out wrong and unsubstantiated...there are no concrete genetic imperatives that stress" or validate the "common stereotypes of any race."

Nevertheless, with this constant misrecognition of Black people, and Blackness more broadly, comes a shame-based feeling on the part of too many Black people of being undeserving of or unwelcomed in supposedly "White spaces." Largely the intended, tangible byproduct of America's social boundaries[38], White

---

[38] Michele Lamont and Virag Molnar defined social boundaries as "objectified forms of social differences manifested in unequal access to and unequal distribution of resources (material and nonmaterial) and social opportunities." Embedded into the sociocultural environment as its status quo, social boundaries establish "identifiable patterns of social exclusion or class and racial segregation."

Social boundaries function as a form of implied social control. Social boundaries, according to Charles Tilly, "separate 'us' from 'them.'" The social construction of threat (to racial hierarchy and privilege) leads to the social construction of boundaries to somehow minimize that threat. The social group currently with the most social power creates boundaries to reject or contain social groups with less power (yet perceived as threatening) in order to maintain intergroup inequalities. And in America, social boundaries, noted Feagin (also White), are largely "grounded in white resistance to substantial changes in the status quo. Central to white concerns is a fear whites have of losing status and power because of black attempts to bring change."

124

spaces, according to Elijah Anderson, are the usually nicer and newer[39] neighborhoods, schools, workplaces, stores, restaurants, and other public spaces that are "overwhelmingly white." These spaces are oftentimes a stress-inducing environment in which Black people are "typically absent, not expected, or marginalized when present;" thus, we "typically approach that space with care" (i.e., hypervigilance). Black people are often required to navigate White spaces in order to access nicer and newer locales and opportunities.

"When present in the white space blacks reflexively note the proportion of whites to blacks, or may look around for other blacks with whom to commune if not bond, and then may adjust their comfort level accordingly; when judging a setting as too white, they can feel uneasy and consider it to be informally 'off limits.' For whites, however, the same settings are generally regarded as unremarkable."

When the anonymous Black person enters a White space, the White people there tend to automatically "try to make sense of him or her—to figure out 'who that is,' or to gain a sense of the nature of the person's business and whether they need to be concerned. In the absence of routine social contact between blacks and whites, stereotypes can rule perceptions, creating a situation that estranges blacks. In these circumstances, almost any unknown black person can experience social distance, especially a young black male—not because of his merit as a person but because of the color of his skin" and the stigma America has socioculturally attached to

---

Michael Schwalbe et al. added that "dominant groups maintain boundaries between subordinate groups to protect their access to resources and maintain their social, economic, and political advantage. These boundaries can be symbolic, interactional, spatial, or all of these. By preserving these boundaries, dominant groups protect the material and cultural capital they have acquired and upon which they rely to preserve their dominance."

[39] Mostly due to relatively recent creation or renovation attributable to phenomena like suburbanization and urban gentrification along with the greater sociopolitical power and income/wealth of White people collectively.

Blackness. "Defensive whites in these circumstances may be less consciously hateful than concerned and fearful of 'dangerous and violent' black people."

For many of them, Black people "in the white space may be viewed as a spectacle of black advancement at the expense of whites. Black presence thus becomes a profound and threatening racial symbol that for many whites can personify their own insecurity and sense of inequality. While certainly not all are guilty of such acts, many can be mobilized in complicity to 'protect' the white space, which blacks must navigate as a condition of their existence, and where whites belong and black people can so easily be reminded that they do not."

Accordingly, we're tolerated as long as we don't dare "disturb the implicit racial order—whites as dominant and blacks as subordinate" and are sometimes even willing to tacitly negotiate or "perform to be accepted" (i.e., confirm that the more threatening anti-Black stereotypes don't necessarily apply to us). *No worries White folks, no Nat Turner here. Please carry on...*

This "performance can be as deliberate as dressing well and speaking in an 'educated way' or as simple as producing an ID or a driver's license in situations in which this would never be demanded of whites." And most of the time we have no desire whatsoever to do all this for you (and your sense of security), but we usually lack an alternative or the ability to not do it (which is stressful). "Depending on how well the black person performs or negotiates, he or she may 'pass inspection,' gaining provisional acceptance from the immediate audience" into the White space.

"When venturing into or navigating the white space, black people endure such challenges repeatedly" and a "degree of scrutiny that a 'normal,' white person would certainly not need to endure." Typically, we "take this sort of racial profiling in stride; they expect it, treat it as a fact of life, and try to go on about their business, hoping to move through the world uneventfully. And most often, with the help of social gloss to ease their passage, they do; however, on occasion they experience blatant discrimination,

126

which may leave them deflated and offended. White salesmen, security guards, and bouncers repeatedly approach black persons with a disingenuous question, 'Can I help you?' The tone of voice and the circumstances belie a true offer of help and define the situation as slightly ominous. Most defenders of such spaces prefer to be more indirect in their challenges and queries to avoid offending" or, more likely, infuriating us "or incurring lawsuits."

When in these White spaces, it's hard for us to not sense the White gaze on our Black bodies as it confirms the continuing significance of race in this country. When in these White spaces, it's hard for us to not feel the abundant anti-Black emotional reactions toward us of so many of the White people there: the annoyance, the avoidance, the apprehension, the disdain, and, of course, the disgust. They're usually expressed very subtly and possibly even unconsciously, but my spirit still can't help but cumulatively experience each of these unwarranted emotions. "These people," to quote James Baldwin, "have deluded themselves for so long that they really don't think I'm human. I base this on their conduct, not what they say." I *personally* can confirm this from conduct I have experienced repeatedly, not just what Mr. Baldwin wrote years ago.

In these White spaces, "small issues can become fraught with racial meaning or small behaviors can subtly teach or remind the black person of his or her outsider status" and that he or she will probably not "be regarded and treated as a full person in the white space." We ultimately may conclude that the real problem is that we are not White "and that being white is a fundamental requirement for acceptance and a sense of belonging in the white space." Once this point is reached, performing for acceptance into a White space becomes more or possibly too difficult and White spaces are now forever approached ambivalently and with a certain degree of defensive callousness. The many highly negative feelings that could accompany such a conclusion (i.e., disappointment, frustration, anger, powerlessness) may be too much to cope with and cause psychological harm (i.e., chronic stress, possibly even traumatic stress) as well as maladaptive neuroplasticity. Never knowing with certainty "whether or not we may be truly welcome" or constantly feeling unwelcomed probably because we are Black could become a chronic racism-related stressor for Black people.

The perceived need for Black people to develop adaptive strategies (i.e., somehow change ourselves, like using our fake "White voice") just to prepare ourselves for negotiating these "White spaces" in anticipation of (usually microaggressive) acts of cultural and interpersonal racism itself can be a chronic racism-related stressor. This perceived need, noted Hicken et al., "may be due to previous interpersonal experiences with prejudice and discrimination, but may also be due to vicarious experiences. In sum, engagement in chronic vigilant thoughts and behaviors in order for one's humanity to be properly recognized is an important source of racism-related stress."

Any type of "anticipatory stress is the activation of the biological stress response system in anticipation of a potentially stressful situation" (e.g., entering a "White space" as a Black person). Notably, research shows that the anticipation of the situation alone—even in the absence of the actual situation—is enough to activate the stress response system. This is a normal, healthy part of human physiology. However, chronic anticipatory stress may result in ultimate dysfunction of the stress response system" along with maladaptive neuroplasticity. Maladaptive neuroplasticity are those brain changes that somehow instigate negative outcomes (e.g., diminished ability to regulate negative emotions and impulsivity, increased reliance on self-handicapping, chronic hypervigilance, etc.).

Overt race relations in America may have improved, wrote Timothy Wilson, "but unconscious racism, in a culture rife with stereotypes, is less controllable and more difficult to avoid or influence." Unconscious racism, as a form of contemporary racism, is more prevalent in American society and far more impactful as a stressor for Black people in America than generally acknowledged.

Anti-Blackness remains rampant but is now normally buried deep in the unconscious of White America. "The vast majority of white Americans harbor unconscious negative associations about and feelings toward Black people," suggested John Dovidio and Samuel Gaertner. So, whenever their anti-Blackness is acted out in the form of racial discrimination, hostility, violence, exclusion, inequality, or injustice, in many cases the perpetrator "may not even be aware of how their implicit beliefs about race influence their judgments and actions," explained Lincoln Quillian. However, being unconscious doesn't make this particular form of racism somehow *less racist* or tolerable or excused. Any act of racism is still an act of racism. And with regard to racism, impact is greater than intent.

Brent Staples recognized that "very few Americans make a conscious decision to subscribe to racist views. But the toxic connotations that the culture has associated with blackness have been embedded in thought, language, and social convention for hundreds of years." Many of the implicit cognitive associations and attitudes that cause unconscious racism can and have been learned, according to Hal Arkes and Phillip Tetlock, "from the broader culture." Much of what enters our unconscious mind comes from the culture around us. As we are socialized in the norms of our national culture, we are also psychologically inundated by the stereotypes and prejudices explicitly or implicitly included in these norms.

Unconscious racism is fundamentally a consequence of the neural structures and circuitry involved in the processing and categorizing of racially biased (i.e., anti-Black) external stimuli[40]. The process of categorizing racial outgroup members based on racial stereotypes creates automatic associations in the human

---

[40]   In America, "negative Black stereotypes," wrote Stanley Tookie Williams, "are broadcasted or implied by the news media, magazines, institutions, television, newspapers, books, and every other medium you can think of."

brain based on the strengthening of specific neural circuitry (how we perceive racial others is determined by connections embedded in neural circuitry). This reaction, especially when repetitive, eventually becomes patterned neuronal activity. Patterned neuronal activity changes the neural structure and functioning of the brain by triggering neuroplasticity. Eventually, our brain changes to automatically associate mostly negative attributes, assumptions, expectations, and emotions with "Blackness" (i.e., being Black in America).

Research recently completed by Patricia Devine and Andrew Elliot confirmed that the brain of most Americans tends to change to automatically associate mostly negative stereotypes with Black people. Our neural responses are informed and formed by a lifetime of repetitive exposure to rather consistent yet mostly implicit cultural cues. Simply existing in the anti-Black stereotype-laden culture of America maintains our brain's vulnerability to being rewired to automatically activate these stereotypes whenever we think about or interact with Black people. This happens regardless of the extent of our explicit racial bias, mere "*awareness* of these stereotypes is sufficient."

Robin Phillips proposed that "the messages we are exposed to in our culture actually change [or strengthen] the neurocircuitry of our brains." That's because culture creates or sustains patterned neuronal activity by creating or confirming repetitive thinking. Humans "all have what might be called a culturally modified brain," according to Norman Doidge. "Neuroplastic research has shown us that every sustained activity ever mapped—including physical activities, sensory activities, learning, thinking, and imagining—changes the brain. Cultural ideas and activities are no exception." The cultural ideas and activities we are most consistently exposed to instigates the most profound neuroplasticity.

One of the most consistent ideas of American culture is that all people (i.e., social or racial groups) are not equal. "Our society assigns value to groups of people," explained Gail Christopher. "It is a process that is embedded in the consciousness of Americans and impacted by centuries of bias," stereotyping, and stigma. All Americans, Kristin Anderson noted, are largely influenced by implicit "cultural messages about who is valued and who is not" as well as what makes certain groups valuable or not.

American culture, according to Cortney Warren, communicates "the traits and characteristics of people that are deemed more desirable and less desirable largely based on who has the most power. We learn these cultural values whether we are consciously aware of it or not. This process of learning about and accepting cultural values through direct (explicit) and indirect (implicit) messages is generally referred to as cultural conditioning."

Historically, American culture teaches all Americans "that being White is better than being non-White. If you were raised in the United States (and many other Western cultures), you learned that being White is better than being non-White—even if you were not consciously aware that you were learning it, or consciously believe it is false. You were conditioned to believe it. And, like all isms of domination, if you are in a position of power (in this case, you are White), you will struggle to see that race matters to the lived experiences of people because it will be mostly invisible to you."

As Americans, we share a common experience with cultural conditioning regardless of our own race, in which racial bias (and anti-Black bias in particular) continues to play a dominant role. "Because of this shared experience," explained Charles Lawrence, "we also inevitably share many ideas, attitudes, and beliefs that attach significance to an individual's race and induce negative feelings and opinions about nonwhites" generally and Black people especially. "To the extent that this cultural belief system has influenced all of us," we are all vulnerable to holding an implicit anti-Black bias. This vulnerability extends to Black people in America as well (in the form of *internalized* racism).

131

We have all been deeply psychically socialized by a culture that is permeated with racism. Therefore, it would be logical, according to William J. Wilson, for us to act according to our culture and "to follow one's inclinations as they have been developed by learning or influence from other members of the community to which one belongs or with which one identifies." This is the process of unconscious cultural transmission, "whereby an individual's exposure to certain attitudes and actions is so frequent that they actually become part of his or her own perspective."

Michael Adams explained that "the individual vision of external reality is mediated—that is, *psychically constructed*—by schemata, categories, or 'types' (be they archetypes or stereotypes), which if not naturally inherited, are so culturally ingrained in the unconscious that they might as well be. Prominent among these are, of course, 'racial' prejudices—biases that through a process of *cultural ingraining* prove especially difficult to modify."

Unconscious racism is uniquely stressful to Black people because it also perpetuates the aforementioned constant "threat of racism," which for us requires, noted Essed, "planning, almost every day of one's life, how to avoid or defend oneself against racial discrimination," hostility, violence, exclusion, inequality, or injustice. Unconscious racism, observed Feagin, "means always having to be prepared for anti-black actions" that in many cases the perpetrator may not even be aware of committing, which, as a specific type of continuous hypervigilance, can be a chronic stressor.

Further exacerbating unconscious racism as a chronic stressor for Black people in America is that we tend to experience unconscious racism cumulatively, "whereby new encounters are interpreted on the basis of past experiences" with unconscious racism, observed Utsey. And because we can experience unconscious racism "almost every day" of our lives, the actual (neuroplastic) impact of unconscious racism as a chronic stressor is oftentimes a "consequence of the cumulative effects of numerous events," explained Carter.

Racism-related stress increases if an experience with any form of racism is "ambiguous, negative, unpredictable, and uncontrollable," and unconscious racism is clearly all of those things. Consequently, unconscious racism can be acutely, chronically, and even traumatically stressful for Black people.

Contemporary racism in America can be *aversive* as well, and oftentimes it is. Adam Pearson et al. noted that "a substantial proportion of Whites in the United States can be characterized as exhibiting reactions toward Blacks consistent with aversive racism."

According to Kristin Henkel et al., "aversive racists sympathize with victims of past injustice, support the principle of racial equality, and regard themselves as nonprejudiced, but, at the same time, possess negative feelings and beliefs about Blacks, which may be unconscious" but not necessarily. Aversive racism features consistently more positive reactions by White people to other White people than to Black people (i.e., an underlying hostility and/or negative orientation toward Black people), in spite of these White people explicitly claiming to not be anti-Black in any way.

Aversive racism is assumed to be "qualitatively different than blatant 'old-fashioned' racism, is more indirect and subtle, and is presumed to characterize the racial attitudes of most well-educated and liberal Whites in the United States. Nevertheless, the consequences of aversive racism are as significant and pernicious as those of the traditional, overt form," including the chronic stress it can cause among Black people by still having the capacity to instigate racist behavior.

"Some Whites may not be racist at all." However, Samuel Gaertner et al. concluded "that given the historically racist American culture and human cognitive mechanisms for processing categorical information, racist feelings and beliefs among white Americans are generally the rule rather than the exception. Many

133

well-intentioned Whites consciously believe in and profess equality, but unconsciously act in a racist manner, particularly in ambiguous situations." They have developed a "value system that maintains it is wrong to discriminate against a person because of his or her race" and "rejects the content of racial stereotypes," but that "nonetheless cannot entirely escape cultural and cognitive forces. Aversive racists recognize that prejudice is bad, but they do not recognize that they are prejudiced."

The "aversiveness" of this form of racism refers to the "inherent contradiction that exists between Whites' denial of personal prejudice coexists with underlying unconscious negative feelings toward, and beliefs about, Blacks. In contrast to the feelings of open hostility and clear dislike of blacks that characterize old-fashioned racism, the negative," anti-Black feelings that aversive racists typically experience are "discomfort, uneasiness, disgust, and sometimes fear," which lead to racial ambivalence, "avoidance, and social awkwardness rather than to open antagonism."

Aversive racists are also more likely to be offended by and defensive of any suggestion that they may still actually be racially biased (i.e., anti-Black) in their thinking and behavior regardless of their rhetoric or intentions. This makes them less likely to adequately reflect on the causes of their anti-Blackness in order to reduce or discontinue its impact, and, if any of these suggestions actually come from a Black person, may reinforce their original anti-Black feelings of anxiety and uneasiness out of a deeper, constant fear of someday being exposed as racist (and/or, to quote Feagin, the "fear Whites have of losing status and power because of Black attempts to bring change"). Experiencing racism from aversive racists is particularly stressful to Black people because of this exaggerated reluctance on the part of aversive racists to admit to and subsequently rectify such experiences. When they are made aware of their racist thinking or behavior, aversive racists tend to "deny that they intended to offend, believe the person of color raising the issue is 'oversensitive,' 'paranoid,' or has simply misinterpreted the situation," noted Derald Sue et al.

Instead of being accountable or corrective, aversive racists are more likely to create ambiguity. Ambiguity causes or increases the stress of an already negative, unpredictable, and uncontrollable act of racism. Ambiguity occurs when numerous interpretations of an experience or situation (or the causes of an experience or situation) are plausible, creating uncertainty. In the case of aversive racism, ambiguity occurs when the target or victim of a racist experience or situation can't identify with certainty that racism is the cause of the experience or situation (i.e., they are, in fact, experiencing racism). It doesn't help that so many people try to claim that racism is over and we're just using it as an excuse for our own presumed laziness, mediocrity, or incompetence.

Whereas "blatant racists exhibit a direct and overt pattern of discrimination," Gaertner et al. described aversive racists' actions as "more variable and inconsistent. Sometimes, they discriminate (manifesting their negative feelings), and sometimes, they do not (reflecting their egalitarian beliefs). Nevertheless, their discriminatory behavior is somewhat predictable. Because aversive racists consciously recognize and endorse egalitarian values and truly aspire to be non-prejudiced, they will *not* act inappropriately in situations with strong social norms when racial discrimination *would be obvious* to others and to themselves. Specifically, when they are presented with a situation in which the normative response is clear (e.g., right and wrong are clearly defined), aversive racists will not discriminate against Blacks. In these contexts, aversive racists will be especially motivated to avoid feelings, beliefs, and behaviors that could be associated with racist intent."

In other situations, the racist thinking and behavior of aversive racists is distinctly unpredictable. The unconscious "feelings and beliefs that aversive racists also possess may produce discrimination in situations in which normative structure is weak, when the guidelines for appropriate behavior are unclear, when the basis for social judgment is vague, or when one's actions can be justified or rationalized on the basis of some factor other than race. Under these circumstances, aversive racists may engage in behaviors that ultimately harm Blacks but in subtle, unintentional, rationalizable ways that allow Whites to maintain a non-prejudiced self-image and insulate them from recognizing that their behavior is not colorblind."

Everyday racism is another form of contemporary American racism commonly endured almost daily as relatively unremarkable events and experiences that are uniquely negative, ambiguous, unpredictable, uncontrollable, and, consequently, chronically stressful for its victims.

A term coined by Philomena Essed, everyday racism is a "process involving the continuous, often unconscious, exercise of power predicated in taking for granted the privileging of whiteness." People of color (especially Black people) are subtly victimized mostly by "systematic, recurrent, and familiar practices" and "conditions of discrimination" rather than "extreme incidents. The crucial characteristic of everyday racism is that it concerns mundane practices." It centers on "injustices recurring so often that they are almost taken for granted—nagging, annoying, debilitating, seemingly small injustices one comes to expect."

Everyday racism is not just about the badness of racists, but more about "racist practice, meaning racism as common societal behavior." Everyday racism is so much more than independent experiences of racial discrimination. It is a manifestation of "systematic, recurrent, and familiar practices that minorities face on an everyday basis" based on the "subtle racist attitudes and actions infused into the fabric of society" that allow the threat of racial discrimination, hostility, violence, exclusion, inequality, and injustice to permeate the everyday life of people of color (Black people especially).

Everyday racism quietly sustains the constant, cumulative disadvantages tangibly associated with being Black in America that oftentimes spawn stressful racism-related experiences.

136

Frances Ansley realized that everyday racism maintains "a political, economic and cultural system in which whites overwhelmingly control power and material resources, conscious and unconscious ideas of white superiority and entitlement are widespread, and relations of white dominance and non-white subordination are reenacted daily across a broad array of institutions and social settings." Everyday racism is not just a singular or exceptional act, but the accumulation of covert (and sometimes quite overt) inequities, injustices, biases, habits, looks, tones, interactions, expectations, and other "everyday practices by which the dominant group secures the status quo of race relations."

The term *everyday* racism "is quite apt, first, because of its reference to the daily occurrences of subtle actions, slights, and microaggressions," explained Eric Grollman, "and second, because it refers to a common, 'everyday' feel of the reality of racism. By attending to the extreme, overt expressions of racism of a few 'bad apples,' we miss the widespread existence of minor, subtle expressions of racism. Though a rare slight here or there has little effect, the everyday exposure to these slights adds up, taking a toll on the health and well-being of each person of color. In fact, the health consequence of everyday racism is comparable to, and may even exceed, those of major events of discrimination."

"This is, in part, due to the heavy cognitive and emotional toll of *processing*—'was that discrimination? was that because I'm Black?' Despite the stereotype that people of color are quick to 'play the race card,' to assume unsatisfactory or differential outcomes are the result of discrimination, most probably go through a series of steps in their heads *before* concluding racism may have been at play. That represents a lot of used up mental and emotional energy, on top of all of the other stressors everyone experiences regardless of race, as well as those disproportionately faced by people of color (e.g., poverty, barriers to important institutions like education, health care, etc.)."

We'd actually rather it *not* ever be racism because Black people in America know intuitively that we lack the social capacity to *control* (i.e., reduce, minimize, or completely stop) most things racism-related. For nearly all forms of contemporary racism, White folks, as their conscious or unconscious creators and beneficiaries, have *that* power (and responsibility) almost exclusively. Uncontrollability increases the stressfulness of any threatening event or experience, especially those (everyday) racism-related.

Ambiguity, as repeatedly abovementioned, also increases the stressfulness of any threatening event or experience, and everyday racism is exceptionally ambiguous. Essed wrote that "everyday racism, though felt persistently, is often difficult to pinpoint. Microinjustices become normal, fused into familiar practices, practices taken for granted, attitudes and behaviors sustaining racial injustice." Continuous contempt and hostilities against people of color, although largely understated, inevitably become endemic to American life. Rules and regulations are oftentimes applied "differently or more strictly to people of color," normalizing racial unfairness in a way that prevents adequate protest and correction because *we* are still doing something wrong.

Is it racism or just that members of America's "dominant racial/ethnic group automatically favor members of their own group, not simply because they want to be with those they feel are their own, but because they believe, deep down, that white lives count more, that they are more human, that theirs is a superior culture and a higher form of civilization than others"? Isn't *that* still racism?

"Yet, it would be incorrect to see everyday racism simply as a white-versus-black phenomenon." One of its greatest cumulative consequences is when people of color, especially Black people, experience White superiority so frequently that we internalize it and ourselves "become agents of everyday racism."

Laura Brown described this as "the process by which a member of an oppressed or stigmatized group internalizes into her or his core identity and self-concept all or part of the negative stereotypes and expectations held by the culture at large regarding that group." This process actually originates as a consequence of the utter pervasiveness of negative cultural messaging and interpersonal aggressions targeting specific oppressed groups. "One need not experience identifiable instances of overt discrimination to internalize racial oppression," the daily occurrences of subtle actions, slights, and microaggressions attributed to everyday racism are sufficient.

Feagin summarized everyday racism as "a system of oppression made up of many thousands of everyday acts of mistreatment of black Americans by white Americans, incidents that range from the subtle and hard to observe to the blatant and easy to notice. These acts of mistreatment can be nonverbal or verbal, nonviolent or violent. Moreover, many racist actions that crash in on everyday life are, from the victim's viewpoint, unpredictable and sporadic. Such actions are commonplace, recurring, and cumulative in their negative impact."

It is in effect these additional characteristics (unpredictable, sporadic, commonplace, recurring, and cumulative) that make everyday racism far more impactful as a stressor for Black people in America than generally acknowledged.

The true (neuroplastic) impact of everyday racism as a racism-related stressor, noted Essed, is not as a "singular act in itself, but the accumulation of small inequities. Expressions of racism in one particular situation are related to all other racist practices and can be reduced to three strands of everyday racism, which interlock as a triangle of mutually dependent processes: (1) the *marginalization* of those identified as racially or ethnically different; (2) the *problematization* of other cultures and identities; and (3) symbolic or physical *repression* of (potential) resistance through humiliation or violence. Accusations of oversensitivity about discrimination, continuous ethnic jokes, ridicule in front of others, patronizing behavior, rudeness, and other attempts to humiliate and intimidate can all have the effect of discouraging action against discrimination" by as well as repeatedly triggering the stress response of the targets of everyday racism.

"Although the term everyday racism has such an informal ring that it may sound as if it concerns relatively harmless and unproblematic events, it has been shown that the psychological distress due to racism on a day-to-day basis can have chronic adverse effects on mental and physical health. The anticipation that discrimination can happen becomes in itself a source of stress. The same holds true for fretting over how to respond, whether the response has been effective, and whether further victimization will follow."

I'd argue that not enough scholarly or conversational attention is given to just how much Black people in this country constantly anticipate racism and the impact on Black people of constantly anticipating racism. We anticipate racism so commonly that anticipated racism is another form of contemporary racism. Far too often after a certain level of cumulative experience, even if unconsciously, we begin to anticipate racism in our interactions with White people and American institutions "regardless of whether we are actually discriminated against on each occasion. This is a strategy of self-protection," but also a dangerous source of chronic stress and maladaptive neuroplasticity.

I cannot accept that Black folks anticipate racism simply because we prefer a negative experience or outcome be rooted in racism in order to then use racism as a substitute or an excuse for our own presumed laziness, mediocrity, or incompetence (being the real reason behind the negative experience or outcome). The main reason why I cannot accept this is because I've *felt* (and, unfortunately, still feel) anticipated racism and am convinced that the feeling of constantly anticipating racism is much worse than the feeling of needing an excuse like racism for something bad happening in my life.

It's worse because the threat of racism is greater and more uncontrollable, which makes the stress and general feeling of it worse. I can *possibly* do something to control, reverse, or stop a negative, non-racism related experience or outcome. However, I already *know* that racism is beyond my control, I can't *stop it*, and the notion of "reversing racism" is fundamentally flawed. It's also easier, as a Black person in America, to convince yourself that you're not inherently lazy, mediocre, or incompetent just because of the color of your skin than it is to convince yourself that it's no longer necessary or beneficial to anticipate the possibility of racism in your everyday life. Racism can be acutely or cumulatively terrifying. Believing that certain negative experiences and outcomes are the consequences of my own inadequacy and, hence, my fault is disappointing but tolerable.

"Counter to the common belief that people of color are overly sensitive to discrimination, research has indicated that most people of color are reluctant to label a given situation as racism before carefully considering all other possible explanations to account for unfair treatment." I believe this reluctance is our brain's cognitive and emotional response to the perception of uncontrollability associated with racist experiences. Once we acknowledge an experience as racist, the perception ensues that we have no control over that experience (which is even more threatening/stressful).

Nevertheless, *anticipation* is a heuristic-like[41], survival-oriented reaction (in this case against the *threat* of racism or an act of racism). And it's necessarily stressful.

Stress is essentially an interaction between an external, negative stimulus (or threat) and our brain's response, a response largely determined by the magnitude of the stimulus as compared to our personal (or social) competence or ability or resources for dealing with the stimulus. Whenever we perceive (consciously or unconsciously, accurately or inaccurately) a negative discrepancy between the magnitude of the negative stimulus (or threat) and our personal (or social) competence or resources to cope, we experience stress; if we perceive this discrepancy recurrently, then we experience chronic stress.

---

[41]   Heuristics are described by Gerd Gigerenzer as "efficient cognitive processes, conscious or unconscious, that ignore part of the information" for the sake of speed and expediency.

However, the overwhelmingly negative stimulus (e.g., a racist experience) does not necessarily have to actually occur in order for us to experience stress, the mere threat or anticipation of such an experience can be enough to trigger the stress response. For the most part, Black people in America have relatively few places where we can go and be assured of not possibly experiencing an act of racial discrimination, hostility, violence, exclusion, inequality, or injustice. This reality may leave us feeling that we must be constantly "on" and vigilant against racism. The chronic stress caused by this continual vigilance against racism may trigger our racism-related stress response so frequently (or chronically) that it becomes stuck "on" (i.e., the brain becomes trapped in perpetual allostasis).

Anticipating racism may largely be why, according to recent fMRI studies, the amygdalae of African-Americans tend to be disproportionately hyperactivate and hypertrophied. Researchers using fMRI demonstrated that seeing or considering interacting with someone from a racial outgroup causes neuronal hyperactivation in our amygdala specifically. This is because we automatically see them as a threat. For Black people, this implies that after centuries of racism as lived experience we now tend to react unconsciously to interracial situations (specifically with White people) by anticipating the threat of racism.

Anticipation is linked to hypervigilance, and anticipated racism is associated with chronic hypervigilance. Anticipated racism, observed Feagin, "means always having to be prepared for anti-black actions," which, as a specific type of constant hypervigilance, can certainly be stressful. "Merely the anticipation of racism," Jason Silverstein explained, and not necessarily experiencing an act of racism, is "enough to trigger a stress response. Just the fear of racism alone should switch on the body's stress-response systems. This makes sense—if we think our environment contains threats, then we will be on guard."

Anticipated racism is a chronic stressor. Chronic stress is stress resulting from repeated or constant exposure to circumstances and experiences anticipated to be or perceived as threatening enough to trigger the stress response and the subsequent oversaturation of stress hormones, primarily cortisol, in the brain. The neural circuitry and structures responsible for producing the stress response are altered to become the dominant areas of the chronically stressed individual's brain. Chronic stress, according to Machiko Matsumoto and Hiroko Togashi, changes the human brain by creating long-lasting negative "alterations in the neural circuits underlying emotional regulation and increase the subsequent reactivity to stress later in life." Continuous cortisol overproduction increases the size and activity of the amygdala (i.e., neuronal hypertrophy). Consequently, negative emotional reactions (e.g., anxiety, anger, frustration, shame, hopelessness, helplessness) are easier to generate and harder to regulate in the future.

Anticipating racism, fundamentally, is another specific type of negative emotional reaction. More precisely, anticipating racism involves a combination of dysregulated negative emotional reactions to past experiences, both direct and vicarious, with racism. We anticipate racism *because* we are overly afraid or anxious of, angry about, frustrated with, shameful[42] of, feel hopeless, and/or helpless about experiencing racism in the future. We anticipate racism because we have so frequently and profoundly (and perhaps even traumatically) experienced racism-related stress in our past.

The more we deploy our brain's racism-related stress response, the more hyperactive it (along with the neural structures and pathways associated with it, e.g., the amygdala) becomes until we find ourselves constantly hypervigilant about the

---

[42] Shame comes with the idea that somehow experiencing racism or not being able to prevent this experience is our fault or indicative of something being wrong with us. Self-blame is a common, maladaptive way to cope with the actual powerlessness or uncontrollability we may feel with regard to experiencing racism.

possibility/threat of encountering racism. In other words, the more we encounter the stress of experiencing, perceiving, or anticipating racism in our past, the more our brain changes to continue to increasingly anticipate racism in the future and experience anticipated racism as a chronic stressor.

A chronically stressed brain houses an overactivated (and *changed*) amygdala. This amygdala is on constant (albeit unconscious) alert for possible danger (e.g., acts of racism) and, as a result of chronic hypervigilance, is more vulnerable to frequently perceiving danger (e.g., acts of racism) that may not actually exist.

Perceived racism, according to Elizabeth Brondolo et al., refers to an "individual's self-reports of exposure to racist interactions." In other words, perceived racism occurs "when racism is believed to be the motivation for a specific experience," explained Teresa Marino, especially an otherwise ambiguously negative (interpersonally or institutionally) interracial experience. Whenever we believe we've experienced racism, *we immediately experience perceived racism* even if we haven't actually experienced an act of racism (i.e., racially motivated discrimination, hostility, violence, exclusion, inequality, or injustice).

Dennis Combs et al. confirmed that "perceived racism acts as a stressor for African Americans." Perceived racism is actually more of a *chronic* stressor for Black people in America than *actual* racism.

If there's enough external stimuli for us to perceive that we are threatened—physically or psychologically—by a situation or experience, our stress response will initiate whether or not the threat is real. Survival, not accuracy or confirmation, is our brain's priority at that moment. Accordingly, our brain's stress response is triggered by perceived stressors more often than actual (legitimate) stressors. More specifically, especially for Black people in America, our brain's racism-related stress response is triggered by experiences of perceived racism more often than experiences of actual racism.

144

As a consequence of the pervasiveness of actual, oftentimes ambiguous manifestations of contemporary racism, perceived racism has become a significantly common psychosocial stressor for African-Americans. Clark et al. realized that perceived racism includes our "perceptions of prejudiced attitudes and discriminatory behaviors, and is not limited to more overt expressions or behaviors (e.g., being called a 'nigger'). That is, perceived racism may also include perceptions of subtler forms of racism," such as institutional, aversive, or everyday racism.

Racism must not be "objectively defined to produce a stress response in a victim," acknowledged Thema Bryant-Davis and Carlota Ocampo. "If the victim perceives the event as potentially racist, a stress response may occur." In other words, *merely perceiving* a highly negative experience as racism-related could cause stress, regardless of the correctness of the perception. Nicole Jagusztyn noted that "as long as a person feels they are subject to differential treatment based on group membership, this perception may have adverse effects."

According to Carol Miller and Cheryl Kaiser, the mere "perception of racism by African Americans, for example, results in negative emotions such as anger, anxiety, frustration, hopelessness, helplessness, resentment, and fear."

Elizabeth Pascoe and Laura Richman added that "if an individual perceives discrimination on a regular basis, these stress responses should be activated more often, potentially leading to a consistently negative emotional state. Chronic, heightened physiological stress responses, such as cardiovascular reactivity and cortisol responses, are also included in this pathway. Experiences of perceived discrimination may contribute to health problems," many of them deadly, disproportionately experienced by Black people because of "allostatic load developed by heightened stress responses and negative emotional states," including heart disease, cancer, stroke, diabetes, hypertension, increased susceptible to infectious viral diseases (e.g., COVID-19), and early health deterioration[43] (i.e., "weathering"). In other words, the chronic stress of *perceived racism*, in particular, is "literally killing" Black people in America.

With contemporary racism, racist behavior is generally more ambiguous and, as a result, necessarily more perceptual than explicit, which may result in a far more chronic stress response than we experienced historically. The human brain is naturally survival-oriented. Accordingly, after generations of racism our brain would now instinctively prefer to presume an ambiguously negative interracial experience is probably racism-related and react in whatever way we can to best survive the experience than regretfully assume that it is not. And every time this process repeats itself, we experience perceived racism negatively as a threat to our physical (i.e., potential bodily harm) or psychosocial (i.e., damage to our self-concept, self-esteem, or social self[44]) well-being.

The human brain, when faced with a real or imagined threat to our physical or psychosocial well-being, readies the human being

---

[43] To account for early health deterioration disproportionately experienced by Black people in America relative other racial/ethnic groups, Arline Geronimus proposed the "weathering" hypothesis, which posits that "Blacks experience early health deterioration as a consequence of the cumulative impact of repeated experience with social or economic adversity and political marginalization. On a physiological level, persistent, high-effort coping with acute and chronic stressors can have a profound effect on health. The stress inherent in living in a race-conscious society that stigmatizes and disadvantages Blacks may cause disproportionate physiological deterioration, such that a Black individual may show the morbidity and mortality typical of a White individual who is significantly older. Not only do Blacks experience poor health at earlier ages than do Whites, but this deterioration in health accumulates, producing ever-greater racial inequality in health with age through middle adulthood."

[44] Threats to our social self, observed Tara Gruenewald et al., feature "situations that contain the potential to devalue one's social self by calling into question abilities, competencies, or traits on which a positive social image is based, or situations characterized by potential or explicit rejection" or inequity. "Such situations are provocative because they contain social information pertinent to a primary human goal: that of achieving and maintaining a positive 'social self.'"

to confront the threat or promptly get as far away (physically or psychosocially) from the threat as possible. Whether the threat is ultimately real or just imagined is irrelevant; it's the perception of threat that triggers the stress response. This "fight or flight" response is a reflexive reaction by our brain to rapidly provide our body with those resources (e.g., increases in the release of certain hormones and neurotransmitters to enhance pro-survival functioning) required for either resisting or running from a threat. Whether this threat is physical or psychosocial, the same brain responses to threat occur, and because they have become automatic (or hardwired due to past utility), these responses typically supersede critical thought or active choice for the sake of rapidity (and ensured survival).

Consequently, we experience and are neuroplastically impacted by the stress of perceived racism far more frequently than we most likely realize.

Sue et al. explained that people of color must "rely heavily on experiential reality that is contextual in nature and involves life experiences from a variety of situations." We begin to identify (and accumulate as emotional memories) anticipatory cues in our lived experience with racism. Because of this lived experience and the pervasiveness of verifiable racism, individual incidents of perceived racism oftentimes become perceived as "nonrandom events" with "the only similarity 'connecting the dots' to each and every one of these incidents being the color of our skin." Thus, the inclination to automatically perceive racism even when racism is not applicable.

Conversely, "most White Americans do not share these multiple experiences, and they evaluate their own behaviors in the moment through a singular event. Thus, they fail to see a pattern of bias, are defended by a belief in their own morality, and can in good conscience deny that they discriminated." In other words, they tend to not perceive racism as quickly or consistently as Black people, even when the possibly ambiguous behavior or experience is *actually* racist.

147

"Numerous psychological stress responses may follow perceptions of racism," concluded Clark et al. These responses include "anger, paranoia, anxiety, hopelessness, helplessness, frustration, resentment, and fear." I have personally experienced every single one of these responses repeatedly with regard to perceived racism. I suppose at this point I just know too much about racism through lived experience and writing so much about it to somehow stop seeing or, more accurately, *feeling* the possible influence of racism on many of my daily interactions and experiences.

Remember, there's so many forms of racism nowadays it's kind of hard to not at least perceive it in one form or another. Contemporary racism can be experienced or just perceived as systemic, individual, institutional, cultural, unconscious, aversive, everyday, anticipated, internalized, or as microevents, which radically increases the probability and regularity of experiencing racism-related stress at least as a consequence of perceived racism.

Honestly, not cool. And if I'm wrong, I'd rather not perceive racism. I'd rather not have to try to cope with that stress unnecessarily. As I mentioned previously, I've struggled with stress my entire life. Much of which was probably racism-related; battling microaggressions mostly while also having to "determine on a regular basis if an event is related to my race or not." Not cool at all.

The "perception of an environmental stimulus as racist" can result in an acute, chronic, or even traumatic stress response. "There is a tendency to discount perceptions of racism as stressful," observed Rodney Clark et al., yet "this denial is inconsistent with the stress literature, which highlights the importance of the appraisal process. The perception of (environmental) demands as stressful is more important in initiating stress responses" than the actuality of it.

"Given that psychological stress responses are more sensitive to an individual's perception of stressfulness than objective demands, there is no a priori way of determining if an environmental stimulus will be perceived as racist by an individual." All racism is perceived, if we're being technical. "The individual who experiences racism does so as a result of their subjective perception of the actions of others" as racist. Accordingly, "the initiation of psychological stress responses as a result of perceiving environmental stimuli involving racism would qualify race-based stimuli as stressors" that could possibly even reach the threshold for being chronic or traumatic.

Whenever racism-related stress is "prolonged, extreme, or repetitive, the neuron pathways in the amygdala lose their 'elasticity' or ability to recover." As a result, "the brain keeps sensing danger, sending out stress response signals," and releasing certain neurotransmitters and hormones such as cortisol. When neural structures and pathways are chronically awash with these brain chemicals and hormones, these neural structures and pathways (e.g., the amygdala, hippocampus, and prefrontal cortex) can be significantly changed structurally or functionally.

It has been theorized that perceived racism, explained Jessica Graham et al., has a unique capacity to drastically increase our feelings of uncontrollability with regard to racism as a negative experience relative to other forms of racism. Many researchers have proposed that "an individual's perception of lack of control over the environment and potentially threatening experiences (which racist experiences are) play a key role" in the chronicity and neuroplastic impact of racism-related stress. This sense of uncontrollability can overwhelm our ability to cope with the negativity of the stressor (e.g., racism) and ultimately trigger a more incessant stress response (and maladaptive neuroplasticity) than experiencing the stressor itself.

Exposure to the uncontrollability of perceived racism can cause an accelerated loss of PFC size and function and increase in amygdala size and function relative to "normal" racism-related stress. According to Avis Hains et al., "when we feel stressed and out of control, high levels of norepinephrine and dopamine release

149

rapidly weaken PFC, while strengthening more primitive emotional responses and habits mediated by the amygdala."

Chronic exposure to the stress of uncontrollability induces greater "loss of PFC pyramidal cell spines and atrophy of dendrites...PFC gray matter decreases and PFC connectivity" weakens quickly. "This can save our lives when we are in danger and rapid, reflexive responding is needed, but can be detrimental when more thoughtful solutions are needed."

A greater sense of sustained controllability increases the prefrontal cortex's ability to regulate and calm the amygdala, specifically as it relates to our perception of negative experiences. Uncontrollability, particularly when persistent, decreases that ability and, consequently, makes the amygdala far more active than necessary. More cortisol is released, eventually leading to prolonged cortisol saturation in certain brain areas and subsequent brain changes.

Constant cortisol saturation, as aforementioned, significantly changes neural structures like the hippocampus and prefrontal cortex, both of which are gradually reduced in size and activity as cortisol annihilates hippocampus and PFC neurons via prolonged overactivation. Conversely, continuous cortisol production increases the size and activity of the amygdala. The now hyperactive and hypertrophied amygdala promotes persistent states of hypervigilance and heightened emotional reactivity, including an exacerbated racism-related stress response. The hypervigilant amygdala is constantly perceiving racism and activating the racism-related stress response, and every activation makes a future activation stronger and more likely (as it becomes brain-changing patterned neuronal activity).

In other words, the more our brain changes to continue to increasingly perceive racism in otherwise ambiguously negative interracial experiences and situations, feel that racism as overwhelmingly uncontrollable, and experience perceived racism as a chronic and possibly even traumatic stressor.

Internalized racism (also often referred to as internalized racial subordination or oppression) is another far too common and stressful yet drastically underacknowledged form of contemporary racism. The vast majority of Black people in America presumably experience internalized racism as a chronic stressor to some degree.

Internalized racism features the process through which people of color tend to unwittingly *internalize* (i.e., accept as valid, then incorporate into our self-concept and self-esteem) the highly negative, uncontrollable racism-related attitudes, prejudices, cultural messages, expectations, and stereotypes we regularly experience in a radical attempt to cope with these experiences as a chronic stressor.

Psychologically rooted in overwhelming feelings of inferiority, frustration, and powerlessness that accompany being racism's consistent targets and victims, internalized racism establishes certain inauthentic yet persistent behaviors and characteristics among racially oppressed people that negates and devalues how we feel about ourselves individually and collectively. Within the lived experience of racism, people of color (especially Black people) habitually "internalize messages of subordination," noted Teeomm Williams, through which we become increasingly vulnerable with regard to thinking, behaving, and understanding "the world in ways that maintain and perpetuate our oppression." Most of the aforementioned forms of contemporary racism feature this type of messaging along with constant anti-Black "stereotyping, scapegoating, and blaming the victim."

The ultimate result of internalized racism is that Black people begin to "perpetuate, collude with, and contribute to the systems of oppression that target them. This collusion occurs despite the fact that there is no member of the dominant group present to ask for, expect, demand, or enforce this behavior. When collusion occurs, it may be conscious or unconscious, intentional or unintentional. The net effect, however, is the same: the perpetuation and

151

maintenance of oppression, in part, through the actions of subordinant groups."

"Like *all* forms of internalized domination," explained Karen Pyke, "internalized racism is *not* the result of some cultural or biological characteristic of the subjugated. Nor is it the consequence of any weakness, ignorance, inferiority, psychological defect, gullibility, or other shortcoming of the oppressed." It is a psychological consequence of (i.e., maladaptive attempt to cope with) prolonged racial oppression. It's not like "to be Black is, by definition, to be self-hating;" however, internalized racism does lead to increased "feelings of self-doubt, disgust, and disrespect for one's race and/or oneself."

We are all vulnerable, perhaps to varying degrees, of internalizing racist conceptions of our intrinsic worth and abilities as promoted by our most consistent sociocultural experiences and perceptions. Lawrence Bobo asserted that "Black people in this country have had to fight a pervasive ideology that blacks are inferior to whites. When an entire society is built around it, it becomes exceedingly difficult to surmount."

It's also worth noting, to quote Pyke, that we "need not experience identifiable instances of overt discrimination to internalize racial oppression." Experiencing most (and perhaps any) of the other forms of contemporary racism can create the chronic stress and psychological vulnerability necessary to instigate internalizing.

Perhaps the most stressful aspect of internalized racism is how it actually exacerbates our experiences with these other forms of racism and, subsequently, racism-related stress by insidiously convincing us to accept racism (in some form) as *inevitable* and somehow deserved as opposed to actively resist it. Feeling that racism is unavoidable increases our tendency to experience anticipated and perceived racism, both of which, as abovementioned, are especially stressful. It also means feeling like you always have to be prepared for anti-Black actions and the "threat of racism," which, as a specific type of constant hypervigilance, can cause even more chronic stress.

Accepting an experience as highly negative and unpredictable as racism as essentially unavoidable, even unconsciously, also further exaggerates the *uncontrollability* of racism. And, as was discussed regarding perceived racism, many researchers have proposed that "an individual's perception of lack of control over the environment and potentially threatening experiences (which racist experiences are) play a key role" in the chronicity and neuroplastic impact of racism-related stress. This sense of uncontrollability can overwhelm our already diminished ability to cope with the negativity of the stressor (e.g., racism) and ultimately trigger a more incessant stress response (and maladaptive neuroplasticity) than experiencing the stressor itself.

Racism-related stress, according to Shelly Harrell, results from "race-related transactions between individuals or groups and their environment that emerge from the dynamics of racism, and that are perceived to tax or exceed existing individual and collective resources or threaten well-being." In addition to the aforementioned various kinds of contemporary racism, racism-related stress itself can be experienced singly or simultaneously in multiple forms.

Through her groundbreaking research, Harrell identified six distinct types of racism-related stressors, including "racism-related life events (significant events that may occur infrequently), vicarious racist experiences (stress induced by other people's racism experiences), daily racist microstressors (frequent experiences of minor racist events), chronic-contextual stress (stress due to the macro environment and atmosphere), collective experiences (perception of racist experiences as a group), and transgenerational transmission (historical events that passed down across generations)."

The first of these stressors is directly experienced incidents of explicit "racism-related life events," wherein stress is triggered as a result of "specific, significant, and relatively time-limited" acts of racial discrimination, hostility, violence, exclusion, inequality, or injustice perceived or experienced as somehow threatening.

These events "may lead to other events, or their effects may be lasting. However, the experience itself has a beginning and an end. The events can occur across various domains of life experience, including neighborhood, work, finances, education, law enforcement/legal, health care, and social; examples include being rejected for a loan, being harassed by the police, or being discriminated against in housing. Personal and environmental characteristics influence the frequency of such experiences. They are unlikely to occur on a daily or weekly basis for most people, and may occur quite infrequently (i.e., less than once a year) or not at all."

Racism can be experienced in a variety of ways. It can be "experienced not only individually and directly, but also collectively and vicariously." Accordingly, vicariously experienced acts of unambiguous racial discrimination, hostility, violence, exclusion, inequality, or injustice are another distinct type of racism-related stressor. Stress is triggered from seeing, hearing, or reading about another Black person's experience of explicit racism from television, social media, or other people or observing obvious acts of racism on a community, national, or even global level.

Contemporary racism continues to exert its influence "not only through direct personal experience, but also vicariously, through observation and report. The inclusion of vicarious experiences is critical in understanding the nature of racism's effect on individuals. Experiences of prejudice and discrimination that happen to members of one's family and close friends, as well as those involving strangers [e.g., the viral 2020 murder of George Floyd by Officer Derek Chauvin in Minneapolis], can be quite distressing. They can create anxiety, a heightened sense of danger/vulnerability, anger, and sadness, among other emotional and psychological reactions. These vicarious experiences can also teach valuable lessons about the places where racism hides and resides."

Stress is the brain's reaction to any information from our external circumstances that reveal or imply threat, especially threat that we feel we don't have the capacity or resources to cope with. I believe that the majority of the stress experienced from vicarious racism is specifically associated with our oftentimes immediate, implicit "realization that we are also vulnerable to the racism that we have vicariously experienced," noted Kimberly Truong et al. Indirectly experiencing "racism that is targeted at other persons of color" (especially other Black people) reminds us of and reinforces the almost constant personal and systemic "threat of racism," which then requires, explained Essed, "planning, almost every day of one's life, how to avoid or defend oneself."

Oftentimes, the level of stress we experience from vicarious racism is traumatic. We "don't have to be a direct target of racism" for exposure to an act or repeated acts of racism to leave us "feeling helpless and afraid" and perceiving the act or acts as "something overpowering...on top of the ongoing daily recurrences of racial events that cause us emotional pain." Gail Parker wrote that as we accumulate personal lived experiences with racism, we develop a racial "group consciousness" or empathy. So, whenever we see, read, or hear about another Black person being targeted or victimized by racial discrimination, hostility, violence, exclusion, inequality, or injustice, we identify with that person and maybe even vicariously experience *their* racism-related stress.

Racism-related stressors, however, are now not always (or even typically) overt or unambiguous. *Racial microstressors*, a term coined by Harrell to describe the "subtle or covert forms of degrading and marginalizing incidents that occur often unconsciously as everyday reminders of one's racial status in the world," are all too common. Racial microstressors are understated everyday sociocultural cues (i.e., things done or said) intended to implicitly reinforce the notion that Black people, in particular, are negatively different (i.e., stigmatized); (racial) difference is supposedly hierarchal; and we (i.e., Black people) are on the bottom of this racial hierarchy.

Microstressors feature "routine experiences with racism" that include being negated, excluded, or victimized in "ways that lead to feelings of demoralization and dehumanization." Microstressors casually highlight the constant, cumulative disadvantages associated with being Black in America. "Although major racism-related events may happen infrequently to individuals, racial microstressors occur more commonly. Most people may perceive them as not serious enough to confront; the incidents may even be forgotten unless someone asks about them. The routine and pervasive aspects of this treatment, however, may lead to uniquely high levels of vulnerability." Racial microstressors, primarily because they are especially ambiguous and recurrent, can have a greater maladaptive neuroplastic[45] impact than "major episodic experiences" of racism.

There are five recognized types of racial microstressors: microinsults, microinvalidations, microaggressions, microinequities, and microassaults.

Morgan Hurst wrote that "microinsults and microinvalidations both suggest a hidden demeaning message to the person of color. Microinsults are behavioral and verbal expressions that insinuate rudeness and insensitivity and demean an individual's racial identity. Microinvalidations typically invalidate, negate and diminish the psychological thoughts, feelings, and racial identity of African Americans. These acts may not be confronted often but the accumulation of microstressors can cause a great deal of stress for an individual. In addition, many times these offenses are

---

[45] Maladaptive neuroplasticity are those brain changes that somehow instigate negative outcomes (e.g., diminished ability to regulate negative emotions and impulsivity, increased reliance on self-handicapping, chronic hypervigilance, etc.).

labeled as non-racial and can be minimized by others which increase the stress in ethnic minorities."

Sue et al. added that microinsults and microinvalidations oftentimes occur "outside the level of awareness of the perpetrator, but clearly convey a hidden insulting message to the recipient of color." Research suggests that they are "potentially more harmful because of their invisibility, which puts people of color in a psychological bind: While people of color may feel insulted, they are often uncertain why, and perpetrators are unaware that anything has happened and are not aware they have been offensive. For people of color, they are caught in a Catch-22. If they question the perpetrator...denials are likely to follow. Indeed, they may be labeled 'oversensitive' or even 'paranoid.' If they choose not to confront perpetrators, the turmoil stews and percolates in the psyche of the person taking a huge emotional toll."

Racial microaggressions, explained Kimberly Griffin, can occur as "everyday interactions that signal that a person's identity or social group is less valued or perceived negatively." Peggy Davis believed these "stunning, automatic acts of disregard" ultimately "stem from unconscious attitudes of white superiority."

Sue et al. defined racial microaggressions as "brief and commonplace daily verbal, behavioral, or environmental slights, insults, indignities and denigrating messages, whether intentional or unintentional, that communicate hostile, derogatory, or negative racial slights and insults towards people of color." Studies support the fact that people of color (especially Black people) "frequently experience microaggressions, that they are a continuing reality in their day-to-day interactions." Racial microaggressions usually feature actions or reactions rooted in hostility, exclusion, or negative expectations and result "in a negative racial climate and emotions of self-doubt, frustration, and isolation on the part of victims."

These subtle, recurring actions and interactions signal that the target individual or group's social identity is perceived negatively and merits less valued treatment than "normal" people. Racial

157

microaggressions are "often unconsciously delivered in the form of subtle snubs or dismissive looks, gestures, and tones. These exchanges are so pervasive and automatic in daily interactions that they are often dismissed and glossed over as being innocent and innocuous."

"Note that the denials by perpetrators are usually not conscious attempts to deceive; they honestly believe they have done no wrong. Microaggressions hold their power because they are invisible, and therefore they don't allow Whites to see that their actions and attitudes may be discriminatory. Therein lays the dilemma. The person of color is left to question what actually happened. The result is confusion, anger and an overall draining of energy. Ironically, some research and testimony from people of color indicate they are better able to handle overt, conscious and deliberate acts of racism than the unconscious, subtle and less obvious forms. That is because there is no guesswork involved in overt forms of racism."

Debra Roberts and Sherry Molock argued that the most "dangerous thing about microaggressions is while they may be small intentional or unintentional offenses, they can accumulate and become burdensome over time for those who experience them. One of the most insidious features of microaggressions is that sometimes it is hard to confront because it is so subtle" and ambiguous; ambiguity usually increases the stressfulness of a situation. "Because they tend to involve small incidences or indirect insults, it is easy for the perpetrators of microaggressions to dismiss or negate your perception that the behavior or comment was racist. After a while, you may begin to question whether you are being overly sensitive," while also starting to *anticipate* future incidents which can in itself become chronically stressful.

Sue et al. also acknowledged that "microaggressions result in high degrees of stress for Blacks because of denigrating messages: 'You do not belong,' 'You are abnormal,' 'You are intellectually inferior,' 'You cannot be trusted,' and 'You are all the same.' Feelings of powerlessness, invisibility, forced compliance and loss

158

of integrity, and pressure to represent one's group are some of the consequences." These messages and resultant feelings are constant, which makes the stress of microaggressions chronic and cumulative.

Mary Rowe defined microinequities, an additional type of chronic everyday racism-related stressor, as "apparently small events which are often ephemeral and hard-to-prove, events which are covert, often unintentional, frequently unrecognized by the perpetrator, which occur wherever people are perceived to be 'different.'" They are seemingly innocuous yet persistent "messages of devaluation" that include casual discriminatory behaviors "such as being ignored, avoided, excluded, belittled, or treated with less courtesy and respect" or negative expectations.

By definition, microinequities are fundamentally "unfair, demeaning, and discriminatory to those whom they affect" as well as "fiendishly efficient in perpetuating unequal opportunity" and "making that person less self-confident." Not limited to interpersonal behavior, microinequities can be "damaging characteristics of an environment." Terribly pervasive, racial microinequities "grow in infinite variety," which may cause many people of color to be "too alert for some new kind of insult because of past frustration" from previous conscious or unconscious experiences with microinequities.

Then there are also microassaults, which, according to Sue et al., are usually "conscious and intentional discriminatory actions characterized primarily by a violent verbal or nonverbal attack meant to hurt the intended victim through name-calling, avoidant behavior or purposeful discriminatory actions."

"Microassaults are most similar to what has been called 'old fashioned' racism conducted on an individual level. They are most likely to be conscious and deliberate, although they are generally expressed in limited 'private' situations (micro) that allow the perpetrator some degree of anonymity. In other words, people are likely to hold notions of minority inferiority privately and will only display them publicly when they (a) lose control or (b) feel relatively safe to engage in a microassault."

White Americans tend to automatically disregard their role in and the daily reality of racial microstressors. Sue et al. noted that they generally argue (even if they don't fully believe) that "minorities are doing better in life, that discrimination is on the decline, that racism is no longer a significant factor in the lives of people of color, and that equality has been achieved. More important, the majority of Whites do not view themselves as racist or capable of racist behavior" even at the "micro" level.

Conversely, people of color (especially Black people) generally notice the pervasiveness of microstressors within contemporary racism (even if we don't articulate it as such), perceiving many White people as "(a) racially insensitive, (b) unwilling to share their position and wealth, (c) believing they are superior, (d) needing to control everything, and (e) treating them poorly because of their race. People of color believe these attributes are reenacted everyday in their interpersonal interactions with Whites," oftentimes in the form of microaggressions, microinequities, microinsults, microassaults, or microinvalidations.

The fourth racism-related stressor described by Harrell is *chronic-contextual stress.* Chronic-contextual stress is the consequence of institutional or "structural inequalities reinforced through everyday practices and interactions that maintain the social oppression of racial minorities," according to Essed. Harrell explained that this specific stressor "occurs when non-whites are forced to live in a society in which they are subjected to differential treatment and an unfair distribution of resources and opportunities. Nonwhite families are forced to cope with the unfair treatment and adapt to an environment in which they are given less of an opportunity for success." And as the name implies, it's an explicitly *chronic* stressor.

"This source of stress reflects the impact of the social structure, political dynamics, and institutional racism on social-role demands and the larger environment within which one must adapt

160

and cope. Unequal distribution of resources and limitations on opportunities for people of color influence the living conditions and quality of life for individuals and families. Some chronic-contextual stressors likely reflect an interaction of race and class. However, the dynamics of racism suggest that race influences the distribution of economic resources. Chronic-contextual stress may or may not be perceived as related to racism by those who most intensely experience it." There is a significant degree of ambiguity associated with this specific stressor, which can intensify its impact as a stressor.

To verify that certain stressful experiences are actually racism-related, "one must have the time, energy, and resources to question the multiple influences on one's life circumstances. Severe and chronic life stress can keep people so immersed in the process of day-to-day survival that such analyses may be unlikely to occur" and racism-related stress could be internalized, inaccurately downplayed, or outright denied as opposed to strategically coped with or reduced.

It should also be noted that chronic-contextual stress is typically triggered by the shame-based feeling on the part of too many people of color (especially Black people) of being undeserving of or unwelcomed in supposedly "White spaces." Largely the intended, tangible byproduct of America's social boundaries, White spaces, according to Elijah Anderson, are the usually nicer and newer[46] neighborhoods, schools, workplaces, stores, restaurants, and other public spaces that are "overwhelmingly white" and socioemotionally anti-Black. These spaces are oftentimes a stress-inducing environment in which Black people are "typically absent, not expected, marginalized when present," or treated with unwarranted suspicion and/or hostility; thus, we "typically approach that space with care" (i.e.,

---

[46] Mostly due to relatively recent creation or renovation attributable to phenomena like suburbanization and urban gentrification along with the greater sociopolitical power and income/wealth of White people collectively.

hypervigilance). Black people are often required to navigate White spaces and endure that accompanying stress in order to access nicer and newer locales and opportunities.

Hurst further described chronic-contextual stress as being reflective of the "impact of social structure, political dynamics, and institutional racism on social-role demands and the larger environment where individuals must adapt and cope. This may include unequal distribution of resources and limitations on opportunities for ethnic minorities. Unequal distribution of resources or limitations on opportunities may negatively influence living conditions, medical interventions, educational opportunities, and quality of life," while sustaining our disproportionate exposure to traditional life stressors, including inadequate family income, homelessness or residential instability, or being a victim or witness to community or familial violence.

Collective experiences, an additional racism-related stressor, impact individual people of color "in their observation of how their group is collectively impacted through stereotypic portrayals, lack of political representation, or economic conditions." This distinct type of stress is triggered when we acknowledge that "nearly every aspect of our lives is mediated by race" or, more specifically, disadvantaged by our Blackness. Or when we realize just how highly doubtful it is that every Black person in America will ever be able to *expect* fairness or justice. Or when we (perhaps hastily) conclude, to quote Derrick Bell, that "Black people will never gain full equality in this country."

"Experiences of racism at the collective or group level involve perceptions of its effects on members of one's same racial/ethnic group, regardless of direct personal experience," explained Harrell. It's not quite the same as vicariously experienced racism because collective experiences "do not involve witnessing or hearing about a specific incident of racism associated with an identifiable individual. Racial disparities in educational achievement, unemployment rates, incidence and prevalence of disease, and treatment in the criminal justice system are examples of potential stimuli for collective racism-related stress. The well-being of those with limited personal experiences of racism can nonetheless be affected by observation of how racism affects the lives of others with whom they feel a sense of connection and identification" (i.e., other or all Black people).

Not enough attention is probably given to how acts of racism against Black people as a group can initiate or sustain the stress response in Black people personally, especially considering that so much of our experience of racism is experienced collectively. Various studies have confirmed that "people perceive discrimination toward their group significantly more often than they do personal experiences of discrimination."

The final, and perhaps most fascinating, racism-related stressor described by Harrell is *transgenerational transmission*, which basically refers to how the collective effects of historical racism (and racism-related stress) can be passed on intergenerationally and, as a result, impact the current generation of Black people in America. John Crocker wrote that "historical injustices aimed at specific racial groups can be transmitted to new generations. Transgenerational transmission of stress can affect an individual who perceives that the group with which they identify has been historically mistreated or oppressed."

Historical, high-stress experiences such as the various horrors of almost three centuries of enslavement, epidemic violence targeting Black communities from the Reconstruction to the Civil Rights era, explicit and implicit racial segregation circumscribing Black existence *nationally*, or the enormity of COINTELPRO covertly destroying various anti-racist leaders and organizations can make Black people *now* uniquely (i.e., neuroplastically) vulnerable to racism-related stress.

Monnica Williams described how because the stress of these past experiences was never adequately coped with it was generally internalized, resulting in the "development of traits and patterns that can be characterized as manifestations of internalized racial oppression, which are then passed on to subsequent generations."

The stress associated with contemporary racism can be unknowingly *added to* the lingering stress associated with past generations of racism-related experiences, potentially triggering a traumatic stress reaction based on the *cumulative* stress.

"What is clear from all historical evidence is that the millions of lives lost thru mass murder, war, the forcible transfer of populations, and the brutal rigors of the Middle Passage and of enslavement as well as the attendant dehumanization and cultural destruction represent one of the most catastrophic events in the history of humankind," asserted Maulana Karenga.

By all odds, noted John Blassingame, "the most brutal aspect of slavery was the forced separation of families. This was a haunting fear which made all of the slave's days miserable…Death occurred too frequently in the master's house, creditors were too relentless in collecting their debts, the planter's reserves ran out too often, and the master longed too much for expensive items for the slave to escape the clutches of the slave trader. Nothing demonstrated his powerlessness as much as the slave's inability to prevent the forcible sale of his wife and children."

David Pilgrim explained how "Whites, including non-enslavers, fearing rebellion among the slaves, used many strategies to ensure that angry slaves did not rebel: slaves were routinely searched for weapons; rebellious slaves were punished, publicly and harshly—including cropping ears, castrating, hanging, burning, and mutilating; the all-white army and militias were constantly on guard; and anyone, black or white, advocating rebellion among the slaves could be lynched. Despite these measures and others, slavers lived with the constant fear that slaves would rise up and kill whites."

Manfred Berg added that Slave Codes "singled blacks for extremely cruel punishment, thus marking black bodies as innately inferior" and "legitimate objects of excessive violence." These codes "allowed for horrible corporal punishment short of death, including savage whipping, branding, castration, nose slitting, and the amputation of toes, fingers, feet, or hands." This excessive interracial violence could be "carried out not only by the authorities" (e.g., slave patrols), "but rather by all white men in the country, who not only felt, but actually were privileged and entitled to do so." In this way, Slave Codes "set clear patterns for future racial violence in America."

Throughout our ancestor's American enslavement, according to bell hooks, "rape was a common method of torture slavers used to subdue recalcitrant black women. The threat of rape or other physical brutalization inspired terror in the psyches of displaced African females." White male slave owners often raped Black slave women or took them as concubines. Slave women had no rights or protection against the sexual desires of their "masters." This disgraceful, tragic situation resulted in the births of 410,000 "mulatto" slaves by 1860.

Evelyn Young described how "slave narratives attest to the heinous abuses inflicted on those of African descent, such as being stripped and sold as chattel, whipped to death by a blood-stained cowskin, and raped at the master's leisure. Even after the emancipation of the slaves, African Americans found themselves unprotected and unjustly treated. The Jim Crow era barred blacks from equal access to public property, legalized hate crimes, and denied them their voting rights. Lynching became prevalent, and the ghastly sights of Black men and women hanging limply on nooses scattered across the countryside became commonplace."

Jennifer Taylor realized that "these lynchings were not isolated hate crimes committed by rogue vigilantes; they were targeted racial violence perpetrated to uphold an unjust social order. Lynchings were terrorism. This violence left thousands dead; significantly marginalized black people politically, financially, and socially; and inflicted deep trauma on the entire African American community."

In other words, explained Jamelle Bouie, "not only could you be killed for transgressing the nebulous and arbitrary social requirements of the Jim Crow, but you could *also* be killed for starting a business, accumulating wealth and otherwise trying to improve your situation. Together with state and federal discrimination against blacks, you had—until the middle of the twentieth century—a country where the government worked to prevent black economic advancement, with an assist from widespread violence from private actors. With few exceptions, this predicament was unique to African Americans, and a critical part of understanding the 'wealth gap' as it developed through the twentieth century and into the present. Unfortunately, this is one of those things that doesn't have a place in the public conversation, in part because most Americans either can't or won't imagine an America where—if you were the wrong color—pulling yourself up by your bootstraps was punishable by death."

Additionally, wrote James Loewen, "lynchings offered evidence of how defenseless blacks were, for the defining characteristic of a lynching is that the murder takes place in public, so everyone knows who did it, yet the crime typically goes unpunished. Lynch mobs often posed for pictures. They showed no fear of being identified because they knew no white jury would convict them."

And then there were the "race riots," which were really *massacres*, during which White mobs collectively attacked entire Black neighborhoods. These notoriously destructive events started en masse just one year after the end of the Civil War and continued into the mid-20th century. "White mobs killed African-Americans across the United States." Some historians have claimed that there were anywhere from 250-300 race riots over this period, most of which have been conveniently forgotten about by the American academia and press and "completely vanished from our history books." Over 25 so-called race riots broke out between April and October 1919 *alone*, a six-month period poet James Weldon Johnson labeled the "Red Summer."

Jerrold Packard added that "hordes of maniacal white Americans took up racial violence" against people who "weren't usually suspected of or charged with any particular act—other, of course, than that of bearing a black skin. The goal of race rioting

166

was typically twofold. First, the white participants—primarily young, working-class males—appeared to actually enjoy these occasions, as though they were a kind of sporting event, a combined chase and slaughter aimed at African-Americans. Second, the white leaders of the riots and the men who led the leaders regarded the terror generated by a race riot as fair warning to blacks to never forget or overstep their place in the American social order."

Black communities were typically outnumbered and outgunned by their White antagonists. Ultimately, the very real fear of members of entire communities being lynched, burned alive, bullet riddled, stoned, bombed (sometimes aerially), axed, castrated, drowned, dismembered, raped, or fatally dragged—all because of achieving a level of affluence deemed intolerable—proved to be a competent deterrent to collective African-American wealth building (particularly through entrepreneurship and professional services).

Just a few decades later, J. Edgar Hoover and the FBI would secretly instruct its field offices to propose schemes under COINTELPRO (i.e., Counterintelligence Program) to "misdirect, discredit, disrupt and otherwise neutralize" specific individuals and groups within the Civil Rights and Black Power Movements. Hoover's ultimate goal at the time to "prevent the rise of a 'messiah' who could unify and electrify the militant black nationalist movement."

In order to "weaken groups the FBI thought were too revolutionary," explained Rebecca Rissman, more than 2000 individual actions were officially approved under COINTELPRO, which included: infiltrations into organizations in order to discredit or disrupt via divide and conquer; psychological warfare from the outside through bogus publications, forged correspondence, anonymous letters and telephone calls, and similar forms of deceit; and various forms of harassment, defamation, intimidation and violence, such as illegitimate evictions, job dismissals, break-ins, vandalism, false arrests, entrapment, and

167

physical violence (including numerous assassinations) were threatened, instigated, or directly employed, in an effort to frighten activists and disrupt their organizational effectiveness.

While this may now seem ridiculous and terribly unethical, Hoover's actions against the Civil Rights and Black Power Movements were fully sanctioned by Presidents Kennedy, Johnson, and Nixon.

"It's important to remember that the civil rights movement and these other movements did not die natural deaths, noted Joseph Barndt. "They did not run out of gas. They did not give up the fight. Their demise was neither accidental or coincidental. Rather, they were systematically and intentionally dismantled, through acts of police violence and oppression, which were mostly coordinated by the U.S. government."

Brian Glick explained that "when traditional modes of repression (exposure, blatant harassment, and prosecution for political crimes) failed to counter the growing insurgency, and even helped to fuel it, the FBI took the law into its own hands and secretly used fraud and force to sabotage constitutionally-protected political activity."

COINTELPRO officially began in 1956 and was initially designed to "increase factionalism, cause disruption and win defections" inside the Communist Party U.S.A. The program was soon enlarged to include disruption of the Socialist Workers Party, Ku Klux Klan, Student Nonviolent Coordinating Committee, Congress of Racial Equality, Organization of Afro-American Unity, Southern Christian Leadership Conference, Poor People's Campaign, Nation of Islam, Black Panther Party, Revolutionary Action Movement, Black Liberation Army, American Indian Movement, Republic of New Afrika, and various anti-war groups.

However, "the most intense operations were directed against the Black Power Movement, particularly the Black Panther Party. This resulted from FBI and police racism, the Black community's lack of material resources for fighting back, and the tendency of the media—and whites in general—to ignore or tolerate attacks on Black groups."

"Sometimes people" or programs "try to destroy you," warned bell hooks, "precisely because they recognize your power—not because they don't see it, but because they see it and they don't want it to exist." Accordingly, damn near every Black person in America who ever dared to tangibly (not just rhetorically) and appreciably rebel against systemic or institutional racism and racial inequality has been killed, overincarcerated, discredited, impoverished, or discreetly co-opted—many of them directly via COINTEPRO.

It's not really a secret at this point, admitted Malcolm X, "that societies often have killed the people who have helped to change those societies." Throughout American history this has been especially applicable to those whose actions could somehow "lead to changes aimed at destroying the inferior status of black Americans." Black people, explained Huey P. Newton, "who refuse to live under oppression are dangerous to white society because they become symbols of hope to their brothers and sisters, inspiring them to follow their example." Consequently, many of them were secretly targeted by COINTELPRO and killed.

There is substantial documentary evidence that COINTELPRO directly facilitated the assassinations of Malcolm X, Martin Luther King, Jr., and Black Panther Party leaders Fred Hampton, Mark Clark, and George Jackson. Nevertheless, not even one of the hundreds of local, state, and federal government officials associated with COINTELPRO were ever significantly punished (e.g., charged, convicted, incarcerated) or even harshly reprimanded for their involvement.

Before his untimely death, Amos N. Wilson sparked this suspicion by audaciously declaring in his definitive work *Black-on-Black Violence* that Black people "kill each other because they have not yet chosen to challenge and neutralize on every front the widespread power of White men to rule over their lives."

White privilege "by its very nature and intent requires the continuing oppression and subordination of Black people and, in time, may require their very lives. Subordination of a people requires that that people in some way or ways be violated, dehumanized, humiliated, and that some type of violence be perpetrated against them. The violently oppressed react violently to their oppression. When their reactionary violence, their retaliatory or defensive violence, cannot be effectively directed at their oppressors or effectively applied to their self-liberation, it then will be directed at and applied destructively to themselves." In other words, it is not coincidental that the demise of the Black Power Movement coincided with the rise of so-called Black-on-Black violence.

For every year of the 21st century the average rate of intraracial homicidal violence among Black people in America's ten largest cities has increased significantly. While White males mostly die from automobile accidents, most of us currently die because other inexcusably violent Black males (e.g., competitive drug dealers, rival gang members, enraged community members with an underdeveloped capacity to regulate negative emotions and impulsivity, the occasional sociopath, etc.) kill us. As long as there is tangible inequity with regard to intergroup access to wealth, power, resources, and opportunity—in other words, as long as there is White privilege—most Black people exist within an imposed reality that fosters levels of stress, frustration, underdevelopment, and aggression that oftentimes become a catalyst for homicidal violence.

Black people are not disproportionately killing each other simply because we are somehow innately violent. We are not any more genetically predisposed to kill each other than any other human being. Being murderous isn't a "racial trait," to quote Na'im Akbar, "attributable to some type of moral weakness in African-American people. Such conclusions fail to identify the real origin of such traits." These killings are oftentimes (but not always) based on a festering frustration that unconsciously

170

accompanies Black people's collective and individual sense of social powerlessness and insignificance. It appears that this frustration quietly accumulates in most of us. For some of us, it warps our psychological capacity to regulate our impulsive reaction to situations involving negative emotions so much so that we potentially become homicidal.

Some of us *are* violently sociopathic criminals, some of us *are* brutal drug dealers, some of us *are* criminally active street gang members involved in destructive turf wars, but most incidents of intraracial homicidal violence among African-Americans start as relatively trivial conflicts. "A fight over a girlfriend, a couple of words, a dispute over a dice game," observed Vaughn Crandall. "Long-running feuds," defensive aggression, retaliation when "somebody else gets shot. These are men who do not trust the police to keep them safe, so they take matters into their own hands."

These murders take place everywhere, explained Sharon LaFraniere et al., "but mostly outdoors: at neighborhood barbecues, family reunions, music festivals, basketball tournaments, movie theaters, housing project courtyards, 'Sweet 16' parties, public parks, endangering innocent people. Where motives could be gleaned, roughly half involved or suggested crime or gang activity. About a third were provoked by arguments that spun out of control, typically drug- or alcohol-fueled, often over petty grievance...minor dust-ups answered with bullets."

The economic motivation of contemporary intraracial homicidal violence among African-Americans is rooted in us having been forced for generations "to live in marginal social conditions that produce pathological, survival behavior," according to Claud Anderson, and our communities lacking "an accountability mechanism that could establish, reward, and punish behavior that is detrimental to them. Since the late 1960s, blacks have been so overexposed to black crime within their communities that they now accept it as normal black behavior." Moreover, "more than 50 percent of eligible black youths can't find jobs.

171

Though this systematic black unemployment often criminalizes blacks and renders them noncompetitive, neither the government nor larger society has demonstrated a willingness to use their vast resources to eliminate the causative factors."

Black people disproportionately kill and commit other criminal activities against each other "in direct proportion to blacks' becoming obsolete and expendable as a labor force in the early 1960s. We have been placed in impoverished positions to encourage our criminality by preying upon our moral vulnerability, despair, and dependency. As black wealth, income, employment, business, educational and male role model opportunities diminished throughout the country, black criminal activities increased." Conversely, White people's relatively "privileged status, contacts, options, and wealth gives them greater access to basic necessities and resources of the society, without their having to commit criminal acts."

However, "the criminalizing of blacks does not excuse blacks who are engaging in criminal activities from being held accountable for their behavior."

According to a recent report commissioned by *The Washington Post*, unarmed Black men are seven times more likely than unarmed Whites to be shot and killed by police. It seems like now you hear or read about some unarmed Black person being shot and killed by a White cop almost every other day. White police have been killing Black people in America with almost absolute impunity since their origination as slave patrols allegedly commissioned to enforce fugitive slave laws in the early 1700s to their evolution into state troopers used to repress civil rights protesters in the 1950s and 1960s. Yet, these police officers are rarely ever criminally charged for killing Black people, and in those rare cases that they are charged, a conviction is even rarer (despite repeatedly incriminating video evidence, conflicting accounts, the victim typically being unarmed, etc.). Consequently, there is now a far more consistent (and stressful) expectation of death and injustice for us than justice for all.

Police brutality is a term used to describe the excessive, and oftentimes lethal, use of physical force, assault, verbal attacks, and threats by police officers and other law enforcement officers. Americans of any race can become victims of police brutality, but federal statistics show that 87% of all documented police brutality cases since 1995 involved Black people, most of which received little if any media coverage. The failure of government to protect Black people in this country from persistent police brutality is a historical reality that we've been actively protesting against for almost a century. During the 1930s, the National Negro Congress (NNC) organized massive rallies against this form of terror. In 1938, the NNC stated in a Petition Against Police Brutality that "our lives, our homes, our liberties each day are made less secure because of unrestrained and unpunished police brutality."

"White people, by and large, do not know what it is like to be occupied by a police force," noted Khalil Muhammad. "They don't understand it because it is not the type of policing they experience. Because they are treated like individuals, they believe that if 'I am not breaking the law, I will never be abused.'" But for Black people, concluded William Jones, "it's like we are seen as animals."

It is problematic that police officers across this country, according to a recent report by the Police Executive Research Forum, are being trained to "draw a line in the sand" and resolve confrontations quickly rather than to become proficient in de-escalation tactics that could bring hostile incidents to peaceful conclusions. It is problematic that new police officers spend an average of 58 training hours on firearms proficiency (i.e., how to shoot successfully) but just 8 training hours on de-escalation tactics that would reduce their overreliance on firearms in potentially antagonistic situations. It is equally problematic that experienced officers are provided annual training that is skewed toward using their firearm to "aim at center mass to neutralize a threat" more than scenario or stress training that would increase their capacity to regulate their own emotions (and bias) in perilous circumstances and properly utilize the force spectrum.

Increasingly, in African-American communities, people fear the police more than the criminals. Racialized police violence has never been properly problematized, so it was almost inevitable, to quote Themal Ellawala, that "police shootings and killing of African American targets has reached epidemic proportions." A solution to these killings has never been perceived as *necessary*; thus, "state-sanctioned violence, as practiced by law enforcement, continues to target Blacks with a vengeance for crimes both real and imagined," explained Peniel Joseph.

And then there's the White civilians now legally authorized to shoot us (e.g., Trayvon Martin) dead while supposedly just "standing their ground." Since 2005, at least 33 states have adopted Stand Your Ground laws and several more have pending legislation to enact such laws, according to the American Bar Association.

These laws, noted Mark Hoekstra and Cheng Cheng, "widen the scope for the justified use of lethal force in self-defense by stating the circumstances under which self-defense is justified and removing the duty to retreat from a list of protected places outside the home. In addition, in many cases they also establish a presumption of reasonable fear and remove civil liability. Thus, these laws could hypothetically deter crime or, alternatively, increase homicide. Results presented indicate that expansions to Castle Doctrine [i.e., "Stand Your Ground" laws] do not deter crime" and actually appear to be another catalyst for the disproportionate killing of African-Americans nationally.

These laws, added Patrik Jonsson, "upset a basic social order by, in essence, deputizing citizens. Not only does that raise the risk of minor disputes and misunderstandings becoming deadly incidents, but it also provides some legal cover for Americans to take deadly action based on their own subjective, and possibly racially tinged, views."

174

And when we are not being killed, Black people in America have been overly incarcerated since the Black Codes were established throughout the Postbellum South (and similar de facto policies in the North).

These new Black Codes consisted of sometimes strategic, oftentimes absurd state laws that applied only to or were only enforced with Black people. The underlying goal of each Code seemed to be to somehow compel all Black people to continue to work willingly in a labor economy where they'd be restricted to slavery-like conditions, terribly low wages, and perpetual debt. Michelle Alexander wrote that the purpose of Black Codes "in general and the vagrancy laws in particular was to establish another system of forced labor" via the unequal and unjust incarceration of Black people.

These vagrancy laws, according to Nancy Wagner, "made it a crime not to have a job or be able to show proof of employment"[47] or be working at a job Whites didn't give approval to[48]. Vagrancy laws also allowed local authorities to arrest people for any number of petty infractions and immediately imprison and commit them to involuntary labor. "While these laws did not specifically mention African Americans, they were rarely enforced for whites" and imposed large fines that few newly freed Blacks could afford to

---

[47]　There were Codes that required Black people to keep and be able to present to authorities upon request an annual labor contract, which was written proof of employment by White landowners, or be charged with vagrancy, arrested, beaten, fined, and leased as convict labor.

[48]　Most Southern states established Codes that prohibited Black people from holding any occupation other than farmer or servant for White land or business owners, unless they paid an annual tax that ranged from $10 to $100 (which most Black people simply couldn't afford). These Codes meant that most Black people who somehow had already begun to earn a living post-slavery as an independent former or artisan were now mandated to relinquish their fiscal self-determination and work directly for White people for unjust wages or be charged with vagrancy and forced to work for White people involuntarily.

pay. Failure to pay certain random, disproportionately imposed taxes could also be in violation of vagrancy laws. "The result was a huge increase in the number of blacks arrested and convicted and the rise of the labor system known as convict leasing."

States sold exploitable prisoner labor to private, for-profit entities, such as plantation and business (e.g., railroad, mining, and logging) owners throughout the South, who then took on the unregulated responsibility of feeding, clothing, and housing the prisoners. Financially strapped Southern states benefitted greatly from this new revenue source, and the lessees profited handsomely from direct access to forced labor at far below market rates. Predictably, African-American males made up the vast majority of the convicts leased, explained Leon Litwack, due to "vigorous and selective enforcement of laws and discriminatory sentencing."

For whatever reason, the federal government had created the constitutional basis for the unjust entrapment, conviction, and leasing of Black people as prison laborers with a "loophole" in the Thirteenth Amendment (yes, the one that supposedly abolished slavery): "Neither slavery nor involuntary servitude, except as punishment for crime whereof the party shall have been duly convicted, shall exist within the United States, nor any place subject to their jurisdiction."

So basically, alleged criminals in America can (and continue to) be punished with enslavement, especially Black ones.

Kathy Forde and Bryan Bowman described how Black men— and sometimes Black women and even children—were disproportionately convicted for violations of the Black Codes and subsequently "leased to private companies, typically industries profiteering from the region's untapped natural resources. As many as 200,000 black Americans were forced into back-breaking labor in coal mines, turpentine factories and lumber camps. They lived in squalid conditions, chained, starved, beaten, flogged and sexually violated. They died by the thousands from injury, disease and torture."

"For both the state and private corporations, the opportunities for profit were enormous. For the state, convict lease generated revenue and provided a powerful tool to subjugate African-Americans and intimidate them into behaving in accordance with the new social order. It also greatly reduced state expenses in housing and caring for convicts. For the corporations, convict lease provided droves of cheap, disposable laborers who could be worked to the extremes of human cruelty" without the dread of legal repercussions.

This practice would continue long into the 20th century and evolve into what's now referred to as the Prison Industrial Complex. Bakari Kitwana described the Complex as when "corporations capitalize on cheap prison labor. Federal and state prisons once restricted prison labor to services and products made for government and nonprofit agencies. However, in 1979, Congress created the Prison Industry Enhancement certification program (CPI), which gave private companies access to prison laborers. Major corporations shopping for the cheapest labor have realized that mandatory minimum sentencing and state laws governing private industry's use of prison laborers have created a captive, non-unionized labor pool, where benefits, vacation time, unemployment compensation, minimum wages, payroll and Social Security taxes, and even human rights and anti-sweatshop activists are non-issues."

Immediately following the Black Power Movement, the federal government's so-called "War on Drugs" could arguably be more appropriately labeled as an employee recruitment drive for the Complex. Its policies have had a drastically disproportionate impact on African-American males and have exacerbated the racial disparities inherent to this country's criminal justice system. Clarence Lusane asserted that "the upsurge in drug trafficking and abuse in the Black community was mainly driven by a complex web of economic need meeting economic opportunity. Black males, particularly young ones, had been trapped in a cycle of poverty and unemployment, nothing less than economic genocide.

177

Whether or not there was a conspiracy, Black people's need for money and consequent desire for psychological escape, exacerbated by the alienating and inequitable environment of poor communities, went a long way in explaining" our intergenerational susceptibility to the Prison Industrial Complex.

One of the more insidious consequences of our coerced over-participation in the Prison Industrial Complex has been epidemic levels of Black paternal abandonment, something I personally continue to be psychologically impacted by.

Approximately 70% of all Black people born in America during or after the 1960s have been physically abandoned at some point of their lives by their father and even more have been emotionally abandoned. I'd argue that paternal abandonment has become too commonplace and passively normalized in the African-American community. However, fathers abandoning their children is not at all normal in humanity or indicative of some congenital moral weakness in Black people specifically; it is largely the outcome of concentrated deindustrialization-based joblessness, various consequences of racism, and patterned emotional dysregulation. Nevertheless, we are certainly witnessing the effects of this atrocity in successive generations of Black children.

Welsing explained that typically "the child who eventually is abandoned...becomes convinced that he is worthless and not worthy of his father's love. The child concludes that something must have been wrong with him from birth for the father to have abandoned him...The child summarizes it all as 'I must not be worth anything'...this wound and deep-seated doubt about the self remains with the child for the length of its life, producing a severe distrust of and alienation from others" that exacerbates other stressors (including racism) and negative emotions.

Most of these children consequently develop *father hunger*, defined as the profound, persistent, yet oftentimes unidentified desire for emotional connection with and validation from our missing father. Father hunger is the result of receiving too little quality fathering as a child or adolescent due to physical or emotional paternal abandonment. The greatest problem with father hunger is its victims' subconscious reaction to it, which is largely based on the ego defense mechanism known as "acting out." Rather than admit that we crave paternal attention, affection, affirmation, advice, and accountability as well as need desperately to boost our degraded sense of self-worth, people with father hunger often act out to avoid dealing with the emotional damage of being abandoned. The "acting" done is usually impulsive and destructive to ourselves or others and inhibits the development of more constructive responses to our feelings.

Beyond seeing it in so many students I've taught as well as doing the research in order to publish two books about it, I know this pattern *intimately* because I was that child.

The American economy, explained Jedediah Purdy, still "does not teach us that 'black lives matter,' at least not as much as white lives." The American economy, which essentially originated in the slavery era, continues to privilege Whiteness (e.g., typically provide White people greater access to intergenerational wealth and opportunity in the skilled labor market), while specifically weeding out the African-American as a suddenly obsolete worker with, consequently, little if any contemporary social value (or role).

After decades of an inherited wealth gap, residential segregation, educational inequality, systemic labor obsolescence (via corporate suburbanization, automation, and globalization), calculated welfare dependency[49], affirmative inaction, an

---

[49] Including the strategic increase in African-American welfare dependency as a strategy to thwart the urban uprisings of the late 1960s that literally ignited parts of every American city in hopes of sparking "Black Power." White America was terrified, to quote J. Fred MacDonald, of the "the legitimate anger and frustration of African Americans trapped in the inner city by prejudice, poverty, ignorance, police power, and fear. Faced with unemployment, dilapidated ghettos, unfamiliar and subtle forms of discrimination, and handicapped by

inadequate technical skills, by the mid-1960s many migrants abandoned established leadership and drifted into violence. Looting and burning often replaced passive resistance and religious principle. In 1967 alone, there were eight major disorders, thirty-three serious outbreaks, and 133 minor disorders."

To many Americans "revolution seemed at hand following the assassination of Martin Luther King, Jr. in April 1968. Anger spilled into the streets, and armed troops were needed in many localities to reestablish social order. The image of U.S. Army soldiers bearing rifles in front of the Capitol, while streams of smoke rose in the background from the ghetto of Washington, D.C., told most dramatically the depth of this racial rage. Such pictures also revealed how disenchanted urban blacks had become with the passive resistance tactics of the early civil rights movement."

In response, the federal government initiated various policies, detailed James Button, "to prevent riots through welfare payments, low income housing, jobs programs—especially summer jobs programs for youths, which were seen as 'riot insurance.'" Christina Maimone cited that "cities that experienced a major riot had a significant increase in welfare spending and the number of individuals receiving welfare in the year after the riot."

Following the riots, the federal government continued to pacify Black people with welfare benefits (or remove with mass incarceration) as our socioeconomic obsolescence was drastically accelerated (due to rapid urban deindustrialization), yet the media's reaction was to cleverly advance the "all Blacks are lazy" stereotype. Martin Gilens recognized how "pictures of poor blacks were abundant when poverty coverage was most negative, while pictures of non-blacks dominated the more sympathetic media coverage." The media of the era was largely responsible for "the centuries old stereotype of blacks as lazy [remaining] credible for a large number of white Americans," who also erroneously believed that more Black people received welfare benefits than White.

Douglas Massey and Nancy Denton accurately identified that "as poverty rates rose among blacks in response to the economic dislocations of the 1970s and 1980s, so did the use of welfare programs. Because of racial segregation, however, the higher levels of welfare receipt were confined to a small number of isolated, all-black neighborhoods. By

180

entrepreneurship gap, and endemic joblessness, more and more Black people in America are experiencing intergenerational poverty.

America is *supposed to be* the "land of opportunity," which essentially means that hard work and perseverance should result in intergenerational income mobility (i.e., children will grow up, make significantly more money, and, consequently, escape the confines of poverty experienced by their parents). In other words, America is generally perceived as the exemplar of a "society in which a child's chances of success depend little on his family background," noted Raj Chetty et al.

However, various structural barriers to intergenerational income (or social) mobility create such a consistent inequality of opportunity that the "chances of making it from a childhood in

---

promoting the spatial concentration of welfare use, therefore, segregation created a residential environment within which welfare dependency was the norm, leading to the intergenerational transmission and broader perpetuation of urban poverty."

Instigating welfare dependency concurrently promoted intergenerational poverty. Wilson confirmed that "food stamps, Medicaid, and the Supplemental Security Income program (SSI) do provide some relief, but as currently designed, they have virtually no effect on the continuing poverty rates among the nonelderly. In short, targeted programs for the poor in the United States do not even begin to address inequities in the social class system. Instead of helping to integrate the recipients into the broader economic and social life of mainstream society—to 'capitalize' them into a different educational or residential stratum, as the GI bill and the postwar federal mortgage programs did for working- and middle-class whites—they tend to stigmatize and separate them. As unemployment in the general population rises, the probability of exiting welfare diminishes. It is not surprising that those who are least employable in terms of skills and training are least successful in avoiding welfare."

As Sackrey realized, "the welfare system promises a little help for everyone, but not a lot for anyone, and, therefore, those currently on the bottom will continue to be there for some time."

181

poverty to an adulthood in affluence are lower in the U.S. than in other developed nations." In America, inequality, not mobility, is decidedly inherited. Rather than being the "land of opportunity," reported Richard Wilkinson, the "United States has unusually low rates of income mobility which seem to match its unusually large income difference."

A nation promotes social mobility "if it allows people to escape poverty while limiting the degree to which those who grow up in privileged homes get advantages throughout their lives," explained Emily Beller and Michael Hout. In America, established policies prefer to concentrate economic growth among the already wealthy, so there is very little "difference between a person's current income, wealth, or occupation and that of the family that raised" him or her. These policies have also increased inequality dramatically (i.e., income gap), particularly over the last 30 years. "An increase in inequality over a person's lifetime increases the probability that someone who starts life in extreme privilege will stay there and (simultaneously) increases the probability that someone whose parents were poor will also be poor."

"Black Americans have substantially lower rates of upward mobility and higher rates of downward mobility than whites, leading to large income disparities that persist across generations." Nationwide deindustrialization—the ultimate consequence of systemic labor obsolescence created by structural economic changes including corporate automation, suburbanization, and globalization—caused an unprecedented increase in joblessness (i.e., the permanent disappearance of blue-collar jobs) starting roughly in the late 1960s initially targeting (you guessed it) areas with large African-American populations.

Over the following decades, an income and "employment gap between skilled and unskilled workers" explained William J. Wilson, "is growing partly because education and training are considered more than ever in the new global economy. At the same time that changes in technology are producing new jobs, they are making many others obsolete. While educated workers are

182

benefiting from the pace of technological change involving the increased use of computer-based technologies and microcomputers, less skilled workers, such as those found in many inner-city neighborhoods, face the growing threat of job displacement."

"The steady advance of automation has raised the skill-level required to obtain steady employment," confirmed Louis Knowles. However, "no American institution has taken sufficient steps to ensure" that poor Americans "gain the skills necessary for entry into the modern job market."

Poor people have "traditionally held the jobs which are now being eliminated," noted Robert Allen. And the "pace of mechanization and automation, uneven though it is, cannot be halted because of the competitive need of individual corporations to increase efficiency and reduce costs in order to maintain profits and growth, and improve their relative standing vis-à-vis other companies. On the contrary, it can be expected that the pace of automation will accelerate, putting more minority groups and other workers without special skills out of work."

Regardless of their work ethic or intellect, many African-Americans come into this world effectively excluded from wealth because most wealth is inherited (i.e., intergenerational). In fact, economists have estimated that almost 80% of a family's wealth typically derives from intergenerational transfers (i.e., inheritance).

"Due to the unearned advantages it transmits across generations, inheritance widens inequality and is a key driver of the racial wealth gap." These advantages include the inevitability, according to Thomas Piketty, "that inheritance (of fortunes accumulated in the past) predominates over saving (wealth accumulated in the present)...Wealth originating in the past automatically grows more rapidly, even without labor, than wealth stemming from work, which can be saved."

Wealth significantly determines an individual's life chances, yet Black people on average are five times less likely to inherit money than Whites, White people's inheritances are ten times

183

bigger, and, consequently, their familial wealth is about eight times that of ours. And while it's true that many among the contemporary affluent in America have amassed their impressive wealth via unprecedented opportunities in information technology, mass retail (including e-commerce), and finance, most of them (which excludes newly wealthy professional athletes and entertainers) still had direct access to significant intergenerational wealth for start-up capital. This reflects the sobering truth, to quote Shannon Moriarty, "that Americans have never had an equal opportunity to become wealthy."

"Wealth is a measure of cumulative advantage or disadvantage," explained Roderick Harrison. "The fact that black and Hispanic wealth is a fraction of white wealth also reflects a history of discrimination in which Whites have had more opportunities to accumulate wealth." Or as Dalton Conley recently phrased it, contemporary wealth reveals "the cumulative disadvantage of race for minorities or cumulative advantage of race for Whites," which originated during the American slavery era.

Personal attributes and behavioral choices are not as influential to the racial wealth gap as the "configuration of both opportunities and barriers in workplaces, schools, and communities that reinforce deeply entrenched racial dynamics in how wealth is accumulated," concluded Shapiro. "This toxic inequality has historical underpinnings but is perpetuated by policies and tax preferences that continue to favor the affluent."

Douglas Massey and Nancy Denton explained in their *American Apartheid* how "most Americans vaguely realize that America is still a residentially segregated society, but few appreciate the depth of black segregation or the degree to which it is maintained by ongoing institutional arrangements or contemporary individual actions. No group in the history of the United States has ever experienced the sustained high level of residential segregation that has been imposed on blacks in large American cities for the past fifty years. Even within suburbs, levels of racial segregation have remained exceptionally high. Residential segregation is the product of systematic racial practices such as restrictive covenants, redlining by banks and insurance companies, zoning, panic peddling by real estate agents, and the creation of massive public housing projects in low-income areas."

"The geographic isolation of black people within a narrowly circumscribed portion of the urban environment forces blacks to live under extraordinarily harsh conditions and to endure a social world where poverty is endemic, infrastructure is inadequate, education is lacking, families are fragmented, and crime and violence are rampant and far removed from the experience of most whites. This extreme racial isolation did not just happen; it was manufactured by whites through a series of self-conscious actions and purposeful institutional arrangements that continue today. Not only is the depth of black segregation unprecedented and utterly unique compared with that of other groups, but it shows little sign of change with the passage of time or improvements in socioeconomic status."

Needless to say, American history as lived experience somehow rooted in racism has always been highly stressful for Black people. And this stress has been insidiously accumulating across generations.

This may get too "sciency," but I believe it's also worth noting that transgenerational transmission of racism-related stress is connected to and may cause *epigenetic neuroplasticity*.

Epigenetics refers to changes to the external structure of DNA (i.e., the epigenome) and the chemicals surrounding DNA that result in changes to how cells read genes and determine gene expression (i.e., which genes are physically activated or not throughout our lifetime). However, these changes do not include modifications to the primary DNA sequence. DNA throughout the human body, including the brain, is susceptible to epigenetic changes.

In several instances, epigenetic changes are durable and heritable, even though the underlying DNA does not change. The

185

passing of epigenetic changes (or epigenetic memory) to future generations is known as epigenetic inheritance, which can include the passing of epigenetic changes across multiple generations (i.e., transgenerational epigenetic inheritance). Researchers are still working on figuring out exactly how all this happens. One widely accepted theory, as explained by Kevin Mitchell, is "that epigenetic marks laid down in the cells of one generation (in response to some environmental factor or experience) can be stably passed through meiosis (into the germ cells) and thus affect some traits in the next generation."

Epigenetics is theoretically rooted in the 18th century work of French naturalist Jean-Baptiste Lamarck, who first proposed that external stimuli could alter which characteristics were acquired during an individual's lifetime, characteristics that could then be passed on to that individual's descendants. Contemporary research shows that various behavioral tendencies and health conditions are attributable to inherited epigenetic changes; in other words, it appears that Lamarck, who was actually ridiculed at the time, was right all along.

Epigenetic neuroplasticity is the altering of gene expression in particular cells in the brain through potentially heritable epigenetic changes. Over a third of the 20,000 genes that comprise the human genome are expressed primarily in the brain, which makes it the most genetically active region of the body. Our behaviors, thoughts, and emotions are all ultimately determined by how these genes are expressed.

External stimuli, both positive and negative, have an explicit effect on epigenetic neuroplasticity. Awesome or repetitive experiences or environmental factors have been proven to induce epigenetic neuroplasticity by changing patterns of gene expression in brain cells in a persistent and possibly heritable manner. Consequently, epigenetic neuroplasticity is both a catalyst and consequence of patterned neuronal activity.

Chronic stress (or more specifically, increased amygdala reactivity due to chronic stress) has been proven to induce heritable

186

epigenetic neuroplasticity. These changes actually make the brain (and the amygdala in particular) more reactive to chronic stress and chronic stress-related neuroplasticity. According to research by Yuliya Nikolova et al., epigenetic neuroplasticity caused by chronic stress increases the DNA methylation of the serotonin transporter gene (i.e., a methyl group, CH_3, is added epigenetically), which maladaptively exaggerates our amygdala reactivity and stress response. The epigenetic neuroplasticity of preceding generations of chronic stressed people can be passed on to succeeding generations who now express an increasingly exaggerated reactivity to chronic stress and chronic stress-related neuroplasticity. In other words, to quote Kathleen Hall, "we are a product of our gene pool and how our ancestors handled stress."

If certain brain changes can be inherited (i.e., epigenetic neuroplasticity) and common experiences can create common brain changes among members of a specific social group (i.e., social neuroplasticity), then it's logical that certain emotional reactions and behaviors can be inherited throughout entire social groups (with exceptions, of course). In other words, brain changes caused by racism-related stress may be just as much of a historically sociological phenomenon (i.e., how Black people developed from what we collectively experienced over a historical period) as it is a recently psychological phenomenon (i.e., impacted by our individual lived experiences).

Not as Human Beings[50]
How to Survive the Stress of Still Being Black in America

"The stress of living in a racialized society has significant health impact
that affects African-Americans at every class level."

-Vernellia Randall

"The stress of being Black is literally killing us."

-Steven Kniffley

"The greatest weapon against stress is our ability to choose one thought
over another."

-William James

"A chronically stressed brain tends to reprogram itself and reinforce the behaviors responsible for the stress," concluded Nuno Sousa et al. Surviving the chronic stress of being Black in this country and experiencing contemporary racism requires intentionally rewiring those neural pathways in our brains previously reinforced by a lifetime of reacting recklessly. A different level of thinking is needed to end this terribly harmful cycle. Accordingly, the goal of this book is to provide an

---

[50] Excerpted from the following Audre Lorde quote: "We have had to fight and still do, for that very visibility which also renders us most vulnerable, our Blackness. For to survive in the mouth of this dragon we call america, we have had to learn this first and most vital lesson—that we were never meant to survive. Not as human beings."

actionable, strategy-based approach to positively recognizing and responding to race-based and racism-related stress.

All Black people in America experience some degree of chronic, brain-changing stress related to being Black and/or enduring some type or consequence of contemporary racism. As a Black person in America, it's virtually impossible not to experience anti-Blackness as either race-based stigma, othering, or invisibility. Or to experience either systemic, individual, institutional, cultural, unconscious, aversive, everyday, anticipated, perceived, or internalized racism. Or to experience some specific type of racism-related stress from racism-related life events, vicarious racist experiences, daily racist microstressors, chronic-contextual stress, collective experiences, or transgenerational transmission.

While these experiences can certainly be common (as stressors), they (and the stress they trigger) are experienced differently. Black people are not a monolith. Stress is different for each of us. We all feel and react personally to traditional life stress as well as race-based and racism-related stress. Even when "exposed to the same trigger/stressor, people vary remarkably in their stress response," noted William Salt. We also differ significantly in the efficacy of our coping responses to stress, especially with regard to race-based and racism-related stress.

Stress is the brain's reaction to any information from our external circumstances that reveal or imply threat, especially threat that we feel we don't have the capacity or resources to cope with. So, how Black people in America experience and are (neuroplastically) impacted by race-based and racism-related stress is directly influenced by how strategically (i.e., how evidence-informed are the resources and interventions we're using) we as individuals attempt to cope with race-based and racism-related experiences as stressors.

Most of us, at least prior to reading this book, tend to experience race-based or racism-related stress and not even know it. And because we didn't know it, this stress wasn't ever properly

189

addressed and, consequently, accumulated (i.e., became chronic stress) and possibly evolved into traumatic stress. Becoming more familiar with these types of stressors can help us identify why and when we are experiencing them, which enables us to better practice various positive coping strategies.

Much of this stress has been implicitly normalized (i.e., made normal, natural, typical, tolerable) when it should have been immediately *problematized*. To problematize, by definition, is to make some thing or situation into (or begin to regard it as) a problem requiring a solution, especially when you consider how these chronic stress responses have negatively affected our ability to live optimally.

Perhaps it's the four decades of cumulative stress personally (and mostly *unstrategically*) experienced or maybe I'm just being too rational due to centuries of historical evidence, but I can't foresee a sudden end to who Black people in America are understood or expected to be, or how we are looked at and what people choose to believe they see (even when it's all negative and erroneous). I don't see a forthcoming end to anti-Blackness in this country. Nor can I anticipate an imminent end to contemporary racism in America in any of its aforementioned forms.

I'm sorry, but I just can't yet see the day that nearly every aspect of our lives *won't be* somehow mediated by race or, more specifically, systemically disadvantaged by our Blackness. Nor can I envision the moment when every Black person in America will be able to *expect* fairness or justice. Some of us probably *can*, and that's so cool. I wish I could.

As abovementioned, Black people are not a monolith, and I don't claim to represent anyone's opinion but my own. However, I have concluded (perhaps hastily), to quote Derrick Bell, that "Black people will ever gain full equality in this country." And that "due to racism," explained Donna Bivens, Black people "do not have the ultimate decision-making power over the decisions that control our lives and resources."

190

By admitting this, I'm not trying to be gratuitously pessimistic or play any kind of card, racial or otherwise. I'm not trying to use racism as some kind of excuse for my or our presumed laziness, mediocrity, incompetence, and subsequent lack of success. Have things gotten better for Black people in this country? Has there been *racial progress*? Certainly. Well, relatively.

Racial progress is not the same as *anti-racism* (i.e., opposition to anti-Blackness and racism). There has not been nearly *enough* anti-racism in any of its potential forms—systemic, individual, institutional, cultural, unconscious, aversive, everyday, anticipated, perceived, or internalized—for me to begin believing that Black people will ever be *automatically* recognized as human beings (i.e., as *fully* human) by White America.

White people in America collectively "appear to be more supportive of equal rights in principle than of equal rights in practice," as boldly argued by Kristin Anderson (herself White) in *Benign Bigotry*. "When commitment is required to perform specific actions involving their own lives and the status of their own group, they are much less receptive to the idea of racial equality" or anti-racism.

This lack of receptiveness, noted Joe Feagin (also White), is actually "grounded in white resistance to substantial changes in the status quo. Central to white concerns is a fear whites have of losing status and power because of black attempts to bring change."

While they might not want to appear racist, "most whites—in the elites and the general public—do not seem interested in giving up significant white power or privilege. Thus, the racist ideology was altered in some ways but continues to incorporate many of its old features, and it continues to rationalize white privilege. The acceptance by the white elite and public of the principles of equal opportunity and desegregation in regard to schools, jobs, and public accommodations did *not* mean that most whites desired for the federal government to implement large-scale integration of these institutions."

191

"White attitudes have shifted from an emphasis on strict segregation and overt bigotry to 'laissez-faire racism,' by which whites continue the stereotyping of blacks and blaming of blacks for their problems. Most ordinary whites have given up a commitment to compulsory racial segregation. Yet, they still strive to maintain white privilege and position."

"Acceptance of the principle of racial integration does not mean that whites wish to see government intervene aggressively, or to personally have more contact with blacks. Whites maintain a positive sense of self and their claims to greater privilege and resources while fending off what whites see as illegitimate black demands for a fair share of those resources."

In other words, "too many White people," concluded Neely Fuller, Jr., "have shown that they prefer White Supremacy (racism) to justice and equality. Too many Black people have shown that they do not care enough about justice and equality to make a maximum effort to produce it." And too many of those of us who once adequately cared have been killed, overincarcerated, discredited, impoverished, or discreetly co-opted. "Black men and women who refuse to live under oppression," explained Huey P. Newton, "are dangerous to white society because they become symbols of hope to their brothers and sisters, inspiring them to follow their example," so they are somehow neutralized and instead become popular disincentives to anti-racism.

Ending racism in America requires an unprecedented level of commitment, courage, and *power* on the part of its primary victims. Can't vote it away. Can't protest it away. Can't pray it away. Can't plead it away. Can't shame (White people) it away. Can't social media it away.

Wade Nobles defined power as "the ability to define reality and have others respond to it as their reality. The most important reality to define is the meaning of one's own human beingness." Black people in America currently lack the power to correct White America's intentionally flawed, fractionalizing, and fictionalizing functional definitions of race and Blackness. White

192

people have more than enough power (and incentive) to continue them. These definitions form the foundation of anti-Black stigma, othering, and invisibility and, ultimately, race-based stress. And neither racism (i.e., racial discrimination, antagonism, exclusion, inequality, and injustice) nor racism-related stress could exist without anti-Black stigma, othering, and invisibility.

"The ultimate goal of the dominant race," according to Eduardo Bonilla-Silva, "is to defend its collective interests (i.e., the perpetuation of systemic White privilege)." As long as anti-Black stigma, othering, and invisibility remains "economically or socially advantageous," White people will continue to see us that way. As long as it remains "economically or socially advantageous to see" Black people in this country as innately lazy, violent, unintelligent, criminal, irresponsible, incompetent, dangerous, self-destructive, excuse-dependent, complaint-oriented, etc., Whites will continue to see us that way. Unfortunately, too many of us may also begin to see ourselves that same way and, consequently, continue to react to anti-Blackness in ways that ultimately *perpetuate* the systems of oppression that target and trigger us.

Even when "non-racist" White people don't necessarily want to or realize that they see us that way, they will continue to see us that way as long as it remains "economically or socially advantageous." Because America remains such an inherently anti-Black society, observed Angela Davis, "it is not enough to be non-racist" to stop seeing Black people this way, they "must be anti-racist."

They can still quickly "access stereotypic beliefs without awareness," confirmed Bernard Whitley and Mary Kite and, "therefore, such beliefs influence the behavior even of people low in explicit prejudice. Negative racial stereotypes still exist in American culture and Americans still absorb the negative emotions associated with those stereotypes. These negative emotions form part of what are called implicit prejudices, prejudices that can be assessed through implicit cognition and some behavioral measures,

193

but which people are not aware of having. Despite this lack of conscious awareness, these prejudices affect White people's emotional response to and behavior toward" Black people and *sustain* racism.

"Some Whites may not be racist at all." However, Samuel Gaertner et al. concluded "that given the historically racist American culture and human cognitive mechanisms for processing categorical information, racist feelings and beliefs among white Americans are generally the rule rather than the exception. Many well-intentioned Whites consciously believe in and profess equality, but unconsciously act in a racist manner, particularly in ambiguous situations." They have developed a "value system that maintains it is wrong to discriminate against a person because of his or her race" and "rejects the content of racial stereotypes," but that "nonetheless cannot entirely escape cultural and cognitive forces" to the point of becoming anti-racists.

Contemporary racism, explained Whitley and Kite, is mostly "motivated by a desire (although not necessarily a conscious one) on the part of many White Americans to retain and justify their traditional privileged position in society and the attendant access to the lion's share of societal resources (such as jobs, educational opportunities, and political power) that they see as threatened by Black economic gain. In effect, a significant segment of White America effectively condones as much Black disadvantage and segregation as modern free-market forces and informal social mechanisms can reproduce or even exacerbate."

Black people in America currently (and probably indefinitely) lack the power required to put an end to systemic anti-Blackness and the negative definition of Blackness in America. Consequently, we will continue to be susceptible to race-based stress.

Power, according to Maulana Karenga, can also be defined as "the social capacity of a group to realize its will, even in opposition to others." Regrettably, Black people in America currently (and probably indefinitely) lack the adequate social

194

capacity (or power) to engage in enough anti-racist behavior to end racism (i.e., racial discrimination, antagonism, exclusion, inequality, and injustice) in any of its contemporary forms. We can somewhat problematize racism, but we can't end it. At least at the moment it is not possible. Consequently, we will also continue to be susceptible to racism-related stress.

Oftentimes apathy, to quote Michael Parenti, becomes an "unconscious adjustment to powerlessness," particularly when it's chronic and inequitable. If nothing you do stops something unwanted, then it's terribly logical to start wanting to do nothing. However, "to not actively seek to interrupt racism," argued Robin Diangelo, "is to accept and internalize it."

A stressor is the negative experience, event, condition, or circumstance that causes stress by triggering our stress response. No matter what we do to reduce our stress, it will continue until we put an end to the stressor itself. Problem-focused coping is a specific strategy that requires successfully targeting and ending the stressor (i.e., solving the problem), which consequently reduces/stops the stress associated with the stressor. It is arguably the ideal way to manage stress.

With regard to race-based and racism-related stress, problem-focused coping is not currently a feasible option. Problem-focused coping can't work in situations where we don't have the capacity to eliminate the stressor (i.e., solve or end the problem). Since we are unable to end anti-Blackness and racism in America (as stressors), we can't use problem-focused coping to reduce race-based and racism-related stress.

Black people collectively don't currently possess the social capacity or power to end racial stigma, othering, bias, discrimination, antagonism, exclusion, inequality, and injustice. It's unfortunate, but true. However, a significant part of *interrupting* racism in its various modern manifestations, a critical part of *being anti-racist*, is changing or controlling our response, specifically our stress response, to racism.

195

Even if we can't control who Black people in America are understood or expected to be or stop racism, we can identify and practice evidence-informed strategies for reducing our stress response to race-based and racism-related experiences.

"When we are not able to change a situation, we are challenged to change ourselves. Between stimulus and response there is a space. In that space," noted Viktor Frankl, "is our power to choose our response. In our response lies our growth and our freedom."

Stress is directly associated with our emotional reaction to negative or threatening external stimuli (e.g., racism). *Active emotion-focused coping* features strategies designed to enable us to better control our emotional response to such stimuli, especially when we can't otherwise stop the stimuli. I believe that focusing on this approach will most effectively equip us to survive the stress of still being Black in America, stress that's literally killing us. "When you can't control what's happening, challenge yourself to control how you respond to what's happening. That's where your power is." That's how we evolve from mere victims to empowered survivors.

I don't believe it's defeatist or counterproductive to admit that we (i.e., Black people in America) can't control or stop racial stigma and racism. In fact, with regard to reducing stress, it's actually advantageous to determine what stressors you can and can't control or prevent. We can't control how someone else perceives us (racial stigma) or behaves towards us (racism), especially when bias against us collectively has existed for centuries. We can, however, control how we respond to their perception and behavior and whatever stress they may cause.

So, we should put our effort and energy into becoming more informed about how we respond to race and racism as stressors. We should all develop a toolkit to manage our stress more strategically. We ought to reflect on whatever unhealthy coping patterns we've established and stop them; identify a bunch of positive, evidence-informed strategies to replace them with;

practice as many of these new strategies that we can, even when they make us uncomfortable; and adopt those that seem to work best for us personally. I know, this all may sound a bit trite (are you serious, a freaking toolkit?), but a diverse toolkit of strategies is absolutely essential if we are to better deal with future race-based and racism-related stress.

There are four basic categories of coping responses for any kind of stressor: active, passive, problem-focused, and emotion-focused. These categories typically are merged to create specific approaches to stress, such as active problem-focused, active emotion-focused, passive problem-focused, and passive emotion-focused. We tend to use different approaches for different stressors. An easy way to think about this: anything active is generally good, anything passive is probably bad (or maladaptive). And, as aforementioned, problem-focused can only work when you have control over the stressor (i.e., can solve or stop the problem).

With passive coping, we try to avoid (thinking critically about) the stressor. We also don't attempt to cope more effectively with the stress it causes. We just hope or pray that it will somehow all go away. Or we allow our negative emotional reactions to the stressor (usually anger or fear) to become so intense and frequent that our amygdala (*changes* and) *takes over* whenever we perceive the stressor. As a result of the ineffectiveness of passive coping, we tend to experience continuous or chronic, brain-changing stress. This is bad, by the way.

An almond-shaped neural structure centrally located in the medial anterior temporal lobe of our brain, the amygdala (which is actually Greek for "almond") processes external stimuli and reflexively determines an emotional significance and response to that stimuli (particularly when deemed threatening), which is then sent out to other regions of the brain. The amygdala is directly associated with learned emotional responses (e.g., fear, anger) and is *proportionately plastic*, which means chronic overactivation of neurons in the amygdala enlarges and hypersensitizes the amygdala (by strengthening its internal and outbound neural

197

circuitry) which causes excessive, conditioned emotional reactions to recurrent (and potentially threatening) stimuli (e.g., racism).

In other words, the more we repeatedly overreact emotionally to certain (e.g., racism-related) life circumstances and experiences, the more likely we are to react equally or even more emotionally to those same (or similar) circumstances and experiences in the future because of distinct changes to our amygdala. These overreactions tend to become maladaptive since overreacting emotionally subdues rational thought, active coping, and authentic problem solving (to include figuring out how to reduce stress, not just stopping the stressor itself).

The now hyperactive and hypertrophied amygdala promotes persistent states of hypervigilance and heightened emotional reactivity, even our stress response is exacerbated and more impulsive. The hypervigilant amygdala is constantly activating the stress response, and every activation makes a future activation much more likely (as it becomes patterned neuronal activity). Our stress response to perceived threats is drastically quickened because our ability to moderate this response is linked to the functional efficiency of the hippocampus and prefrontal cortex, both of which are neuronally atrophied by continuous cortisol saturation.

Our capacity for emotional self-regulation depends heavily on the functional efficiency of the neural circuitry connecting the prefrontal cortex and amygdala. This connectivity is compromised dramatically in the brains of people who have experienced chronic stress (partly as a result of passive coping). When we can efficiently regulate our negative emotions, we influence if, when, and how we experience and are affected by them. When we can't, negative emotions can negatively bias our thoughts and actions; they can control us rather than the other way around. Emotional self-regulation is the ability to react to negative emotional stimuli (including stress) without compromising our long-term best interest, which typically means inhibiting our reflexive response in favor of a more appropriate one. When this ability is intact, we can scrutinize and manage our own emotions (including stress), thoughts, and actions as well as constructively modify them when circumstances require it. Our brain's natural capacity for regulating its reaction to negative emotions is essential, not just for survival but for success in anything.

Conversely, with active coping, we try to control the stressor directly in order to reduce the stress it causes. Whenever a stressor can't be controlled, active coping shifts the attention to figuring out ways (e.g., behaviors, resources, etc.) to more effectively cope with or minimize the stress. The implicit goal appears to be keeping the prefrontal cortex and hippocampus more involved in our reaction to stressors than the amygdala (e.g., being more intentional in our stress management), which enables us to better regulate our negative emotions and reduce the neuroplastic impact of stressors we must continue to endure.

Active emotion-focused coping is an approach to stress management that involves deliberately reducing the negative emotions produced by exposure to stressors in order to maintain our emotional and physical well-being. Active emotion-focused coping features the use of a variety of research-based, actionable strategies designed to better regulate the negative emotional responses associated with stress (e.g., fear, frustration, anger, shame, sadness, etc.).

By using these strategies to positively change our response to stressors, especially those stressors that are outside of our control, we can minimize experiencing those negative emotions that would otherwise increase or prolong our stress relsponse. It's not about having no emotional reaction at all, which would be practically impossible, or denying or avoiding our negative emotions. In fact, denying a threat as tangible and ubiquitous as racial stigma or racism can have its own negative consequences. Nor is it simply about being indifferent or helplessly tolerating or justifying those stressors that we can't currently prevent or stop.

The goal is to proactively practice various tools and interventions proven capable of helping us not let those negative emotions overwhelm us and restrict our possible responses to the stressor to only negative, counterproductive reactions. Being overly afraid or angry or sad on account of a particular stressor won't change or increase our control over that stressor and just makes us feel worse (i.e., more negative emotions). The more we can't stop (or regulate) feeling these negative emotions with regard to this particular stressor because we lack the necessary competence or resources, the more stress we experience (or the longer we experience stress).

Shifting our emotional experience relative to certain uncontrollable stressors (e.g., being Black in America) can reduce their ability to trigger chronic stress and, consequently, maladaptive neuroplasticity.

Neuroplasticity is possible because of the capacity of neurons to extend and create connections between brain regions and structures in order to facilitate efficient recall of past experiences along with reflexive instigation of a response. Recurring emotional responses become patterned neuronal activity that can cause us to begin responding to the circumstances of our lives habitually based on these (re)established neural activation patterns (i.e., brain changes). Maladaptive neuroplasticity are those brain changes that somehow instigate negative outcomes (e.g., diminished ability to regulate negative emotions and impulsivity, chronic hypervigilance, weakened capacity to regulate the inflammatory response, etc.).

We can't continue to allow the chronic stress of racial stigma and racism to deny us an equal opportunity to feel happy, safe, relaxed, desirable, and successful. We have a right to live in the present moment as opposed to "always having to be prepared for anti-black actions," to recall Feagin, and experiencing the stress that comes with that constant preparation. We have the *human* right to live happier, healthier, and longer lives, and learning to reduce stress, especially race-based and racism-related stress, positively and proactively will better enable us to realize that right.

Presumably, all Black people in America experience some degree of chronic, brain-changing stress related to being Black and/or enduring some type or consequence of contemporary racism.

Danielle Williams acknowledged that just "being Black in a racist society is stressful." Being Black in America makes us uniquely, highly, and constantly vulnerable to experiencing race-based stress. And we don't necessarily need to experience some form of racism in order to experience race-based stress; merely *being Black* is enough.

Existing in a "social environment in which Black Americans bear the stigma burden of their racial group while White Americans are allowed to view themselves as individuals" is stressful, explained Margaret Hicken et al. Having to deal with, possibly to some degree on a daily basis, the negative assumptions and expectations now associated with being Black in America is stressful. Enduring "unequal life experiences and chances based on the socially constructed racial group membership categories" being "woven into our social structure and institutions" is chronically stressful.

Additionally, we are "exposed regularly to racism, which could represent a continuous stressor," concluded Ma'at Lewis-Coles and Madonna Constantine. Racism creates events and experiences that are uniquely negative, ambiguous, unpredictable, and uncontrollable for its victims. Hence, "racism is stressful."

Moreover, to quote Nia Heard-Garris, "racism is a pervasive stressor." Racism is a normative experience for people in color (especially Black people) in this country and, therefore, a pervasive stressor. Contemporary racism can be experienced as systemic, individual, institutional, cultural, unconscious, aversive, everyday, anticipated, perceived, internalized, or microevents, which radically increases the probability and regularity of experiencing it in some form as a chronic stressor.

Chronic stressors are likely to deplete whatever coping skills and resources we intuitively employ and minimize the efficacy of our approach to stress management. Accordingly, Black people in America should all develop a personal toolkit of various practiced strategies to manage our race-based and racism-related stress more intentionally. This toolkit will enable us to develop a "relaxation response" to race-based and racism-related experiences to counteract and reduce the chronic stress response. Much of the rest of this chapter is dedicated to reviewing evidence-informed strategies in support of you developing your own toolkit.

Research confirms that victims of race-based and racism-related experiences display increased resilience to race-based and racism-related stress when they practice a variety of active coping strategies. *Stress resilience* is our capability and, more importantly, *choice* to cope effectively with stress—especially chronic stress—in a positive, intentional way. It's realizing that you can control the intensity and (neuroplastic) impact of your stress response by consciously regulating your negative emotions relative to experiencing the stressor. Stress resilience is a flexible trait you can cultivate and increase. Having more options in our toolkit when responding to chronic stressors, particularly those that are outside of our control, increases our stress resilience and lessens the likelihood of ruminating[51] or feeling helpless or hopeless in the face of those stressors despite their uncontrollability.

Our chronic stressors, including racism, oftentimes lose much of their power once we decide to lean into developing our capacity to reduce stress strategically. This commitment begins with choosing to see or define yourself as a survivor, not a victim. Survivors are far more inclined to look for ways to resolve a stressor than victims. Even for stressors that ultimately prove unstoppable in the moment, survivors are still more likely to focus their effort on identifying actionable methods that they can control

---

[51] Defined as the process or habit of continuously thinking about uncontrollable negative experiences from our past, rumination actually prolongs and/or exacerbates our stress response by impairing our ability to regulate negative emotions and thinking critically.

in order to create a more positive outcome (e.g., *reducing* stress). The survivor is more likely to accept responsibility and include more options in their toolkit (i.e., create a greater capacity) for responding emotionally to chronic stressors, particularly those that are outside of their control. Conversely, people who see themselves as victims are more likely to accept that uncontrollability over a stressor means they don't have the ability and responsibility to better control their associated stress response and, consequently, are more likely to suffer from the adverse effects of chronic stress.

The biggest thing with confronting race-based and racism-related stress is creating the opportunity for more Black people in America to be able to take a constructive *break* from the stress via active emotion-focused coping strategies. To literally—but positively—*interrupt* the race-based and racism-related stress response. And this should be done as soon as you begin to recognize this type of stress in your life. Doing so will give our brain a chance to recover from previous stress exposure and reduce *allostatic load* caused by uninterrupted (or chronic) stress.

David Borsook et al. explained that "the brain responds to potential and actual stressful events by activating hormonal and neural mediators and modifying behaviors to adapt. Such responses help maintain physiological stability (allostasis). When behavioral or physiological stressors are frequent and/or severe, allostatic responses can become dysregulated and maladaptive (allostatic load). Allostatic load may alter brain networks both functionally and structurally. As a result, the brain's responses to continued/subsequent stressors are abnormal, and behavior and systemic physiology are altered in ways that can, in a vicious cycle, lead to further allostatic load."

Allostatic load (or overload) is the neuroplastic result of our brain's chronic exposure to an exaggerated neural response due to continuous stress and allostasis. Neural pathways and structures (e.g., prefrontal cortex, hippocampus, and amygdala) are maladaptively changed as the brain is burdened by being constantly forced to adapt to abnormally recurrent adverse physical or psychosocial situations.

Javier Gilabert-Juan et al. asserted that chronic "aversive experiences, such as stress, can induce neuronal structural and functional plasticity" as a "neuroprotective mechanism." In other words, chronic stress compels the brain to change in an attempt to preserve relatively normal neuronal structure and/or functioning (i.e., achieve homeostasis via allostasis). However, if these experiences and subsequent changes are too prolonged it makes returning to *normal* much more difficult. A new normal is established that may not provide adequate or appropriate adjustment to past experiences and may promote increased vulnerability to comparable experiences in the future.

For instance, when functioning properly (i.e., without the burden of chronic stress), the amygdala directs incoming emotional information to the prefrontal cortex (or PFC) where it is logically evaluated for response or repression. The primary functions of the highly plastic PFC are the regulation of emotional behavior and the processing of external information in order to decide reasonable cognitive, behavioral, and emotional responses to the information. However, the altered neural circuitry of a chronically stressed or anxious amygdala experiencing allostatic load blocks the flow of information to the PFC. Instead, the amygdala's function is modified to now include the processing of external information in order to decide cognitive, behavioral, and emotional responses to the information (in lieu of the PFC).

This is particularly maladaptive considering how inherently irrational any decisions led by the emotion-based amygdala must be. This functional change inevitably limits most cognitive, behavioral, and emotional responses to incoming emotional information—especially negative emotional information—to the repeated activation of the stress response, which only aggravates the cumulative impact of additional chronic stress on allostatic load.

Hans Selye proposed that "stress is a major cause of disease because *chronic stress* causes long-term chemical changes," primary the overproduction of cortisol in the brain during allostasis. Recent research conducted by Sheldon Cohen et al. confirmed Selye's proposal by identifying that chronic stress causes disease because too much cortisol causes the brain to lose its capacity to regulate the inflammatory response. This inability to regulate inflammation triggers the development and progression of disease.

Most importantly, chronic stress "over time, can cause damage that leads to premature death," noted Patricia Celan. Any type of stress causes the release of cortisol, a hormone designed to enable the brain to elevate blood sugar and pressure levels in order to enhance our ability to respond to danger. However, with chronic stress there is so much cortisol constantly being produced that it becomes toxic and creates a significantly higher risk of serious health issues including stroke, heart attack, diabetes, and cancer.

"Inflammation is partly regulated by the hormone cortisol and when cortisol is not allowed to serve this function, inflammation can get out of control." Chronic stress "alters the effectiveness of cortisol to regulate the inflammatory response because it decreases tissue sensitivity to the hormone. Specifically, immune cells become insensitive to cortisol's regulatory effect, and consequently, produce levels of inflammation that promote disease. The evidence is compelling and growing," wrote Camara Harrell et al., that anti-Black stigma and "racism is pathogenic with respect to a variety of physical and mental health outcomes" for Black people.

In addition to its impact on our health, the chronic stress associated with race and racism can also prompt "antisocial behavior, lowered self-esteem, lowered levels of general happiness and life satisfaction, and poor academic performance," noted Shawn Utsey and Joseph Ponterotto.

I'd be remiss if I failed to emphasize that certain Black people constantly exposed to the possible stress of race-based and racism-related experiences can adapt appropriately and cope effectively. Our response to race-based stressors is not monolithic. Some of us can somehow prevent or reduce the maladaptive neuroplasticity described above. We (or more specifically, our brains) are exceptional, but only because we are informed and intentional in our response to race-based and racism-related experiences. More often than not, Black people exposed to the chronic stress caused by these experiences endure lasting adverse brain changes, but only because too many of us are uninformed and, consequently, can't be intentional in our response. Hopefully, this book can help change that.

To paraphrase Selye, it's not just the chronic stress of still being Black in America that's killing us, it is our unstrategic, habitual reaction to that stress. And while we currently may not be able to control experiencing racial stigma or racism in this country, we can better inform and control our response to the stress triggered by these experiences. Our future response should develop stress resilience while also give us chances to take a break from constant stress. Many of us have been experiencing race-based and racism-related stress so constantly that we don't realize just how stressed we are, which prevents us from even aspiring to reduce the stress strategically.

Approaching race-based and racism-related stress from a *proactive* position can further help reduce their impact as chronic stressors. "Traditional forms of coping," noted Esther Greenglass and Lisa Fiksenbaum, "tend to be reactive. They deal with stressful events that have already occurred and their purpose is to compensate for past harm or loss. Proactive coping is more future-oriented." With proactive coping, we identify, analyze, and prepare for anticipated (or probable) stressors. Accordingly, this approach would better enable us to minimize the triggering of race-based and racism-related stress by using certain strategies to prime a relaxation response to race-based and racism-related experiences in advance of the actual experience.

"The motivation for proactive coping is more positive" than traditional coping, and positivity increases our stress resilience. This positive motivation "results from perceiving situations as challenging, whereas reactive coping emanates from risk appraisal, that is, environmental demands are appraised as threats."

Proactive coping could be either problem-focused, in which we anticipate and act in advance of a potential but controllable stressor to prevent it, or emotion-focused. *Proactive emotion-focused coping* features the use of strategies designed to enable us to more effectively regulate our emotional response in anticipation of experiencing certain stressors, especially when we can't otherwise avoid or stop the stressor. By deliberately regulating our emotional response in advance of race-based and racism-related experiences that are fairly certain to occur, we can minimize experiencing those negative emotions that would otherwise increase or prolong our stress response.

Proactive emotion-focused coping is particularly effective with stressors that (neuroplastically) impact us the most through ambiguity and cumulative or chronic exposure, which include just being Black in America or enduring some type of contemporary racism.

Stress is basically an interaction between an external, negative stimulus (i.e., a stressor) and our brain's response, a response largely determined by the magnitude of the stimulus as compared to our capacity or resources for dealing with the stimulus. Whenever we perceive a negative disparity between the magnitude of the stimulus and our resources to cope, we experience acute stress; if we perceive this disparity recurrently, then we experience chronic stress.

With proactive emotion-focused coping, we accumulate resources (e.g., evidence-informed stress management strategies) and proactively take steps to avoid the resource gap that would otherwise lead to emotional dysregulation and, subsequently, increase or prolong our stress response. Essentially, as we expand our stress toolkit, we are also increasing our overall resistance to chronic stressors—especially those stressors we can anticipate and target specifically with the strategies in our toolkit. Even those future stressors that are inherently ambiguous are covered by this cumulative resistance because the same established set of strategies can be applied to them as well.

As aforementioned, just being a Black person living in an anti-Black, racialized society is still stressful. "The stress of living in a racialized society," concluded Vernellia Randall, "has significant health impact that affects African-Americans at every class level."

Rodney Clark et al. recognized that the mere "perception of an environmental stimulus as racist results in exaggerated psychological and physiological stress responses," which "over time, these stress responses influence health outcomes" far more than we typically fathom or strategically counteract. Stressors are more likely to negatively affect our health when they are "chronic, highly disruptive, or perceived as uncontrollable," according to Ellen Pastorino. Racial stigma and racism regularly create stressful experiences for people of color in this country (especially Black people) that are "chronic, highly disruptive, or perceived as uncontrollable."

The chronic stress of experiencing racial bias, discrimination, antagonism, exclusion, inequality, and injustice, especially when not adequately managed or reduced, can definitely lead to allostatic load, which drastically increases our susceptibility to a number of health problems. Constantly elevated levels of stress hormones, particularly cortisol, in our brain makes us significantly more vulnerable to infectious viral diseases like the common cold, influenza, and the coronavirus; high blood pressure; cancer; diabetes; heart disease; migraine headaches; depression; obesity; erectile dysfunction; irregular and painful menstruation; sterility/infertility; accelerated aging; and Alzheimer's disease.

Most of these conditions, if not properly treated, can shorten our lifespan (i.e., literally kill us). Even if properly treated, they can potentially make life miserable. However, our vulnerability to any of these conditions can be lowered considerably with an immediate commitment to identifying and strategically reducing the chronic stress we tend to experience from both traditional life stressors as well as race (especially being Black) and racism as stressors.

The statistical fact that today Black people in America as a whole, regardless of economic status, suffer and die more frequently from chronic illness than the poorest White Americans may be the most irrefutable evidence available of the differential impact of chronic race-based and racism-related stress.

Recent studies show that African-Americans tend to have significantly flatter diurnal cortisol slopes (i.e., production of cortisol during the day) than White Americans—an indication of increased allostatic load. Several of these studies, like the one led by O. Kenrik Duru et al., have also confirmed that Black people generally have a higher allostatic load score than White people "after adjustment for socioeconomic status and health behaviors."

As aforementioned, a higher allostatic load is the result of experiencing chronic stress over a prolong period. In this situation, Black people would need to experience chronic stressors that White people, irrespective of socioeconomic status and health behaviors ("traditional sociobehavioral risk factors"), *cannot experience.* Those stressors are race-based and racism-related experiences.

"Chronic stressors such as food insecurity, living in substandard housing, inadequate access to health care, and greater exposure to violence are greater among persons with low socioeconomic status, regardless of race. However, both poor and nonpoor blacks may share other stressors not generally experienced by whites, such as interactions with institutionalized racism, which could lead to increased allostatic load."

"Psychological stressors that disproportionately affect blacks may help explain racial differences in allostatic load as well as racial differences in mortality. As an example, perceived racial discrimination as experienced in interpersonal interactions or as a result of institutional racism could potentially result in elevation of primary (e.g., cortisol) and secondary (e.g., systolic blood pressure) biomarkers in this population, leading in turn to subclinical disease, overt disease, and, ultimately, death from a variety of conditions. Furthermore, internalized racism and the acceptance of negative societal beliefs about oneself may lead to similar outcomes."

David Williams and Selina Mohammed realized that "for most of the 15 leading causes of death including heart disease, cancer, stroke, diabetes, kidney disease, and hypertension, African Americans have much higher death rates than Whites." Perhaps not at all coincidentally, a recent study led by Bruce McEwen and Teresa Seeman revealed that chronic stress increases our susceptibility to heart disease, cancer, stroke, diabetes, kidney disease, and hypertension. The logical conclusion: Black people in America, *because* we are Black in America, are experiencing significantly more chronic stress than White Americans and disproportionately getting sick and dying prematurely as a result of it.

Of course, most "experts" aren't publicly endorsing this sort of thing; preferring instead to rely on theoretical or fabricated differences in genetics[52], cultural norms, economic class status, or irrational tendencies toward unhealthy life choices to rationalize interracial health disparities.

Arline Geronimus explained how "there have been folk notions and laypeople who have thought that health differences between populations—such as black versus white in the U.S.— were somehow related to differences in our DNA, that we were, in a sense, molecularly programmed to have this disease or that

---

[52] "It is important to bear in mind that *race* is a social category, not a biological one," wrote Bernard Whitley and Mary Kite. For example, "genetic studies find more differences within traditionally defined racial groups than between them. In statistical terms, the differences between races that do exist are trivial relative to the genetic factors common to all people." However, "its social nature does not diminish the psychological importance of race. It remains a fundamental basis for how people think about and interact with each other."

disease. But what I've seen over the years of my research and lifetime is that the stressors that impact people of color are chronic and repeated through their whole life course, and in fact may even be at their height in the young adult-through-middle-adult ages rather than in early life. And that increases a general health vulnerability—which is what weathering is."

Weathering is a direct consequence of continually experiencing race-based or racism-related stress. It is a "physiological process that accelerates aging and increases health vulnerability spurred by chronic toxic stress exposures over the life course and the tenacious high-effort coping that families and communities engage in to survive them."

"Persistent, high-effort coping with acute and chronic stressors," especially maladaptive coping[53], "can have a profound effect on health. The stress inherent in living in a race-conscious society that stigmatizes and disadvantages Blacks may cause repeated stress response activation and, consequently, disproportionate physiological deterioration, such that a Black individual may show the morbidity and mortality typical of a White individual who is significantly older. Not only do Blacks experience poor health at earlier ages than do Whites, but this deterioration in health accumulates, producing ever-greater racial inequality in health with age through middle adulthood."

"Weathering emphasizes that population differences in the early onset of chronic disease result from the qualitatively different life experiences, exposure to stressors, and access to coping resources associated with socially constructed categories, such as race, from conception onward."

Anderson argued that "racial health disparities need to be analyzed and understood by taking into account the social conditions which created them and the hostile racial climate of the

---

[53] "The emotional weight of racism," noted Monnica Williams, "can lead African-Americans to engage in maladaptive coping, such as remaining in denial, engaging in substance use, displaced aggression, self-blame—even in extreme cases suicide."

United States which allows such conditions to flourish. They need to be understood, not only in terms of individual characteristics, but also in light of patterned racial inequalities in exposure to societal risks and resources." In other words, "racism and racist structures within society are a central explanatory factor for racial differences in health."

Poverty is most often used in lieu of racism to explain away why we have much higher morbidity and mortality rates than White people. Poverty, not racism, is purportedly killing Black people. However, historical and contemporary racism (and the current and cumulative racially inequitable distribution of resources, income, and opportunity) are the root causes for why Black people are more likely to be poorer than White people.

Moreover, the poverty argument does not account for the aforementioned fact that poor White people are appreciably healthier on average than more affluent Black people. African-Americans have more negative health outcomes than Whites on their same income level. It appears that the impact of racism on health is actually independent of economic class status.

Pamela Sawyer et al. reported that "some mediators of the relationship between race/ethnicity and health include reduced access to health care, housing, and employment opportunities. Nevertheless, large racial/ethnic differences in health are still evident even after controlling for these factors. Scholars assert that higher stress levels among minorities caused by exposure to prejudice and discrimination may contribute to health disparities."

Race in and of itself cannot be an adequate justification of these disparities either. If we recall Glenn Loury's recognition that "the enduring and pronounced social disadvantage of African-Americans is not the result of any purportedly unequal innate human capacities of the 'races.' Rather, this disparity is a social artifact—a product of the peculiar history, culture, and political economy of American society."

We must bear in mind that "*race* is a social category," as explained by Whitley and Kite, "not a biological one. For example, genetic studies find more differences within traditionally defined racial groups than between them. In statistical terms, the differences between races that do exist are trivial relative to the genetic factors common to all people."

Moreover, noted Duru et al., "while racial differences in allostatic load may be influenced to some extent by genetic differences between racially designated groups, this is unlikely to be the sole or predominant explanatory factor for observed black/white disparities in the United States. Adults in sub-Saharan Africa have much lower rates of hypertension, diabetes, and obesity than do blacks in the United States" as their genetic descendants. While we may share a genetic legacy, Black people in America and Black people in Africa typically don't share chronic stressful experiences with racial stigma and racism. Those are uniquely American.

So, to quote Troy Duster, "the impact of race on disease is not biological in *origin* but in *effect*."

Conversely, there are few, if any, competent arguments against Lee Pachter et al.'s claim that "racism is a chronic stressor that causes allostatic load" and, consequently, increased morbidity and mortality, "since racial and ethnic minorities tend to have worse health outcomes even while controlling for other social factors."

Ryan Blitstein described in *Racism's Hidden Toll* how the chronic stress of "living in a white-dominated society makes African Americans get sick and die younger than their white counterparts. American minorities face a bevy of chronic obstacles that whites and the socioeconomically advantaged cope with far less often: environmental pollution, high crime, poor health care, overt racism, inferior educational opportunities, concentrated poverty. Over the course of a person's life, the psychological and physiological response to this kind of stress leads to dire health problems, advanced aging, and early death."

"Although most stressful experiences do not increase vulnerability to illness," according to Pascoe and Richman, "certain kinds of stressors—those that are uncontrollable and unpredictable—are particularly harmful to health," and these characteristics are common to racism. They set "into motion a process of physiological responses (e.g., elevated blood pressure, heart rate, cortisol secretions) that over time can have negative effects on health."

"Evidence also suggests that repeated exposure to discrimination may work in ways that prepare the body to be more physically reactive in stressful or potentially stressful social situations." The chronicity of the stress of being Black makes it even more detrimental to our long-term health as it progressively perpetuates allostatic load; erodes our protective resources; and increases our susceptibility to heart disease, cancer, stroke, diabetes, kidney disease, and hypertension. It also appears to be directly responsible for shortening the average lifespan of African-Americans.

A recent study led by David Chae concluded that "multiple levels of racism, including interpersonal experiences of racial discrimination and the internalization of negative racial bias, operate jointly to accelerate biological aging among African-Americans, especially African-American males."

Because we typically experience racism "on a routine, chronic, everyday basis, it wears out our biological systems because they are being continually engaged…and it can lead to this accelerated physiological wear and tear." Specifically, Chae's study revealed that because of the chronic stress of everyday racism Black Americans as a whole tend to have significantly shorter telomere lengths than White Americans.

Admittedly, when I first discovered this it didn't mean much to me because I had no clue of what a *telomere* was and why it should be longer versus shorter. I mean, how bad could this be in comparison to all the other bad stuff associated with being Black in America? After digging a little further, its significance soon became a life or death situation, literally.

Telomere length is a primary indicator of cellular (or biological) aging. Similar to how an aglet at the end of a shoelace prevents it from becoming damaged or unraveled, a telomere is a repetitive sequence of DNA located at the ends of each of our chromosomes that protects them from damage and deterioration. Telomeres reduce the loss of genetic information, which is required to sustain a cell's stability and vitality.

Masood Shammas explained that "telomeres shorten with age and rate of telomere shortening may indicate the pace of aging. Telomere length may therefore serve as a biological clock to determine the lifespan of a cell and an organism. Accelerated telomere shortening may increase the pace of aging. Telomere length, shorter than the average telomere length for a specific age group, has been associated with increased incidence of age-related diseases and/or decreased lifespan in humans."

This is because shorter telomeres inhibit the capacity of cells to divide properly, which causes cells in our body and brain to either to die off or malfunction and cause a physiological imbalance. Ultimately, this physiological imbalance substantially increases an individual's susceptibility to heart disease, cancer, stroke, diabetes, hypertension, and premature death.

The quicker we age biologically (as evident by the shorter our telomeres), the sooner we die, essentially.

Chronic stress appears to aggravate the rate of telomere shortening. Chronic stress, as aforementioned, significantly increases cortisol production in the brain. Cortisol saturation reduces the "levels of antioxidant proteins and may therefore cause increased oxidative damage to DNA and accelerated telomere shortening." Accordingly, because of the chronic stress of contemporary anti-Blackness and racism Black people in America as a whole tend to have significantly shorter telomere lengths than White Americans. And we don't even have to be conscious of this stress for it to have the same telomeric impact.

Generally, according to Cohen et al., "stressful events are thought to influence the pathogenesis of physical disease by causing negative affective states (e.g., feelings of anxiety and depression), which in turn exert direct effects on biological processes or behavioral patterns that influence disease risk. Exposures to chronic stress are considered the most toxic because they are most likely to result in long-term or permanent changes in the emotional, physiological, and behavioral responses that influence susceptibility to and course of disease."

Selye not only "discovered" stress but also was the first known scientist to realize the relationship between chronic stress and disease. He also hinted at the relationship between chronic stress and shorter telomeres, writing that "every stress leaves an indelible scar, and the organism pays for its survival after a stressful situation by becoming a little older."

Selye proposed that "stress is a major cause of disease because *chronic stress* causes long-term chemical changes," primary the overproduction of cortisol in the brain during allostasis. Recent research conducted by Cohen et al. confirmed Selye's proposal by identifying that chronic stress causes disease because chronic stress causes the brain to lose its capacity to regulate the inflammatory response. This inability to regulate inflammation triggers the development and progression of disease.

"Inflammation is partly regulated by the hormone cortisol and when cortisol is not allowed to serve this function, inflammation can get out of control." Chronic stress "alters the effectiveness of cortisol to regulate the inflammatory response because it decreases tissue sensitivity to the hormone. Specifically, immune cells become insensitive to cortisol's regulatory effect, and consequently, produce levels of inflammation that promote disease. The evidence is compelling and growing," wrote Harrell et al., that anti-Black stigma and "racism is pathogenic with respect to a variety of physical and mental health outcomes" for Black people.

Apparently, Steven Kniffley was terribly accurate in concluding that the "stress of being Black is literally killing us." However, it doesn't have to *continue* killing us. We could live

216

healthier, longer if we had less of this stress in our lives. That's why practicing proactive stress-reducing strategies is so important, as opposed to simply maintaining a victim mentality in which we choose tolerating over preventing our own demise.

The first step toward reducing race-based and racism-related stress is candidly understanding how we currently react to those specific stressors, especially emotionally, and making changes (e.g., adding new evidence-informed strategies to our stress toolkit) if necessary. (Hint: It will most likely be necessary.)

A key difference between those of us who effectively reduce our race-based and racism-related stress and those who are less effective is the *practiced* ability to monitor and subsequently regulate negative emotions relative to our race-based and racism-related experiences. We've consciously *cultivated* more stress resilience through consistent practice. Practice creates confidence in our stress resilience. Stress resilience is our capability and, more importantly, *choice* to cope effectively with stressors—especially chronic stressors—in a positive, proactive way.

Negative emotional awareness and regulation—accurately understanding what we're feeling and why and what we should do about it—is the foundation of stress resilience. Relative to our race-based and racism-related experiences, we have to get increasingly comfortable noticing that "this frightens me" or "this makes me angry" or "I feel ashamed when." And when we feel this way (or can anticipate feeling this way), what can we do that's positive to stop (or prevent) feeling this way. Even if we can't reduce our stress by getting rid of the stressful situation or experience, we can reduce our stress by practicing creating a more positive emotional (or relaxed) response to it. To *deliberately* feel less frightened, not as angry, not so ashamed by doing something constructive when we experience or anticipate stress.

With proactive emotion-focused coping, we accumulate resources (e.g., evidence-informed stress management strategies) and proactively take steps to avoid the resource gap that would otherwise lead to emotional dysregulation and, subsequently, increase or prolong our race-based and racism-related stress responses. By deliberately regulating our emotional response in advance of race-based and racism-related experiences that are fairly certain to occur, we can minimize experiencing those negative emotions that would otherwise increase or prolong our stress response.

Far too often we rely on negative coping responses, comforting habits, or self-defeating or destructive behaviors in reaction to the emotions of stressful situations and experiences involving race or racism. Adequate stress resilience typically doesn't just happen. Clark et al. observed how experiences of "racism that engender anger may lead to coping responses that include anger suppression, hostility, aggression, verbal expression of the anger, or the use of alcohol or other substances to blunt angry feelings." Similarly, "chronic feelings of helplessness and hopelessness may evoke feelings of frustration, depression, resentment, distrust, or paranoia that lead to passivity or avoidance."

Negative coping increases experiencing those negative emotions that would otherwise increase or prolong our stress response. Negative coping prevents a relaxed response to certain stressors. Negative coping disincentivizes practicing evidence-informed stress management strategies. Negative coping promotes chronic stress and, ultimately, allostatic load. Negative coping is also catalyst for maladaptive neuroplasticity.[54]

Unfortunately, negative coping has apparently been normalized throughout the African-American community. For much of my life, I personally relied on negative coping to deal with chronic race-based and racism-related stress. For a long time, I actually rationalized rage as an appropriate response to my negative experiences of being Black.

---

[54] Maladaptive neuroplasticity are those brain changes that somehow instigate negative outcomes (e.g., diminished ability to regulate negative emotions and impulsivity, chronic hypervigilance, weakened capacity to regulate the inflammatory response, etc.).

It wasn't until I randomly came across the following quote from James Baldwin that I even began to consider that rage may not necessarily be the best (or even a good) response and that finding a better approach for me to cope with race and racism may be unavoidable: "To be a Negro in this country and to be relatively conscious, is to be in a rage almost all the time. So that the first problem is how to control that rage so that it won't destroy you."

I never considered this rage was capable of destroying me. If anything, I assumed it was protecting me. I was so full of anger that for as long as I can remember my favorite superhero was unquestionably the Hulk. To me being a "Black Hulk" was an appropriate response to any experiences of stigma, othering, bias, discrimination, antagonism, exclusion, inequality, and injustice. I was so full of uncontrolled anger. It was until much later in life that I realized that this rage was intuitive camouflage for worse feelings like fear, disappointment, sadness, helplessness, invisibility, and, most importantly, the constant stress of "always having to be prepared for anti-black actions."

Race and racism, combined with other traditional life stressors, left me with a short temper, argumentative disposition, and general irritability that was oftentimes embodied and acted out or projected onto innocent people who actually cared about me. I had subconsciously learned early on to be afraid because "if you try to help Black people, you will be killed." And perhaps too late in life I discovered firsthand, to quote Amos N. Wilson, that "the White American community severely punishes through social ostracism, ridicule, mockery, employment discrimination, physical assault and denial of fundamental civil rights, those African-Americans who openly identify with and espouse African culture, history, values, autonomy, and liberation." Being anti-racist in this country is actually dangerous.

Knowing I should be afraid of and acquiescent to anti-Blackness only increased the anger. I secretly was never not angry. That anger intensified my consciousness of racial stigma and the many ways I was probably experiencing contemporary racism. That consciousness exacerbated the stress I felt being Black in America and, over time, it started to kill me too (via various chronic illnesses). What I didn't know until much later in life was how exactly to control the anger and, ultimately, survive the stress.

If we are unfamiliar or uncomfortable with producing an adequate relaxation response, the chronic stress of race and racism may motivate us to continually lash out at others; engage in risky, escapist, or hypersexual behaviors; automatically expect the worst or exaggerate the negative aspects of any unfavorable situation; overeat; overwork; feel hopeless; wallow in self-pity; sleep too much; become apathetic; spend money compulsively and create unnecessary debt; use drugs or alcohol addictively to avoid painful thoughts and emotions; suppress or repress negative thoughts and emotions; disengage mentally or behaviorally (i.e., give up); or ignore, deny, or passively complain about the stress (or the stressor).

None of these things are healthy nor will they somehow reduce the stress. If anything, they have become unhealthy *habits* that tend to increase or prolong our stress response until it becomes overwhelming.

Our brain forms habits, both beneficial and harmful to us and others, automatically. Once we do something (e.g., suppress negative thoughts and emotions) enough times, we become effortlessly capable of continuing to do that thing, even if we shouldn't. A habit, according to Liesl Ulrich-Verderber, is a "behavior that has become almost involuntary. Essentially, it's a habit if you don't have to think about it to do it. What's incredible about habits, and can make them difficult to break, is that they actually rewire our brains."

The rewiring that ultimately creates or changes habits occurs in what Charles Duhigg refers to as a three-step loop. First, "there is a cue, a trigger that tells your brain to go into automatic mode and which habit to use." This cue could be an action, thought, event, or emotion—experienced consciously or unconsciously—

that initiates an internal craving to get the reward at the end of this specific habit's loop.

Then, "there is the routine, which can be physical or mental or emotional." The routine is the behavior associated with the trigger that we actually *do*. It is the mental, physical, or emotional action we repeatedly engage in to secure the reward at the end of this specific habit's loop.

Finally, "there is a reward, which helps your brain figure out if this particular loop is worth remembering for the future." If this specific behavior or routine consistently enables us to experience positive emotions (e.g., happiness, excitement, joy, hope) or alleviates stress, the pleasurable release of dopamine in our brain will make us want to repeat the behavior. High levels of released dopamine make us literally feel good, so good that it motivates us to do more of whatever stimulated the release of dopamine initially (i.e., the routine).

"Over time, this loop—cue, routine, reward—becomes more and more automatic. The cue and reward become intertwined until a powerful sense of anticipation and craving emerges." Ultimately, this is the reason that the routine becomes a habit. Once a habit develops, it becomes instinctive for us to complete the routine whenever our brain recognizes the cue and begins to crave the reward. "When a habit emerges, the brain stops fully participating in decision making. It stops working so hard, or diverts focus to other tasks. So, unless you deliberately fight a habit—unless you find new routines—the pattern will unfold automatically."

"Each time a cue precedes a behavior," observed Connie Stemmle, the "link between the behavior and its cue is strengthened. As this connection increases, the behavior becomes increasingly ingrained in your brain to the point that you eventually engage in the behavior without even giving it a second thought after you're triggered to do so."

As our brain unconsciously creates habits, our habits are subtly changing neural structures and pathways, comprised of neurons connected by dendrites. Each repetition of the habit increases the number of dendrites within these pathways, which strengthens the capacity of the neurons to communicate with each other (known as *neuronal firing*) and speeds up this communication. Stronger and faster communication among specific neural pathways and structures creates more automatic behavior, or habits.

Even though our brain forms most habits unconsciously, it is possible to consciously change (as well as create) certain habits. Doing so initially requires merely paying more attention to the specific habit we'd like to change. "Just the act of paying attention to our habits can start shifting them," noted Micaela Higgs. Increased attention to the habit enables us to then begin rearranging the three steps of the habit-forming loop that previously created the habit.

First, scrutinize the routine, or the specific behavior you want to change. Identify whether or not the negative consequences of the behavior are greater than the *why* (i.e., reasons for doing) of the behavior, and thus worthy of change. Is the only why getting the reward? If so, is that enough to continue the routine?

Next, recognize the reward you get following the routine. Then, evaluate the reward. Is the reward worth continuing the negative consequences of the routine? What positive consequences could you instigate by discontinuing or changing the routine? Are the positive consequences for discontinuing or changing the routine greater than the negative consequences for continuing it, and thus worthy of change?

Lastly, identify the cues, or triggers, for the behavior. What consciously compels you to continue the behavior? What may unconsciously be compelling you to continue the behavior? Figuring out our unconscious motives can be difficult but is absolutely necessary for changing habits. Most habits are unconsciously formed *and motivated*, so if we only address the explicit motivation, we'll continue to be motivated unconsciously to maintain the habit (without knowing that or how we are still

222

being motivated). What were you doing, reacting to, expecting, and/or feeling just before *doing* the habit (i.e., reacting to the cue)? Is there a positively different way to respond to the cue? How willing are you to respond positively differently, especially when you are experiencing (or being triggered by) negative emotions?

It would be nice if we could just control our habits and end or change them instantly whenever we deemed it beneficial. Unfortunately, research has confirmed that the "brain networks associated with self-control (e.g., the prefrontal cortex) are the first to go 'offline' when faced with triggers such as stress" and other highly negative emotions, noted Jud Brewer.

Moreover, we commit to a habit, even the worst habit, largely because we crave its highly positive (to us) emotional reward. A habit's *reward value* is the degree of positive emotion (e.g., happiness, excitement, joy, hope) or stress relief we experience from completing the habit. The higher the reward value, the more likely we are to repeat the habit (regardless of its negative consequences to ourselves or others). "How *rewarding* a behavior is drives how likely we are to repeat that behavior in the future, and this is why self-control as an approach to breaking habits often fails." Identifying a habit's *true* reward value, which could be partly or mostly experienced unconsciously, is key to possibly changing that habit.

Most of our unhealthy habits are essentially behaviors our brains have been rewired to repeat with conscious thought in order to help us cope with stress or other negative emotions. Stress and other negative emotions bias our brain towards repeating old habits rather than attempting new actions because it remembers that the old habit (regardless of its negative consequences to ourselves or others) somehow successfully alleviated the stress or other negative emotions. Consequently, in order to stop repeating these habits, our brain has to override its now default response and create (or rewire) a new response to situations that typically triggered the use of the old, unhealthy habits.

In other words, we intentionally introduce our brain to a new routine that will replace the old, negative one (e.g., passively complaining about racism). Once a habit loop is established, it becomes instinctive for us to complete its routine when our brain recognizes the cue and begins to crave the reward. We usually can't control the cue (or triggering circumstances) and will continue to crave the reward (e.g., negative emotion and/or stress reduction), so we don't try to change those parts of the loop. We focus only on what we can change, and that's deliberately inserting a new, positive routine (i.e., stress reducing strategy) into the habit loop. And doing so consistently and repeatedly until a new habit loop becomes wired in our brain via positive neuroplasticity. Assuming you're adequately motivated to stop the old habit, the real trick then becomes identifying and gaining confidence in practicing positive alternative routines (i.e., responding differently to race-based and racism-related experiences).

Identifying and practicing alternative routines will concurrently increase your awareness of the established habit along with its consequences. Increasing your awareness of a habit and its consequences can ultimately transform the habit from an automatic, unconscious decision into a deliberate, conscious (i.e., "choosable") behavior. "Cultivating awareness will help your prefrontal cortex override default patterns." Increasing your awareness can enable you to make a conscious decision with regard to accepting the consequences that accompany perpetuating the habit. Most people will not continue to consciously choose to do harm to themselves or others and will begin to choose their future behaviors accordingly.

"To break a destructive coping habit," noted Debbie Hampton, "very rarely can you just stop doing it because you're still left with the original stress" from the triggering circumstances (e.g., race-based or racism-related experience) in your brain. "You have to replace the undesirable habit with another, more positive one and take measures to reduce the stress that triggers the unwanted habits. You can stop the bad habit spiral by building more positive habits in your brain" (e.g., practicing proactive emotion-focused coping strategies).

All negative habits seem to both cause and be a consequence of maladaptive neuroplasticity (i.e., brain changes that somehow instigate negative outcomes). We change our habitual behavior by "building alternate pathways in our brain." Changing a habit "involves weakening connections" between the neural circuitry associated with the habit "through disuse" and conscious decision making (i.e., consciously deciding to change). Conscious, positive choices can trigger enduring, positive neuroplasticity. The brain regions and structures (e.g., the amygdala, hippocampus, prefrontal cortex) negatively changed by the chronic stress of being Black in America can also be positively changed by other, more positive stimuli (e.g., practicing proactive emotion-focused coping strategies).

When initially trying to insert a new, positive routine into the habit loop, "it's going to require conscious effort, intention, and thought until you've done it enough for the connections to be made and strengthened in your striatum." Creating a positive neuroplastic impact specifically in your striatum[55] is critical to

---

[55] Habits are developed in the striatum, which is a cluster of neurons situated in the region of our brain known as the basal ganglia. Our basal ganglia are capable of taking a repeated behavior and transforming it into an automatic routine. Functionally, our striatum unconsciously processes external stimuli in order to prompt us to react by repeating our most repeated past response to the same or similar stimuli.

The nucleus accumbens is a major part of the striatum. Functionally, the nucleus accumbens motivates us to repeat past behavior that we specifically found to be pleasurable (i.e., triggered positive emotions). This is based on its unique craving for the neurotransmitter dopamine, which is released whenever we do, think, or feel something we find pleasurable. The first times we do, think, or feel this pleasurable thing, dopamine is released shortly afterwards.

However, after this pleasurable thing is adequately repeated, dopamine begins to be "released earlier and earlier until just thinking about something in anticipation causes a dopamine reward," explained Hampton. "The dopamine preceding the action motivates us to perform the behavior in the future. Every time we act in the same way" in pursuit of more dopamine, a "specific neuronal

changing the negative habit. "This means that in the beginning, your prefrontal cortex has to use conscious will to override the old patterns until the burden of action shifts to become the unconscious default of your striatum."

We do this by engaging our prefrontal cortex "by actively paying attention" to our behavior. "Intentional actions," such as practicing alternative routines, are "handled by the brain's prefrontal cortex." The human brain has limited cognitive resources. When you stop paying attention to your behavior because you're emotionally distracted or experiencing stress, "your brain reverts back to old patterns" and habits. Every time you consciously perform the new routine, you're making the neural circuitry associated with the old habit weaker in your brain.

When you first start to change a habit, "you have to enlist your prefrontal cortex and insert conscious effort, intention, and thought into the process. When you've performed the new routine enough times for connections to be made and strengthened in your brain, the behavior will require less effort as it becomes the default pattern." Conversely, continuing to deny, defend, or disregard our use of unhealthy coping behaviors will minimize our awareness and easily maintain the habitual use of those unhealthy coping behaviors.

All Black people in America experience some degree of chronic, brain-changing stress related to being Black and/or enduring some type or consequence of contemporary racism. "A chronically stressed brain tends to reprogram itself and reinforce the behaviors responsible for the stress," Nuno Sousa et al. People are more negatively affected by chronic stress when they haven't yet established a toolkit to manage their stress more strategically. Our goal now should be to stop reacting to race-based and racism-

---

pattern is stimulated." This pattern becomes increasingly wired in (as it changes) our brain and easier to activate perpetually. Eventually, this action and its associated neural pathway becomes the "unconscious default," and our brain, seeking cognitive efficiency, repeats it without much thought or cognitive resources regardless of how maladaptive or constructive it may be.

related stress with unhealthy habits and instead begin to respond habitually with proactive emotion-focused coping strategies designed to reduce or stop our stress response and increase our stress resilience. Since we can't currently eliminate race and racism as chronic stressors, *self-care* is how we'll develop enough resilience to survive the stress of still being Black in America.

Prioritizing self-care through proactive emotion-focused coping is a decision we all must make for ourselves, and changing our unhealthy stress habits will require lots of information, effort, and persistence. Making even small changes in our approach to race-based and racism-related stress can go a long way in reducing that stress and improving our physical and mental health. Honestly, the hardest part about change and creating new habits is *starting*. Procrastination, pessimism, and complaints about not having enough time to start oftentimes prevent us from ever starting.

One way to make starting easier, according to Stephen Covey, is to "schedule your priorities." Find the time now to start (or continue) learning about and then practicing those proactive emotion-focused coping strategies capable of managing your race-based and racism-related stress response.

Set specific goals about what strategies you'd like to try. Make a plan of incremental steps on how and when you will meet these goals. Writing this plan down, even if you just type it as a note in your phone, increases the odds of achieving your goals by 30%. Telling people close to you about your plan increases your chances of success even more. Finding external support, like from a friend or mentor, certainly helps. Reward yourself for taking positive steps toward meeting your goals. And when you have setbacks, rather than beat yourself up explore them for feedback on how to be better in the future.

There are several evidence-informed, proactive emotion-focused strategies for coping with the stress of race and racism. Some of them at first may seem frivolous or not capable of effectively coping with something as significant as the specific stress of race and racism, but they are definitely appropriate. (I'll do my best to explain how.)

Accordingly, the rest of this chapter is dedicated to introducing these strategies, most of which are very digestible and practical. Please note that these strategies are neither miraculous, instantaneous, nor absolute, and typically multiple strategies must be used consistently, concurrently, and confidently in order to see significant impact. Most of them I have tried or continue to practice in my own struggle for survival.

I'd argue that the first or a foundational proactive strategy for coping with and surviving the chronic stress of race (i.e., being Black) and racism in America is vehemently, or at least candidly, acknowledging that you have experienced this stress in some way probably on a daily basis and tended to self-blame, normalize, or somehow avoid (i.e., just live with or get over) it. But now, you recognize and want to problematize[56] this stress and ultimately reduce it by replacing unhealthy habits with proactive emotion-focused coping strategies.

Talking about your race-based and racism-related experiences and the stress and other negative emotions these experiences triggered is a simple yet often overlooked emotion-focused coping strategy. Talking about your feelings to a trustworthy, empathetic support system (of friends, peers, family, educators, community members, and/or professional therapists who listen and offer advice and perspective based on their own experience) can help reduce your stress by assuring that you're not oversensitive or overreacting (unless you are, which is a whole other thing) and validating your experience and feelings.

Talking with others can also help you increase your understanding of the stressor and different ways to respond to it that could trigger less stress and other negative emotions based on shared experience with your support system. Talking about your feelings also helps you specify (or name) and, subsequently,

---

[56] To *problematize*, by definition, is to make some thing or situation into (or begin to regard it as) a problem *requiring* a solution or end.

228

release those feelings (along with some of the stress that came with them). Clarifying our emotions can help us figure out how to change our behavioral and emotional reactions to those emotions as needed as opposed to just repeating them. Research shows that naming our stress-related emotions can increase our stress resilience.

Although we tend to freely discuss our experiences with racism, most Black people don't talk nearly enough with each other (or anyone else) specifically about our experiences with the stress of race (i.e., being Black in America) and racism. Think about it. Prior to reading this book, when was the last time *you talked about* feeling race-based or racism-related stress with someone else.

Men generally don't talk much about any of our feelings. Too many of us are afraid of being embarrassed or appearing weak (or less manly) if we do. We also tend to believe that talking about our feelings won't do anything to change or stop those feelings, so what's the point. And that talking about our feelings, especially the negative ones, may actually reinforce these feelings and make us feel worse.

Black men are especially terrible at talking about this particular feeling, perhaps due to accompanying feelings of fear, anger, helplessness, etc. In my forty-four years of being a Black man in America, I can only remember having one conversation (just two years ago) with other Black people explicitly about the stress of still being Black in America. Not coincidentally, Black men seem to rely far more than Black women on negative coping responses, comforting habits, or self-defeating or destructive behaviors in reaction to the emotions of stressful situations and experiences involving race or racism.

In fact, realizing the rarity of that conversation ultimately inspired the writing of this book.

Talking specifically about the stress of being Black in America is not easy for Black men *and* women (and, for that matter, children). I think most of the difficulty comes from an intuitive feeling of anger or sadness-laden helplessness relative to race and racism as

229

uncontrollable, ubiquitous stressors. We may be reacting to a subconscious logic of "if we can't stop it, what's the point in talking about it." Without us knowing, our ego defense mechanisms may also be working overtime to repress these emotions especially, supposedly to protect our self-concept. This makes it a challenge to even know what we feel.

It also doesn't help that nobody (like a parent or teacher) usually models or teaches us *how* to talk about the stress of race and racism. It's hard to do (or even want to do) something you haven't really been exposed to. Just in writing this book, I realized that there is a special language required to accurately articulate these kinds of feelings that most Black people simply never learn. I taught mostly Black students for well over a decade, and even though I was the "why he teach us all this Black stuff" kind of teacher, I don't recall ever teaching that lesson. I wish I would have. So, we continue to ignore, deny, and avoid talking about it, all the while letting the unmanaged stress accumulate and perhaps ultimately kill us.

Talking about the chronic stress of race and racism is such an impactful yet doable strategy for self-care that I'd advise you to create your own discussion group to have those candid, empathetic conversations. Or join and promote an already established group if you're fortunate enough to find one. Start with a manageable number of people, people you know or who are recommended by other people you trust. Consider even inviting professional therapists to add their expertise. You could meet in-person or virtually (using one of the billions of free virtual meeting platforms that suddenly exist). Perhaps most importantly, be very explicit in the purpose of your discussion group and stick to that purpose as you meet.

It's also never too early to talk with children of color (especially Black children) specifically about the stress of race and racism. As aforementioned, there is a special language required to accurately articulate these kinds of feelings that most Black people simply never learn. Talking with (your own or, if you're in a position to do so appropriately, other people's) children about the stress of race and racism can help break this cycle of ignorance and get more of us on the path to improved stress resilience.

There's no age requirement to start having stressful race-based and racism-related experiences. You'd probably be surprised at just how early and frequently Black children and adolescents experience the stress of still being Black in America. And because of their relative lack of exposure, they tend to struggle more with identifying feelings and causes of race-based and racism-related stress as well as how to manage this stress effectively. So, they can benefit greatly from talking about it with older, more informed people as long as we're willing to listen actively, encourage them to speak candidly, respond positively and thoughtfully, and model successful coping strategies.

Basically, these conversations *teach* young people of color about race-based and racism-related stress and possible coping strategies for it they should practice. The more they learn about this specific type of stress, their resilience to it is improved proportionately. Stress resilience is our capability and, more importantly, *choice* to cope effectively with stress—especially chronic stress—in a positive, intentional way. It's realizing that you can control the intensity and (neuroplastic) impact of your stress response by consciously regulating your negative emotions relative to experiencing the stressor. Stress resilience is a flexible trait you can cultivate and increase. Research confirms that victims of race-based and racism-related experiences display increased resilience to race-based and racism-related stress when they practice a variety of active coping strategies.

Another recommended proactive emotion-focused coping strategy for race-based and racism-related stress is *journaling*. Some people are better at or just more comfortable expressing themselves in writing than talking with others, especially with regard to such complicated stressors and emotions. As long as you journal consistently and candidly, writing can be just as, if not

231

more, beneficial for self-care than talking about the chronic stress of race and racism.

Ideally, you would take a five to fifteen preplanned minutes every day to reflect on and write about your thoughts and feelings relative to any race-based or racism-related experiences you either had that day or past (or recurring) experiences that you're still processing. Journaling can be a healthy outlet for processing and releasing the negative emotions connected to these experiences that would otherwise do harm if allowed to accumulate and fester. You don't have to share your journal with anyone else, so be transparent, emotive, and as detailed as possible (write like you would talk in a therapy session). And don't worry about your spelling or grammar or being wordy or whatever, just write whatever comes to mind.

Putting these thoughts and feelings on paper (or on your phone or iPad, etc.) can have a clarifying, calming, and cathartic effect in the moment, which will, in turn, assist in reducing chronic race-based or racism-related stress. Journaling can help you recognize those aspects of the stressor that you could actually control or change, even if it's just your emotional reaction to it, and by changing produce more positive feelings (and less stress). It's actually a best practice to always take time at the end of your journaling session to write about how and why you will implement those changes. Only writing about negative thoughts and feelings without a plan for optimism can actually cause more stress.

A simple proactive emotion-focused practice I've been doing for a while now to cope with the stress of being Black in America is reciting and posting *positive affirmations or quotes*. Being an author, I obviously believe that words have power. However, I actually first began to understand the stress-reducing power of affirmations and quotes as an educator and seeing their impact on my mostly Black students.

Catherine Moore defined positive affirmations as "positive phrases or statements used to challenge negative or unhelpful thoughts" and feelings and "encourage an optimistic mindset."

Affirmations, according to Kathryn Lively, are "simply statements that are designed to create self-change in the individual using them." Even when in the midst of the most stressful experiences, being able to recall the right words or thought can be calming, deeply transformative, and (stress) resilience building. They help us better regulate our negative thoughts and emotions by introducing a more positive perspective with regard to the ways we tend to think and feel about (and respond to) negative experiences (as stressors).

Positive affirmations and quotes influence our subconscious mind to aspire to new, healthier habitual reactions to race-based or racism-related stress, especially when they are repeatedly spoken, heard, or seen (i.e., *practiced*). By consistently practicing positive affirmations and quotes, we gradually rewire our brains in preparation for replacing reinforced negative coping responses to and limiting beliefs about race-based or racism-related stress experiences with more positive responses and beliefs.

"There are few advantages associated with being Black in America," noted Kathy Russell. And it's the constant, cumulative disadvantages associated with being Black that oftentimes spawn stressful race-based experiences (i.e., negative, uncontrollable things we experience as stressors primarily, but oftentimes ambiguously, because we are Black). Race-based stress is caused by race-based experiences, which for Black people in America can occur at any time on any given day because we currently lack the individual and collective capacity and resources to stop the stigma and disadvantages of being Black in America.

"African-Americans in the United States are exposed regularly to racism, which could represent a continuous stressor," concluded Ma'at Lewis-Coles and Madonna Constantine. Racism-related stress is stress specifically triggered by experiencing some form of racism or racist behavior, inclusive of any act of racial discrimination, hostility, violence, exclusion, inequality, or injustice perceived or experienced as somehow threatening.

233

Racism has the additional capacity, according to Amos N. Wilson, to produce and perpetuate conditions that disproportionately increase our exposure to traditional life stressors—such as "inadequate family incomes, health care, education, job training, housing, employment, and economic development—which strain the Black community's coping mechanisms. The effects of these stressors are amplified by the relatively dependent and reactionary orientation of the Black community."

"One of the many byproducts of negative thinking is stress, which then leads to more negative thinking," noted Terry Small. In order to reduce stress, we must practice replacing negative thinking with positive thinking. Doing so initiates *positive neuroplasticity*. "Brains are designed to respond to experiences," confirmed Eric Jensen, "both good and bad." The brain regions and structures (e.g., the amygdala, hippocampus, prefrontal cortex) negatively changed by chronic race-based and racism-related stress can continue to be changed (or *healed*) by other external positive stimuli, such as practicing positive affirmations and quotes.

So, even though we currently lack the social capacity to engage in enough anti-racist behavior to end racism, practicing positive affirmations and quotes can at least provide us with enough positive thinking that could evolve into a sort of psychological armor or immunity from the chronic stress of still being Black in America.

I've practiced and now recommend the following positive affirmations and quotes with regard to coping with this specific stress. I'm sure you're already familiar with some equally effective options, and the Internet and social media are always willing to provide more. Or you can create your own.

Just remember, the goal is to practice (i.e., learn) *proactively*. You can't efficiently absorb new positive affirmations and quotes when negative emotions and stress are currently triggered. Our amygdala, when activated by the stress response, won't allow our prefrontal cortex to process them or our hippocampus to remember them. In the midst of experiencing stress, we reduce our stress response by being able to recall positive affirmations and quotes, not by suddenly trying to learn them.

- "What matters most is how well you walk through the fire." (Charles Bukowski)

- "If I didn't define myself for myself, I would be crunched into other people's fantasies for me and eaten alive." (Audre Lorde)

- "Life is not the way it is supposed to be. It is the way it is. The way you cope with it is what makes the difference." (Virginia Satir)

- "If you have no confidence in self, you are twice defeated in the race of life. With confidence, you have won even before you have started." (Marcus Garvey)

- "Don't sweat the small stuff...and it's all small stuff." (Richard Carlson)

- "Our deepest fear is not that we are inadequate. Our deepest fear is that we are powerful beyond measure." (Marianne Williamson)

- "The perceptions of reality that you have in your mind will either free you or keep you enslaved." (Anthony Browder)

- "To become free, you have to be acutely aware of being a slave." (Assata Shakur)

- "The only way to deal with an unfree world is to become so absolutely free that your very existence is an act of rebellion." (Albert Camus)

- "If there is no struggle, there is no progress." (Frederick Douglass)

235

- "You may encounter many defeats, but you must not be defeated. In fact, it may be necessary to encounter the defeats, so you can know who you are, what you can rise from." (Maya Angelou)

- "We are what we repeatedly do. Excellence then is not a single act but a daily habit." (Aristotle)

- "The only thing permanent is change." (Heraclitus)

- "To fly we have to have resistance." (Maya Lin)

- "A man can stand a lot as long as he can stand himself." (Axel Munthe)

- "When anger rises, think of the consequences." (Confucius)

- "If you can walk you can dance. If you can talk you can sing." (Zimbabwe proverb)

- "Control what you can control." (Cam Newton)

- "The only real solution to the race problem is a solution that involves individual self-improvement and collective self- improvement." (Malcolm X)

- "We must not let the fact that we are the victims of injustice lull us into abrogating responsibility for our own lives and become an excuse for mediocrity and laziness." (Martin Luther King, Jr.)

- "What we think, we become." (The Buddha)

- "Life isn't fair…and perhaps, it was never intended to be." (Richard Carlson)

- "Your wings work, use them." (Marjorie Harvey)

- "We can only be destroyed by believing that we really are what the white world considers a nigger." (James Baldwin)

- "Do not dwell in the past, do not dream of the future, concentrate the mind on the present moment." (The Buddha)

- "Not everything that is faced can be changed; but nothing can be changed until it is faced." (James Baldwin)

- "When I discover who I am, I'll be free." (Ralph Ellison)

Committing to consistent *physical exercise* is another proactive emotion-focused coping strategy that's certainly applicable to race-based and racism-related stress. Cycling, walking, jogging, swimming, strength training, kayaking (yes, Black folks kayak!), hiking, boxing, martial arts, CrossFit, yoga, dancing, spin, golf, tennis, racquetball, Pilates, kickboxing, bootcamp, Zumba, and playing team sports like basketball and softball are all excellent at reducing stress and improving mental health if done regularly (3-4 times per week for about an hour each time).

Exercise is a type of *physical* stress that can reduce our psychological stress (e.g., race-based and racism-related stress). Various studies have confirmed that routine cardiovascular exercise decreases our brain's production of stress hormones (e.g., cortisol and adrenaline) and increases the production of stress-reducing hormones (e.g., oxytocin).

Physical exercise is also a palpable, practical way of practicing mindfulness. Practicing mindfulness, explained Katharine Blackwell, seems "to put a brake on the amygdala, keeping it from getting overactive." People who practiced mindfulness "in their everyday lives show less activity [and decreased neuronal size] in the amygdala and more activity [and increased neuronal size] in the prefrontal cortex." In other words, "mindful habits tame the amygdala" and enable us to better regulate negative emotions that would otherwise intensify or prolong our stress response. Practicing mindfulness have can a positive effect on our overreliance on the stress response by

237

changing the neurons and neural pathways of the amygdala and prefrontal cortex previously negatively reinforced by chronic stress. In other words, regular physical exercise can trigger positive neuroplasticity.

Using regular physical exercise as a proactive emotion-focused coping strategy can be discouraging to many of us at first. The key is tolerating the initial discomforts and drawbacks of consistent physical exercise, then you'll begin to find pleasure in it and crave the mental distraction and endorphins produced by exercise. If it's been a while since you've engaged in physical exercise or you have health concerns, I'd recommend speaking with your doctor before starting this strategy.

Getting regular *message therapy*, even if it's just you guilting your wife or gaming-addicted son into using an electronic massager on you every few days, is a great release for race-based and racism-related stress.

Having the body's soft tissues vigorously manipulated (i.e., getting a massage) reduces stress by triggering the brain's release of more endorphins, serotonin, and dopamine ("happy hormones") and reducing its production of cortisol (the stress hormone). Increasing the amount of these happy hormones (or neurotransmitters) in our brain reduces felt stress. When we feel stress, it's because we're not having enough of the type of experiences that would trigger our brain to produce more endorphins, serotonin, and dopamine than cortisol. A massage tangibly stimulates the autonomic nervous system, which prompts the brain's release of more of these happiness hormones instead of cortisol. This subsequently creates a "relaxation response" as opposed to increasing or prolonging our stress response.

In other words, message therapy can make us feel happiness and other positive emotions in spite of nearly every aspect of our lives being somehow mediated by race or, more specifically, systemically disadvantaged by our Blackness. Being Black in America, observed Feagin, "means always having to be prepared for anti-black actions," which, as a specific type of constant

238

hypervigilance, can be a chronic stressor. Message therapy can physically interrupt this constant hypervigilance with compelled relaxation, which gives our brain an opportunity to recover from the neuroplastic impact of race and racism as chronic stressors.

Race-based and racism-related experiences tend to trigger our chronic stress response and the subsequent overproduction of stress hormones, primarily cortisol, in the brain. The neural circuitry and structures responsible for producing this response are altered to become the dominant areas of the chronically stressed individual's brain. Chronic stress, according to Machiko Matsumoto and Hiroko Togashi, changes the human brain by creating long-lasting negative "alterations in the neural circuits underlying emotional regulation and increase the subsequent reactivity to stress later in life." Continuous cortisol overproduction increases the size and activity of the amygdala (i.e., neuronal hypertrophy). Consequently, negative emotional reactions (e.g., anxiety, anger, frustration, shame, hopelessness, helplessness) are easier to generate and harder to regulate in the future.

Anything that decreases our brain's production of cortisol, including message therapy, will increase our ability to regulate or cope with negative emotions, including those associated with stressful race-based or racism-related experiences. The more regularly we engage in message therapy, the lower our brain's cortisol production gets, and the more proactive this strategy becomes with regard to helping us better regulate potential negative emotions that would otherwise intensify or prolong our stress response.

Getting your massage therapy from a trained massage therapist once or twice a month would be an ideal practice. If your disposable income is really limited, I'd recommend budgeting for at least one monthly massage with a professional therapist. Since we can't currently eliminate race and racism as chronic stressors, prioritizing self-care by as many means possible is how we'll develop enough resilience to survive the chronic stress of still being Black in America.

Another very practicable strategy to reduce our brain's cortisol production is *drinking more water* throughout the day, every day. Drinking more water can drastically reduce any type of chronic stress, including race-based and racism-related stress.

Chronic stress significantly increases the level of cortisol in our brain by overproducing it. Studies have confirmed that not regularly drinking enough water can actually perpetuate this stress-induced cortisol overproduction, which in turn makes it harder to regulate the negative emotional responses normally associated with race-based and racism-related stress (e.g., fear, frustration, anger, shame, sadness, helplessness, etc.). "Studies have shown that being just half a liter dehydrated can increase your cortisol levels," according to Amanda Carlson. Dark colored, pungent smelling urine is a clear indication that you're already dehydrated.

Drinking more water can help our brain better cope with and recover from chronic stressors by flushing out the excess cortisol. Less cortisol enables improved regulation of negative emotions by shrinking the amygdala and causing it to be less active and dominant. By proactively using this simple strategy, we can minimize ever experiencing those negative emotions that would otherwise increase or prolong our stress response.

For some mysterious reason, drinking more water isn't all that appealing to many people. Adding a little fruit or some veggie slices (lemons, limes, pineapples, strawberries, oranges, cucumbers, etc.) to flavor your water may help you drink more of it. Keeping a pitcher of water with those things already added is a good strategy. Making it a habit to drink a glass of water before you go to sleep and right after you wake up is really effective. Using one of the phone apps to track your water intake and remind you periodically to drink water is also helpful. Switching from juice or soda to a glass of water with meals is another great tip for drinking more water.

In addition to drinking more water, *drinking (a little) more wine* can also help reduce race-based and racism-related stress. Numerous studies have confirmed the stress-reducing capability of wine, especially red wines. (I can hear my dear wife cheering loudly as I write this.)

Drinking wine depresses (i.e., reduces the level of activity in) our central nervous system and, by doing so, enables us to slow down our negative (emotional) thinking enough to reduce or prevent it. "One of the many byproducts of negative thinking is stress, which then leads to more negative thinking," noted Small. In order to reduce stress, we must practice replacing negative thinking with positive thinking. Doing so initiates positive neuroplasticity.

Several recent studies have realized that the plant compound resveratrol, which is found in red wines (from the skin of grapes used to make red wines), reduces stress by blocking the expression of an enzyme that controls stress in the brain. Resveratrol also stimulates a "stress response gene" and activates PARP-1, a stress reducing protein, which helps protect our brain cells from being saturated by corticosterone, a very damaging stress hormone comparable in effect to cortisol. Reducing the impact of corticosterone enables improved regulation of negative emotions that would otherwise increase or prolong our stress response.

You only need to drink a glass or two of red wine to evoke this protective, stress reducing effect. Drinking too much wine actually has a detrimental effect when experiencing stress and other negative emotions. "When our blood alcohol content increases, we become emotional—or more emotionally unstable—as we experience impairments to memory and comprehension," explained Lauren Wolfe. "This makes managing stress while intoxicated even more challenging than it already is when we are clear-headed." This strategy also only works in combination with other proactive emotion-focused coping strategies.

Despite lingering anti-cannabis stigma, various studies suggest that CBD oil can significantly reduce chronic race-based or racism-related stress when used on a regular basis. CBD (short for cannabidiol) oil is a natural chemical (or cannabinoid) extracted from the cannabis plant (either hemp or marijuana). Although it comes from cannabis, CBD doesn't get you "high," that feeling/psychoactive effect comes from THC (tetrahydrocannabinol), which is another cannabinoid found in cannabis. CBD is completely non-psychoactive.

Once ingested (directly or through CBD-infused foods and drinks), CBD oil reduces the feeling of chronic stress and other negative emotions by increasing the hypothalamus' ability to detect and stop the brain's overproduction of cortisol sooner. Chronic stress would normally (i.e., without CBD oil) cause the hypothalamus to become less sensitive to cortisol and allow its prolonged overproduction. The excess cortisol would then saturate and alter the neural circuitry of other areas of the brain, like the amygdala, prefrontal cortex, and hippocampus.

Prolonged cortisol saturation, as aforementioned, significantly changes neural structures like the hippocampus and prefrontal cortex, both of which are gradually reduced in size and activity as the cortisol annihilates hippocampus and PFC neurons. Conversely, prolonged cortisol overproduction increases the size and activity of the amygdala. Our capacity for negative emotional self-regulation and, consequently, reduced stress depends heavily on the functional efficiency of the neural circuitry within and connecting the prefrontal cortex, hippocampus, and amygdala. The cortisol-enhanced amygdala promotes persistent states of hypervigilance, dysregulated negative emotional reactions, as well as an exaggerated and extended stress response to race-based or racism-related experiences.

Regularly *reading for pleasure* (i.e., not required reading for school, work, research, or other adult responsibilities) is another excellent stress management strategy. This is a proactive strategy, so don't wait until you have a race-based or racism-related experience to start reading; read daily regardless of what you may experience with regards to race or racism. Reading habitually can offer a relaxing, healthy distraction from past and anticipated stressors. Reading is essentially meditative. Distracting yourself with a good book can be a great way to reduce stress because it keeps your brain actively and fully engaged in positive emotions while reading.

Ideally, we should read something we are eager to read for thirty minutes to an hour every day in a private, quiet place. No music, television, social media, pets, or other people around. Reading before bedtime is a common, sustainable practice. And after reading, dedicate a little more time to reflecting on what you just read and then noticing how you feel. You should feel a little less stressed in general, which should encourage you to pick up that book again tomorrow.

The chronic stress of still being Black in America is killing us prematurely. Chae concluded that "multiple levels of racism, including interpersonal experiences of racial discrimination and the internalization of negative racial bias, operate jointly to accelerate biological aging among African-Americans."

Conversely, people who read books regularly live almost two years longer on average than nonreaders. Avni Bavishi et al. referred to it as a "23-month survival advantage," which could somewhat counter the abovementioned impact of chronic race-based and racism-related stress. Of course, using reading regularly in addition to other proactive emotion-focus coping strategies will increase its effectiveness.

The same study that identified this survival advantage also noted that printed books are more advantageous than newspapers, magazines, and any type of online or digital reading. Apparently, the tactile sensation of physically holding of a book and turning its pages keeps our brain more actively and fully engaged while reading, which reduces more stress.

Printed books also keep us more engaged by enabling us to mark it up and use active reading strategies like underlining or highlighting key text, asking questions about the text, or summarizing parts of the text in the margins. "Why is marking up a book indispensable to reading," asked Mortimer Adler. "First, it keeps you awake. (And I don't mean merely conscious; I mean *awake*.) In the second place, reading, if it is active, is thinking, and thinking tends to express itself in words, spoken or written. The marked book is usually the thought-through book. Finally, writing helps you remember the thoughts you had, or the thoughts the author expressed."

Social media or news articles should be avoided when using this strategy. I know that this is most of what we now call reading, but this type of content is typically negative emotion-laden and inherently anti-Black and, consequently, could be more stress-inducing than reducing. It also makes you more vulnerable to experiencing the stress of vicarious racism.

I recommend reading books on historical Black successes and self-efficacy in spite of racism, especially autobiographies and nonfiction books about ancient Black civilizations (e.g., *Stolen Legacy* or *The African Origin of Civilization*), anti-slavery and decolonization leaders (e.g., *Narrative of the Life of Frederick Douglass* or *I Write What I Like*), the Black Power Movement (*Revolutionary Suicide*, *Assata*, or *The Autobiography of Malcolm X*), and Black wealth creation (e.g., *Black Fortunes* or *Why Should White Guys Have All the Fun*).

Reading purposeful fiction by Black authors like James Baldwin, Ralph Ellison, Zora Neale Hurston, Toni Morrison, and Octavia Butler is also highly recommend for this strategy. Reading fiction, noted Jenni Ogden, "enhances our ability to empathize with others; to put ourselves into another's shoes; to become more intuitive about other people's feelings (as well as our own); and to self-reflect on our problems as we read about and empathize with a fictional character who is facing similar problems. When we find ourselves weeping with (or for) the character in the story, we are also weeping for ourselves—it can be a sort of catharsis. When our character finds happiness in the end, we think that, perhaps, we can as well. We may discover ourselves coping in ways that we can only have learned from that novel we read years before."

Even if it's not necessarily written by or related to Black people or racism in anyway, routinely reading whatever seems

244

beneficial to you and piques your interest can still help you better cope with the negative emotions and chronic stress of being Black in America.

You should also strongly consider joining or starting a book club or discussion group in person or online. Doing so is a great way to motivate you to read regularly, introduce you to new books, and provide a way to talk with others about not only what you're reading but how it makes you feel, which has additional stress-reducing benefits.

Cinema therapy, which was defined by Birgit Wolz as "watching a movie for a needed emotional release," is another evidence-based stress reduction strategy applicable to race-based and racism-related stress. Watching movies as therapy can help us learn more about ourselves and our stressors "in more profound ways based on how we respond to different characters and scenes."

According to Delphine Tobias, "identifying with a character in a movie is a way to experience empathy and bonding. Movies can help us better understand some situations or people in our own lives. They allow us to confront real issues by experiencing 'reality' in a safe distance on the screen because our emotional responses feel real. Observe people (even fictional) with the same problems (or in worse situations) can make people feel less isolated in their own struggles. Some people enjoy sad movies as a way to reflect on their problems."

In terms of emotion-focus coping, certain movies "can open up different levels of our psyche" and evoke a cathartic exploration and release of those stressor-related negative emotions that would otherwise increase or prolong our stress response. Cinema therapy, when used appropriately, can provide a form of emotional distraction or break that could be a healthy coping strategy.

Even movies that would be considered stressful, scary, or sad could actually trigger positive emotions like happiness and hope. Watching movies that are suspenseful or stressful causes our brain to at first release cortisol just like in real life, but, unlike in real life, this cortisol is quickly offset by the release of an even greater amount of dopamine. Dopamine triggers positive emotions like happiness and hope and, consequently, is naturally stress-reducing.

Watching scary movies allows us to practice actively regulating our own negative emotions within the safety of a fictitious experience. Watching a scary movie is like *choosing* to trigger our stress response and, ultimately, practicing to control the triggering of our stress response in real life. Horror movies makes feeling stress safe, and in doing so, allows us to develop a healthier relationship with stress along with the ability to manage it (and accompanying negative emotions) more effectively.

Watching horror movies can also provide us with a rare respite from the constant hypervigilance toward anti-Black actions caused specifically by chronic race-based or racism-related stress. These movies force us to "focus on one thing, not the thing you're currently worrying about," (e.g., a past, current, or anticipated race-based or racism-related experience) but "the monster in the room or whatever it might be," explained Coltan Scrivner. "So in watching a horror movie, your perceived threat shifts from whatever thing you're worrying about to whatever the character in the movie is worrying about. And then when the movie ends, the feelings of anxiety go away because the threat goes away." And our brain can briefly apply that sense of calmness and safety to all of the threats it's dealing with, not just the fabricated one in the movie. Consequently, watching a scary movie can actually make us happier and less stressed.

Watching horror movies, as a "high-arousal negative stimuli," can provide significant stress relief and boost our stress resilience. This specific effect, explained Margee Kerr, is due to the "different neurotransmitters and hormones released during the experience," primarily endorphins and dopamine. Sad movies have a similar effect in our brain.

Watching sad movies, according to Debbie Hampton, also tends to make us "more appreciative of the blessings and important relationships in our lives which translates to feeling happier." These movies subconsciously encourage us to reflect on the more positive aspects of our lives, which counteracts some of the negative thinking and emotions dedicated to race-based or racism-related experiences. Although these experiences are often psychologically (and sometimes even physically) devastating, watching sad movies can shift our thinking into being grateful because, as displayed by the movie's tragic plot, things could be a lot worse. This therapeutic effect has been referred to as the "tragedy paradox."

Much like the aforementioned reading strategy, with regard to using cinema therapy for race-based and racism-related stress, I recommend watching movies that feature various aspects of the lived experience of Black people and Black success in spite of racism. Biopics of Black historical figures are my favorite, but fictional films about Black folks (especially those that are novel-based) can be just as impactful.

Laughing more is another proactive emotion-focused coping strategy capable of significantly reducing race-based or racism-related stress. By practicing ways to *make* ourselves smile and laugh more, humor therapy promotes positive neuroplasticity with regard to better regulating those negative emotions that would otherwise increase or prolong our stress response.

Finding a way to laugh in the midst of a typically stressful race-based or racism-related experience enables us to think more positively about the experience, especially how we perceive the threat within it[57], and feel more in control of (and capable of changing) our response to it. "When you can't control what's happening, challenge yourself to control how you respond to what's happening. That's where your power is." That's how we evolve from mere victims to empowered survivors. Making ourselves laugh more, as counterintuitive as it may initially seem, is an awesome way to trigger this evolution.

---

[57] Research reveals that a negative experience can be less stressful if perceived more as a challenge than a threat. Humor therapy can oftentimes change our perspective of these experiences and help us see them more positively as challenges than threats, thereby reducing our stress response.

Laughter can create the psychological distance from otherwise stressful experiences we need to become resilient enough to normalize a relaxation response to these experiences capable of counteracting and reducing the chronic stress response. As opposed to complaining or ruminating, finding whatever humor is accessible in these experiences and *talking about* (a previously mentioned strategy) that found humor with members of your support team can both validate the experience and provide release emotionally in the form of shared laughter. Looking back on these experiences and finding something to laugh about in them will help you assume less stress and other negative emotions in those same experiences.

Sometimes in looking back we may have to *fake laugh* at the experience just enough to still trigger a relaxation response. Fortunately, the human brain can't differentiate between fake laughter that we compel ourselves to do and genuine laughter that comes from actual humor. Consequently, the benefit with regard to reducing stress is exactly the same, and typically when you can force yourself to laugh, you'll eventually start laughing organically.

Humor therapy, when used appropriately, can provide a positive distraction from those negative emotions associated with race-based and racism-related stress (e.g., fear, frustration, anger, shame, sadness, etc.). This distraction can significantly reduce the intensity and duration of our stress response. Laughing more can also decrease our brain's production of stress hormones like cortisol and adrenaline while increasing the production of stress-reducing "happiness hormones" like endorphins, serotonin, and dopamine. This subsequently creates a relaxation response as opposed to increasing or prolonging our stress response.

Chronic stress appears to aggravate the rate of telomere shortening. Chronic stress, as aforementioned, significantly increases cortisol production in the brain. Cortisol saturation reduces the "levels of antioxidant proteins and may therefore cause increased oxidative damage to DNA and accelerated telomere shortening." Shorter telomeres inhibit the capacity of cells to divide properly, which causes cells in our body and brain to either to die off or malfunction and cause a physiological imbalance. Ultimately, this physiological imbalance substantially increases an individual's susceptibility to heart disease, cancer, stroke, diabetes, hypertension, and premature death. The quicker we age biologically (as evident by the shorter our telomeres), the sooner we die, essentially. However, humor therapy, when used regularly, can uniquely reduce telomere shortening by drastically increasing our body's production of antibody-producing, telomere-protective B and T cells.

Using this strategy doesn't mean that you're laughing *at* experiencing anti-Blackness or racism or not taking the experience seriously. It means that you're choosing to strategically regulate those negative emotions typically triggered by race-based or racism-related experiences and stress that would otherwise intensify or prolong our stress response.

Moreover, this is primarily a proactive strategy, which means it's most effective when used habitually and not only as a direct response to a race-based or racism-related experience. *Practice* laughing more. Download a daily joke app onto your phone. Schedule time throughout the week to watch a bunch of funny shows and comedy specials on television and Netflix. Listen to funny podcasts during your daily commute or workout. Challenge friends, family members, and coworkers to make you laugh impromptu. Challenge yourself to make them laugh more (and then laugh at yourself for doing so). Try *laughter yoga*[58]. The more you laugh,

---

[58] Laughter yoga, which can be practiced as a class just like regular yoga, is a "unique concept where we laugh for no reason—no comedy, no jokes, no humor, just laughing for the sake of it," explained Sharon de Caestecker. "If we leave laughter to chance it may not happen, particularly given the current situation. However, laughter yoga provides a time and a space to laugh just for the sake of it. Anyone can laugh when times are good, but laughter yoga teaches people to laugh unconditionally and helps them to keep a positive mental attitude regardless of circumstances." I recommend Googling "laughter yoga exercises by Sebastien Gendry" for drills you can start practicing alone or

even if forced (i.e., laughter without humor), the more your brain will be rewired to automatically reduce your stress response, even in negative experiences.

Studies have suggested that *drawing, painting, photography, sculpting, and coloring (i.e., making art)* as a consistent hobby can have tremendous benefits as a proactive emotion-focused strategy to reduce chronic race-based or racism-related stress.

Using "art as therapy," we create art freely as a way to combat stress by exploring and releasing those negative emotions that would otherwise increase or prolong our stress response. As we make art, we analyze (personally, collaboratively, or with a professional counselor) what we have made, why we might have made it (e.g., causal experiences or emotions), and how creating this art makes us feel now.

You don't have to "be an artist" to use art therapy. Regardless of your skill level, making art can reduce stress. You just do the best you can and create art based on what you feel. No one will judge your artistic ability or lack thereof (and neither should you). The goal is purely to create art—via whatever media you're interested in—that would evoke or emote negative perceptions and emotions we may be repressing internally that are possibly related to race-based or racism-related experiences. Creating this art could then be used to recognize, reflect on, and release those experience-connected perceptions and emotions that would otherwise increase or prolong our race-based or racism-related stress response.

It's actually the *process* of creating art, not the end product, that is most impactful with regard to reducing stress. If done consistently, forty-five minutes of art therapy per week can have a lasting impact of alleviating and preventing chronic stress. This is a proactive strategy, so you shouldn't respond directly to a race-based or racism-related experience by using art therapy. Use this strategy once or twice a week regardless of what you may

---

with others; many of which are super silly but will definitely get you laughing more. Just remember, "choosing to laugh as and when you want to is not a sign of silliness, it's a sign of emotional maturity."

experience with regards to race or racism. Creating art habitually can offer a relaxing, healthy distraction from past and anticipated stressors, especially stressors that are currently uncontrollable like racism.

There is also a meditative quality to making art. Creating art has the ability to calm down the amygdala, which is responsible for triggering our stress response, and reduce our negative thinking. You could become so actively engaged or fully engrossed in the process of drawing or painting or whatever that you experience a state of mindfulness (i.e., living in the present moment) psychologists refer to as *flow*.

Experiencing flow can reduce chronic stress by better enabling us to regulate those negative emotions that would otherwise increase or prolong our stress response. Experiencing flow facilitates the development of our emotional complexity. *Emotional complexity*, according to Anthony Ong and Cindy Bergeman, refers to our "capacity to distinguish between pleasant and unpleasant feeling states" (i.e., recognizing the causes and effects of our positive and negative emotions). "Improved emotion regulation is associated with greater emotional complexity." People with underdeveloped emotional complexity tend to rely on "significantly more maladaptive emotion regulation strategies" (i.e., "remaining in denial, engaging in substance use, displaced aggression, self-blame—even in extreme cases suicide.")

"A lot of stress is caused by ruminating over past events or worrying about the future," noted Anna Willieme. "Shifting attention to our senses can land us more fully in our bodies and in the present, helping us let go of anxious thoughts." This stress-reducing mindfulness can be achieved by bringing our full attention to the process of creating art. "As we do so, we can become more fully present to the moment."

Practicing *mindfulness meditation* is arguably the most effective strategy for proactively recognizing and reducing the negative emotions associated with chronic race-based and racism-related stress.

251

Chronic race-based and racism-related stress does not come from race-based and racism-related experiences as much as it comes from our maladaptive emotional and behavioral reactions to these typically highly negative experiences. Practicing mindfulness meditation enables us to recognize and accept those maladaptive emotional and behavioral reactions in a detached manner, which ultimately thwarts the (neuroplasticity-based) urge to automatically react those ways again.

First off, please don't allow yourself to become (or continue to be) intimidated by the term "mindfulness meditation" or my attempt to explain it as usefully as I possibly can. It's really not that complicated. Trust me.

"Meditation actually alters how the brain reacts to stress," explained Sameet Kumar. Through mindfulness mediation, we can consciously decrease our brain's habitual reaction to race-based and racism-related stress by disrupting the stress pathways. Even though we can't control, stop, or even avoid the stressor (i.e., negative race-based or racism-related experiences) itself, we can practice *improving* our emotional and behavioral reaction to and relationship with the stressor. Improving our emotional and behavioral reaction can minimize continuing those negative emotions and self-defeating or destructive behaviors that would otherwise increase or prolong our stress response.

According to Kirk Brown and Richard Ryan, "the concept of mindfulness has roots in Buddhist and other contemplative traditions where conscious attention and awareness are actively cultivated. It is most commonly defined as the state of being attentive to and aware of what is taking place in the present."

Paul Tingen wrote that "the essence of Buddhist practice is to use mindfulness to develop singularity of thought, which can help us to get out of habitual thinking and feeling and help us to stop triggering our habitual neural pathways of suffering. Mindfulness, in effect, allows us to consciously rewire our brain for improved well-being. We train the brain to create and deepen a neural pathway of well-being that might not otherwise be there.

Conversely, if we focus on the negative, we keep firing and strengthening the neural pathways associated with our suffering" and chronic stress.

Chronic race-based and racism-related stress enlarges and hypersensitizes the amygdala and weakens the prefrontal cortex and hippocampus, which diminishes our ability to regulate habitual emotional reactions to race or racism as stressors. Practicing mindfulness meditation, explained Katharine Blackwell, seems "to put a brake on the amygdala, keeping it from getting overactive." People who practiced mindfulness "in their everyday lives show less activity in the amygdala and more activity in the prefrontal cortex." In other words, "mindful habits tame the amygdala."

Sandra deBlois confirmed that practicing mindfulness, "the simple act of intentionally and nonjudgmentally paying attention moment by moment to our experience, can exact a positive effect" on our overreliance on the stress response by changing the neurons and neural pathways of the amygdala and prefrontal cortex.

"In less mindful states," conditioned emotional or behavioral responses, explained Brown and Ryan, "may occur outside of our awareness or drive behavior before one clearly acknowledges them. Mindfulness is also compromised when individuals behave compulsively or automatically, without awareness of or attention to one's behavior."

"Mindfulness captures a quality of consciousness that is characterized by clarity and vividness of current experience and functioning and thus stands in contrast to the mindless, less 'awake' states of habitual or automatic functioning that may be chronic for many individuals. Mindfulness may be important in disengaging individuals from automatic thoughts, habits, and unhealthy behavior patterns and thus could play a key role in fostering informed and self-endorsed behavioral regulation."

"The big implication here is that if our brain changes itself based on our experiences," described Steven Handel, "then by changing our experiences we can actively reshape our brains. One way to consciously change our experience is to learn how to apply mindfulness, the ability to be intentionally aware of our experience as it is unfolding. And by being more aware of our present experience as it is happening, we begin to form 'response flexibility'—the capacity to pause before we act."

Practicing mindfulness meditation creates an intentional gap between a stimulus/stressor and our brain's response to it, which enables our brain to be more flexible and constructive in its reaction (especially to negative stimuli). This gap is largely based on our capacity to become unconditionally connected to the present moment, which then allows us to recognize and accept the stimulus/stressor for what it is without automatically getting caught up in our conditioned (amygdala-based) emotional responses. This capacity increases the more we actually practice mindfulness meditation.

Practicing mindfulness takes *practice*. John Teasdale described it as "a habit, it's something the more one does, the more likely one is to be in that mode with less and less effort. It's a skill that can be learned. It's accessing something we already have. Mindfulness isn't difficult. What's difficult is to remember to be mindful."

Practicing mindfulness also requires meditation, which starts with somehow calming our brain and relaxing our body with controlled breathing. I recommend using a mindfulness or meditation phone app to help guide your practice. Insight Timer is my favorite. I just find a private place to sit in a relaxed position, put on my noise cancelling headphones (no outside distractions for me), start a guided meditation based on the time I have and topic I find interesting, close my eyes, and then trust the process.

Five to thirty minutes of regular (preferably daily) meditation can have a tremendous impact on our ability to regulate negative emotions and reduce race-based and racism-related stress. You'll become less reactive and more resilient to stress the more regularly you meditate. The goal is to make mindfulness meditation a daily habit regardless of that day's experiences with the stress of being Black in America. This strategy is best when used proactively, but can certainly help manage your emotional response to a current race-based or racism-related experience.

Practicing mindfulness meditation can actually reduce cortisol secretion and reverse the changes to neural circuitry and structures caused by chronic stress. As a result, the stress response is progressively diminished with people who meditate as mindful awareness is increased.

Elissa Epel et al. elaborated on how automatic or conditioned emotional, cognitive, and behavioral responses (e.g., chronic stress) to recurrent, negative stimuli are "reduced following certain forms of meditation practice. One implication of the 'deautomatization' of thought is that it should lead to enhanced ability to notice nuanced details of experience from a fresh perspective and inhibit reliance on memories, expectations, and schemas during information processing. Meditation training has further been shown to reduce elaborative processing of previous stimuli thereby increasing attentional resources to present-moment experience. Enhanced attention-related processes are hypothesized to improve early detection of potential stressors and increase the probability that effective coping will be implemented in a timely manner."

Several fMRI "studies provide neural evidence that mindfulness meditation cultivates interoceptive awareness, which is thought to play a key role in maintaining present moment awareness and regulating emotions. One key way in which mindfulness may protect one from the negative effects of stress is by decreasing rumination. Increasing awareness of present-moment experience may disrupt ruminative thought processes that play a role in prolonged stress reactivity."

"As thoughts and feelings are experienced as transient mental events occurring within a wider context of awareness, attenuation of automatic identification and reactivity to them may occur. Over time, this more objective perspective on mental content may interrupt ruminative thinking, increase the ability to evaluate the accuracy of thoughts, and allow greater freedom of choice in responding to thoughts and emotions."

"Mindfulness practice involves first allowing awareness of thought and then becoming less engaged or attached to the thoughts themselves before attempting to evaluate their accuracy. Mindfulness is theorized to enhance emotion regulation skills by increasing awareness of emotions, increasing the willingness to tolerate and accept distressing or uncomfortable emotions, and reducing emotional reactivity to provocative events and emotions themselves."

"These studies support the notion that mindfulness facilitates interpretation of situations as less threatening, perhaps due to less activation of self-relevant concerns, so that events are responded to more thoughtfully, rather than reacted to through automatic filters of cognitive and emotional processes. Mindfulness may also improve coping with events that are appraised as threatening in which there is little possibility of control. Mindfulness may serve to increase a sense of control, not simply by reacting more 'coolly,' (with attenuated cycles of negative thoughts and emotions), but by lessening one's perceived need to be in control, especially when situations are determined to be uncontrollable" (e.g., the microevents of everyday racism).

Mindfulness meditation can apparently change our brain's typically maladaptive responses to the chronic stress of everyday racism (e.g., internalizing presumed Black inferiority and stereotypically behaving in ways that inadvertently help to maintain White privilege) by changing our brain.

Jessica Graham et al. explained that "through gaining a more accepting relationship with one's internal experiences, mindfulness meditation can provide Black individuals with cognitive and behavioral skills that might help individuals in this community approach the anxiety they experience in the face of racism and gain a sense of agency over their life experiences."

"Specifically, mindfulness meditation might help Black individuals focus their attention on the present moment and learn

256

to approach the anxious thoughts and emotions that arise in response to the experience of racism, instead of avoiding or attempting to control these distressing anxious thoughts and emotions, which may decrease anxiety and avoidance."

"In addition to addressing the anxiety that might come from repeated racist experiences, mindfulness meditation might also help Black individuals cope with the internalization of racism that may also be associated with anxiety. Internalized racism has been defined as the acceptance by the marginalized group of the negative beliefs, words, and images about one's racial or ethnic group as truth and this internalization of negative stereotypes has been associated with feelings of worthlessness and powerlessness in African-Americans."

"A key mechanism of mindfulness meditation is the process of seeing your thoughts and feelings as objective events as opposed to seeing the thoughts and feelings as truths, otherwise described as decentering. The cultivation of a different perspective in which thoughts are held more loosely and the idea that these thoughts are not truth has been theoretically and empirically connected to less anxiety. In the context of racism, mindfulness meditation, more specifically the decentering that is cultivated in mindfulness practice, might help Black individuals see these negative stereotypes and beliefs as objective thoughts instead of internalizing them as truths which can lead to the feelings of powerlessness, worthlessness, and low self-esteem."

"The perception of inability to control or have power over one's situation has been associated with the development and maintenance" of chronic stress. Mindfulness meditation "has been shown to be associated with heightened perceptions of control. Specifically, mindfulness meditation teaches skills that help us gain mastery over our anxious symptomology in the face of external stressors that may be unalterable (i.e., racism). This may seem contradictory because mindfulness meditation places a strong emphasis on relinquishing attempts at rigid control of internal experiences."

However, "rather than focusing on rigid control over one's internal experiences, mindfulness meditation focuses on one's ability to influence one's internal experiences to a degree by using compassion and awareness to decrease the overwhelming nature of anxiety, which leads to heightened perceptions of control, rather than paradoxical effects associated with rigid efforts at control. It is important to note that acceptance should not be confused with resignation. Mindfulness meditation can help Black individuals cope with and function in the face of racism, which might include taking action towards social justice."

On that note, identifying and committing to ways to *actively protest* against racial stigma, inequality, and injustice impacting other people of color (especially Black people) is an incredibly impactful emotion-focused coping strategy for race-based and racism-related stress. It's as close as we can get to problem-based coping with a problem (and stressor) that currently can't be completely solved or stopped.

Knowing that you practiced empathy and compassion and *did something* that, at a minimum, lessened the negative impact of a race-based or racism-related experience on someone else can certainly reduce many of the negative emotions and stress you feel with regard to your own race-based or racism-related experiences. Experiencing a lifetime of chronic race-based and racism-related stress significantly impairs our brain's natural ability to produce the dopamine necessary for positively coping with or reducing current stress. Any type of problem solving (or reducing), including actively protesting, triggers our brain to release more dopamine. Increasing the amount of dopamine in our brain reduces our stress response by counteracting the overproduction of cortisol (and the feeling of negative emotions like anger, helplessness, and hopelessness) that otherwise would have increased or prolonged it.

Active empathy and compassion, explained Elizabeth Segal, promote abilities that help us to better handle stress. "Studies show that when we can regulate our emotions, we are better able to relate to others in positive ways. This is known as emotion regulation, which is the ability to take in the experiences of others without being overwhelmed."

This particular ability, as we've discussed throughout the chapter, is "also imperative for us to de-stress ourselves" by decreasing or discontinuing those negative emotions that would otherwise increase or prolong our stress response. When we actively practice compassion and engage in empathy, "we draw on skills for emotion regulation. In doing so, we are also controlling emotions that can be stressful." The personal benefit of actively protesting is that "we can be exercising good control over our emotions" and, consequently, coping more effectively with our own race-based and racism-related stress.

A slight drawback to using this strategy is that it can make you more vulnerable to the stress of vicarious racism (i.e., stress induced by witnessing other people's racism experiences).

Stress is the brain's reaction to any information from our external circumstances that reveal or imply threat, especially threat that we feel we don't have the capacity or resources to cope with. I believe that the majority of the stress experienced from vicarious racism is specifically associated with our oftentimes immediate, implicit "realization that we are also vulnerable to the racism that we have vicariously experienced," noted Kimberly Truong et al. Indirectly experiencing "racism that is targeted at other persons of color" (especially other Black people) reminds us of and reinforces the almost constant personal and systemic "threat of racism," which then requires, explained Essed, "planning, almost every day of one's life, how to avoid or defend oneself."

To quote the brilliant Lorraine Hansberry, "a status not freely chosen or entered into by an individual or a group is necessarily one of oppression and the oppressed are by their nature forever in ferment and agitation against their condition and what they understand to be their oppressors. If not by overt rebellion or revolution, then in the thousand and one ways they will devise with and without consciousness to alter their condition."

259

"Do I remain a revolutionary? Intellectually—without a doubt. But am I prepared to give my body to the struggle or even my comforts? This is what I puzzle about."

Active protest as a proactive emotion-focused coping strategy for race-based and racism-related stress can involve all sorts of actions. My favorite historical example of active protest against race and racism are the undercelebrated Black Panther Party for Self-Defense's "Survival Programs." These programs, of which there came to be more than 35, were operated by Party members under the slogan "survival pending revolution."

JoNina Abron explained that the "Panthers established a network of community service projects designed to improve the life chances of African American people. Institutional racism relegated a disproportionate number of African Americans to deplorable housing, poor health care services, an unresponsive criminal justice system, inadequate diets, and substandard education. The Party's survival programs aimed to help black people overcome the devastating effects of racism and capitalism."

The most famous and successful of their programs was the Free Breakfast for Children Program, through which the Panthers would cook and serve breakfast to the poor youth of the area. Initially ran out of the St. Augustine's Church in Oakland, the Program became so popular that by the end of the year the Panthers would set up Free Breakfast Programs in cities across the nation, feeding over 10,000 children every day before they went to school.

According to Miriam Monges, "Party members understood that malnourishment impeded the learning process. Yet in the 1960s and early 1970s, poor children attended school hungry and saddled with the unrealistic expectation that they would master the curriculum. Party members and students cooked and served large pots of grits and eggs. We cajoled supermarkets for [food] donations [and community members for financial contributions]...Most importantly, we also nourished their minds with Black history lessons as they ate their meals." The impact of this program was such that the federal government was soon shamed into adopting a similar program for public schools nationally.

Other survival programs were free community services such as classes on politics and Black history, free medical clinics, lessons on self-defense and first aid, free shoe program, free clothing program, free grocery giveaways, Liberation Schools, legal assistance, transportation to prisons for family members of inmates, a free ambulance program, drug and alcohol rehabilitation, escorted senior citizens to banks to cash their checks, free pest control, and testing for sickle-cell disease, which was performed on more than 500,000 Black people before it was recognized by the national medical community as a disease impacting us disproportionately.

Other types of active protest you can do now include volunteering to help meet the needs of other people, especially people seemingly impacted by race and racism, whether that's tutoring or mentoring at-risk students or serving food at a homeless shelter; "tabling," in which you literally set up a table at some public space or social event to talk about and distribute information to get other people engaged in a specific race or racism-related issue; planning a boycott against complicit companies and organizations; establishing a campaign to protest by sending letters, emails, and petitions to complicit corporate, organizational, and elected leaders; lobbying local, state, and national elected leaders for support or in protest of a specific race or racism-related issue; starting your own or promoting investing in and consumer support of specific Black-owned businesses; demonstrating (e.g., planning or supporting marches, rallies, sit-ins, sleep-ins, teach-ins, etc.) in protest of a specific race or racism-related issue; creating, working for, or volunteering with a nonprofit organization dedicated to resolving or reducing the impact of particular race or racism-related issues; or raising funds and/or promoting awareness for public schools predominantly serving students of color and

261

other nonprofit organizations addressing the unmet needs of people seemingly impacted by race and racism.

And just like the other strategies discussed in this chapter, active protest is most effective as an emotion-focused coping strategy when used proactively.

I'd be remiss at this point to not include *speaking with a professional therapist or counselor* as another highly impactful proactive emotion-focused strategy for coping with chronic race-based and racism-related stress. Mental health professionals can provide informed support for your use of the aforementioned self-care strategies as well as help you identify other ways to survive the stress of still being Black in America.

The shortage of Black therapists (or non-Black therapists trained in race-based and racism-related stress) along with the perceived stigma and cost of professional therapy are oftentimes enough to prevent more Black people for seeking this type of support, but they shouldn't continue to be.

Even when non-Black therapists lack the exposure and empathy that would increase your comfort level and enable them to provide you with a more precise approach to resolving your race-based or racism-related stress, they still can use their professional expertise to provide you with evidence-based strategies for general stress recognition and reduction. Professional support to help us reduce the chronic stress of race and racism should be something we prioritize and certainly not be ashamed of. Whenever we need professional help to be successful in other things outside of personal expertise, we typically purchase that help, so why should this type of therapy be so different. There are also different ways of accessing professional therapy, including new smartphone apps and virtual counseling, many of which are very affordable and possibly included in your current insurance package (if insured).

www.ingramcontent.com/pod-product-compliance
Lightning Source LLC
Chambersburg PA
CBHW052123270326
41930CB00012B/2740